He Swore an Oath

Biblical Themes from Genesis 12–50

Second Edition

Edited by

Richard S. Hess,
Gordon J. Wenham,
and Philip E. Satterthwaite

WIPF & STOCK · Eugene, Oregon

Wipf and Stock Publishers
199 W 8th Ave, Suite 3
Eugene, OR 97401

He Swore an Oath, Second Edition
Biblical Themes from Genesis 12-50
Edited by Hess, R. S., Wenham, G. J., and Satterthwaite, P. E.

ISBN 13: 978-1-55635-732-9
ISBN 10: 1-55635-732-X
Publication date 11/28/2007
Previously published by Tyndale House, 1994

CONTENTS

EDITORS' PREFACE

For many years Donald Wiseman, Professor of Assyriology at London University, chaired the Old Testament Study Group at Tyndale House, Cambridge. Through his warm pastoral support of those who attended this group many younger scholars have been encouraged to pursue academic biblical scholarship. He was also Secretary of the Fellowship during the important stages of its development after the Second World War, then Chairman of the Tyndale House Council and its predecessor from 1957 to 1986. In 1980 he was President of the Society for Old Testament Study.

Through his vision Tyndale House has been built up so that it now has the best library and supporting facilities for biblical study in Britain. As an editor of the *New Bible Commentary, New Bible Dictionary,* and the Tyndale Old Testament commentaries he has disseminated the fruit of his own scholarship and that of the wider Tyndale Fellowship to the world-wide church. His concern has always been to encourage individuals, stimulating them to research and publication in order to improve understanding and appreciation of the Scriptures, both as outstanding texts from antiquity and as the Word of God vital for us today.

As an expression of their deep gratitude for all his labours and to celebrate his seventy-fifth birthday, the members of the 1993 Old Testament Study Group at Tyndale House agreed to dedicate the papers read at this year's meeting to Professor Wiseman.

A.R. Millard (Chairman, Tyndale House Council)
R.S. Hess
P.E. Satterthwaite
G.J. Wenham (Editors)

1

ABRAHAM RE-ASSESSED THEOLOGICALLY

The Abraham Narrative and the New Testament Understanding of Justification by Faith

T. Desmond Alexander

Summary

From a survey of the NT it is apparent that the Abraham narrative in Genesis 11:27-25:11 significantly influenced the thinking of the early church regarding its soteriology and the nature of Jesus Christ's mission to the world. This article examines firstly the Genesis account by focusing on the call of Abraham in 12:1-3, the covenants in chapters 15 and 17 and the divine oath in 22:16-18. Attention is then given to the references to Abraham in the NT Epistles in order to see how the Genesis material is interpreted. This highlights a common understanding of the Abraham narrative, derived from a careful exegesis of the Genesis text.

I. Introduction[1]

In the New Testament the patriarch Abraham is often presented as an example of one who exercised outstanding faith in God (*cf.* Rom. 4, Gal. 3-4, Heb. 11 and Jas. 2). This prominence is undoubtedly due to his unique status as the father of the nation of Israel. Yet, the way in which the New Testament writers exegete the biblical account of Abraham presents various problems. On the one hand, it is sometimes difficult to see how a particular exegesis may be sustained in the light of modern principles of interpretation. How, for example, do we explain Paul's bold affirmation in Galatians 3:16 that the 'seed of Abraham' mentioned in Genesis refers to Jesus Christ? On the other hand, aspects of the NT interpretation of the Abraham narrative appear contradictory. This is most apparent in Paul's use of Abraham to support the concept of justification by faith rather than by works of the law (*cf.* Rom. 4:1-5; Gal. 3:1-9), and James' use of Abraham to conclude that 'a person is justified by what he does and not by faith alone' (2:24). To address these particular problems, we shall first examine the Abraham account in Genesis before returning to the NT material.

Any attempt to understand the NT references to Abraham must clearly start with the text of Genesis. It must be recognised, however, that contemporary methods of studying the book of Genesis have been dominated by source and form criticism. While such approaches, used with appropriate care, may shed some light on the process by which the present text was formed, they can never explain fully the meaning of the text as it now stands. Indeed, there is the danger that our understanding of the final text is influenced either consciously or unconsciously by our perception of how the text was composed; what we read is not the text of Genesis as presently constituted, but rather the complex process by which we think it originated. This possibility must be appreciated especially when we come to consider how the NT writers understood the Abraham story. Unaware of modern critical methods, their interest was in the account as it stood before them - an account

---

[1]This present essay is meant to complement an earlier study by D.J Wiseman, 'Abraham reassessed' in A.R. Millard and D.J. Wiseman (eds.) *Essays on the Patriarchal Narratives* (Leicester, IVP 1980) 139-156, which examines the person of Abraham from an historical perspective.

which they viewed as a unity and not as the product of various sources. Thus, if we are to appreciate their perspective on Abraham, it is essential to adopt a pre-critical reading of the text.

II. Abraham in Genesis

In terms of the number of chapters given over to him, Abraham[2] is clearly the most important of all the human characters in Genesis. Moreover, his life marks an important watershed in God's relationship with human beings. Although there are in chapters 3-11 indications that divine mercy will triumph over the consequences of the fall, it is with Abraham that a clearer picture begins to emerge. The divine promises associated with his call (12:1-3) reveal that he is to play a central role in the restoration of humanity's broken relationship with God.[3]

1. Overview of the Abraham narrative

The Abraham narrative falls into two sections separated by a brief genealogy in 22:20-24; the main section consists of 11:27-22:19, with 23:1-25:11 forming an appendix.[4] Running through

---

[2]For convenience the names Abraham and Sarah are used throughout this essay in spite of the fact that these are first introduced in 17:5 and 17:15 to replace the earlier designations Abram and Sarai respectively.

[3]Although this present essay focuses on the Abraham story, it is important that the material in Genesis 12-25 should be interpreted within the context of the whole book of Genesis. Unfortunately, insufficient attention is generally given to the relationship of chs. 12-25 to their wider context.

[4]Three main factors support this proposal. First, genealogies are frequently used in Genesis to separate narrative sections. Although 22:20-24 is short and does not follow the pattern of the main genealogies in Genesis, its contents are clearly genealogical in nature. Secondly, the divine speeches in 12:1-3 and 22:15-18 form an inclusio, framing chs. 12-22. While the speeches differ in their terminology, they are remarkably similar in substance, and, as we shall see below, the divine oath in 22:15-18 forms a very fitting conclusion to the process started by the call of Abraham in 12:1-3; *cf.* R.W.L. Moberly, 'The Earliest Commentary on the Akedah', *VT* 38 (1988) 322-23 = *idem*, *From Eden to Golgotha: Essays in Biblical Theology*, (South Florida Studies in the History of Judaism; Atlanta, Scholars Press 1992) 73. Thirdly, A. Abela *The Themes of the Abraham Narrative: Thematic Coherence within the Abraham Literary Unit of Genesis 11,27-25:18* (Malta, Studia Editions 1989) 9, suggests that the material in 22:20-25:18 is a self-contained unit, forming a palistrophic pattern.

the main section are three closely intertwined themes concerning seed, land and blessing.[5] Not only are these themes significant within the Abraham narrative, but they may also be traced throughout the whole of Genesis.[6]

Within the Abraham narrative the theme of seed centres on the divine assurance that Abraham will have many descendants. The initial promises that Abraham will become a 'great nation' (12:2) and that his 'seed' will possess the land of Canaan (12:7) are set against the background of Sarah's inability to have children (11:30). Later, after the LORD assures Abraham that he will have a son of his own and many descendants (15:1-5), Sarah persuades him to have a child by her maidservant Hagar (16:1-4). By naming him, Abraham claims Ishmael as his own (16:15). Afterwards, however, God reveals on two separate occasions that Sarah will indeed have a son who will be Abraham's true heir (17:15-21; 18:9-15). Eventually, Sarah gives birth to Isaac (21:1-7), and he is established as Abraham's heir through the divinely approved departure of Hagar and Ishmael (21:8-21). Thus, Isaac's birth marks the first step towards the fulfilment of the divine promise that Abraham will become a 'great nation' and have numerous descendants.

The second theme in the Abraham narrative concerns land. Initially, God commands Abraham to leave his own land and 'go to the land I will show you' (12:1). Although it is not mentioned specifically that Abraham will possess this land, the promise that he will become a 'great nation' (12:2) implies that his descendants will possess it; the Hebrew term גּוֹי ('nation') denotes people inhabiting a specific geographical location and forming a political unit.[7] Thus, when Abraham first arrives in

---

[5]Among recent writers to consider the themes of the Abraham narrative Abela, *ibid.*, 15-125, concludes that there are three main themes concerning blessing, son and land. L.A. Turner, *Announcements of Plot in Genesis*, (JSOTS 96; Sheffield, Sheffield Academic Press 1990) 51-114, discusses the same basic themes under the headings of nationhood, land and blessing.

[6]See J. McKeown, *A Study of the Main Unifying Themes in the Hebrew Text of the Book of Genesis* (unpublished Ph.D. thesis, The Queen's University of Belfast 1991).

[7]*Cf.* E.A. Speiser, 'People and Nation of Israel', *JBL* 79 (1960) 157-163; R.E. Clements, *TDOT* 2:426-33; A.R. Hulst, *THWAT* 2:290-325; T.D. Alexander, *A Literary Analysis of the Abraham Narrative in Genesis*, (unpublished Ph.D. thesis, The Queen's University of Belfast 1982) 306.

Canaan, the LORD promises, 'To your offspring (seed) I will give this land' (12:7). Later, following the separation of Lot from Abraham, God repeats this promise, emphasising the extent of the land to be possessed by Abraham's descendants (13:14-17).[8] The topic of land reappears in 15:7-21 where the idea is introduced that Abraham's descendants will only take possession of the land of Canaan after a period of four hundred years during which they will be slaves in another country (15:13-14). This revelation of a delay regarding the acquisition of the land probably explains why the promise of land, which is prominent in chapters 12-15, is mentioned less frequently in the remaining chapters of the Abraham narrative (*cf.* 17:8; 22:17). Although later episodes highlight Abraham's acquisition of a well at Beersheba and a tomb at Hebron, these mark only the beginning of the process by which God will fulfil his promise to Abraham regarding land and nationhood.

The third main strand in the Abraham narrative is the idea that Abraham and his 'seed' will be a source of divine blessing, or possibly cursing, for others. This is highlighted in both the initial call of Abraham (12:3) and the concluding oath in 22:16-18. Although various episodes reflect in part the divine blessing or cursing of others (e.g. the visit to Egypt [12:10-20], the abduction of Lot by the eastern kings [14:1-24], the rescue of Lot from Sodom [18:16-19:29], the abduction of Sarah by Abimelech [20:1-18] and the treaty between Abimelech and Abraham [21:22-34]), it is clear that, like the promise of nationhood, the promise of God's blessing upon all the families of the earth will only be fulfilled in the future (*cf.* 22:18).

This brief survey of the themes of seed, land and blessing establishes their presence within Genesis 12-25. To explore further how they are developed within the Abraham narrative we shall examine in more detail the initial call of Abraham in 12:1-3, the covenants in chapters 15 and 17, and the divine oath in 22:16-18. This will enable us to have a clearer picture of how the overall narrative is structured.

---

[8]Although Abraham is mentioned as possessing the land, there is no suggestion that the present inhabitants of the land will be dispossessed during Abraham's lifetime.

2. The divine call of Abraham in 12:1-3

Within the context of the book of Genesis the divine speech in 12:1-3 is very important. It marks the beginning of a new stage in God's relationship with humanity, and sets the agenda for the entire Abraham story, introducing those themes which will be developed in the subsequent narrative.[9] The LORD says to Abraham,

Leave your country, your people and your father's household and go to the land I will show you, so that I may make you into a great nation and bless you and make your name great. Be a blessing, so that I may bless those who bless you, and curse the one who disdains you, and so that all the families of the ground may be blessed through you (12:1-3; my translation).[10]

---

[9]*Cf.* H. Gunkel, *Genesis: übersetzt und erklärt* (6th ed; Göttingen, Vandenhoeck & Ruprecht 1964) 167; J. Muilenburg, 'Abraham and the Nations: Blessing and World History', *Interpretation* 19 (1965) 393; H.W. Wolff, 'The Kerygma of the Yahwist', *Interpretation* 20 (1966) 137; R.E. Clements, *Abraham and David: Genesis XV and its Meaning for Israelite Tradition* (London, SCM 1967) 15; G. von Rad, *Genesis: A Commentary* (revised ed; Philadelphia, Westminster 1972) 165-67; C. Westermann, *Promises to the Fathers: Studies on the Patriarchal Narratives* (Philadelphia, Fortress 1980) 156; *idem*, *Genesis 12-36: A Commentary* (Minneapolis, Augsburg 1985) 146; E.A. Martens, *Plot and Purpose in the Old Testament* (Leicester, IVP 1981) 26, 32; J. Goldingay, 'The Patriarchs in Scripture and History', in A.R. Millard and D.J. Wiseman (eds.) *Essays on the Patriarchal Narratives* 3. However, it should also be noted that the agenda set in 12:1-3 extends far beyond the Abraham narrative itself; *cf.* J. Bright, *Covenant and Promise* (London, SCM 1977) 24; G.J. Wenham, *Genesis 1-15* (Waco, Word 1987) 283; C.H.H. Scobie, 'Israel and the Nations: An Essay in Biblical Theology', *TynB* 43 (1992) 285-6.

[10]Two aspects of the translation adopted here require clarification. Firstly, the imperative form וֶהְיֵה ('be') in 12:2d is maintained. This is also the conclusion reached by Turner, *op. cit.*, 53-55, who reviews briefly other possibilities. Secondly, special consideration has been given to the fact that the imperatives 'go' and 'be a blessing' are both followed by cohortatives. In such contexts the cohortative normally expresses purpose or result; *cf.* S.R. Driver, *A Treatise on the Use of the Tenses in Hebrew* (10th ed; London, Methuen 1916) 64; P. Joüon *Grammaire de l'hébreu biblique* (2nd ed; Rome, Institut Biblique Pontifical 1947) 314-15; A.B. Davidson, *An Introductory Hebrew Grammar* (26th ed., revised by J. Mauchline; Edinburgh, T. & T. Clark 1966) 197; T.O. Lambdin, *Introduction to Biblical Hebrew* (London, Darton, Longman and Todd 1973) 119; *Gesenius' Hebrew Grammar* (ed. E. Kautzsch; Oxford, Clarendon 1910) 320; M. Greenberg, *Introduction to Hebrew* (Englewood Cliffs, Prentice Hall 1965) 183-84. To

Two features of this speech are noteworthy in the present context. First, the fulfilment of the divine promises is conditional upon Abraham's obedience. By commanding him to leave his homeland and be a blessing, God places the onus on Abraham to obey in order that the promises concerning nationhood and the blessing of others may be fulfilled.[11] Secondly, the climax of the speech comes in the statement that 'through you all the families of the earth will find blessing'.[12] The primary motive behind the call of Abraham is God's desire to bring blessing, rather than cursing, upon the families of the earth. The promise that Abraham will become a great nation, implying both numerous seed and land, must be understood as being subservient to God's principal desire to bless all the families of the earth.[13]

Abraham's positive response to God's call is noted immediately, and his arrival in the land of Canaan is rewarded by the assurance that 'to your descendants (seed) I will give this land' (12:7). The subject of land dominates chapter 13 where, following the separation of Abraham and Lot, God confirms that Abraham's many descendants will take possession of Canaan (*cf.* 13:14-17). The promise of land then comes to an important climax in chapter 15 with God covenanting to give Abraham's descendants the land 'from the river of Egypt to the great river, the Euphrates' (15:18).

---

highlight this syntactic arrangement, the imperatives 'go' and 'be a blessing' are followed by 'so that'.

[11]As it stands the divine speech to Abraham falls naturally into two halves, each introduced by an imperative. Whereas the first half focuses on the promise of nationhood, the second centres on the blessing of others. As we shall observe below, this two-fold division is reflected in the two covenants found in chs. 15 and 17.

[12]There has been considerable debate regarding the correct translation of the verb נִבְרְכוּ. Three possibilities exist: it may be translated as (a) a passive ('they will be blessed); (b) a middle ('they will find blessing'); or (c) a reflexive ('they will bless themselves'). Since the earliest versions (LXX, *Targ. Onk.*, Vg; *cf.* Acts 3:25; Gal. 3:8) reflect the passive sense, that is the translation adopted here (*cf.* O.T. Allis, 'The Blessing of Abraham', *PTR* 25 [1927] 263-98). For a fuller discussion, see H.C. Chew, *The Theme of 'Blessing for the Nations' in the Patriarchal Narratives of Genesis*, (unpublished Ph.D. Thesis, University of Sheffield, 1982) 5-10.

[13]The importance of the theme of blessing is underlined by the five-fold repetition of the root ברך ('to bless') in 12:2-3.

3. The unconditional promissory covenant of chapter 15

Chapter 15 falls into two parts which have in common the subject of inheritance. Whereas verses 1-6 are concerned with Abraham's immediate and future heirs, verses 7-21 focus on what shall be inherited. Abraham is reassured by God (a) that he will have a son of his own from whom shall come numerous descendants, and (b) that after several centuries these descendants will take possession of the land of Canaan. Interestingly, the two parts of the chapter parallel each other structurally.[14] They both begin with a divine statement (15:1; 15:7) followed by a question from Abraham (15:2; 15:8). Next we have God's response involving an appropriate sign (15:4-5; 15:9-17),[15] and finally, a concluding comment by the narrator (15:6; 15:18-21).

Two elements in the chapter deserve special attention. First, verse 6 contains the observation that 'Abram believed the LORD, and he reckoned it to him as righteousness.' The rarity in Genesis of such comments by the narrator makes them all the more important when they occur. Here Abraham is viewed as righteous in God's sight because he believes unreservedly that the LORD will fulfil his promise regarding a son and numerous descendants. Thus, Abraham is reckoned righteous on account of his faith in God's promise, rather than due to any deeds performed by him.[16]

---

[14]See Wenham, *op. cit.*, 325-326.

[15]The first sign, the stars in the heavens, conveys the vast number of Abraham's descendants. The second sign is more complex. According to G.J. Wenham, 'The Symbolism of the Animal Rite in Genesis 15: A Response to G.F. Hasel', *JSOT* 22 (1982) 134-137, the sacrificial animals probably represent Abraham's descendants, the birds of prey are the Egyptians and 'the smoking brazier with a blazing torch' indicates God's presence. The sign thus looks forward to the release of the Israelites from slavery in Egypt and the subsequent presence of the LORD in their midst. After the exodus God's presence was indicated by the pillar of cloud by day and the pillar of fire by night (Ex. 13:21; 19:18; 20:18).

[16]R.W.L. Moberly, 'Abraham's Righteousness (Genesis xv 6)' in J.A. Emerton (ed.) *Studies in the Pentateuch*, (VTS 41; Leiden, Brill 1990) 103-130 = *idem, From Eden to Golgotha*, 29-54, helpfully reviews recent studies on 15:6. He concludes, however, that the Genesis writer viewed the righteousness of Abraham in terms of the later Jewish concept of the 'merit of the fathers' (זְכוּת אָבוֹת); that is, Abraham's faith was rewarded by God bestowing divine blessings upon his descendants. While the entire Genesis account clearly associates Abraham's obedience with divine

Secondly, the LORD makes a covenant with Abraham which affirms that his 'seed' will possess the land of Canaan. This marks the climax of the earlier divine promises regarding land and descendants found in 12:7 and 13:14-17. Several features of the covenant are worth noting. (a) It guarantees unconditionally what the LORD has stated to Abraham. Nowhere is it indicated that the fulfilment of the covenant is dependent upon the actions of either Abraham or his descendants; God covenants unreservedly to fulfil his promise that Abraham's descendants will possess the land of Canaan. For this reason it may be designated an unconditional promissory covenant.[17] (b) The structure of the chapter suggests that there is a link between the making of the promissory covenant in verses 7-21 and the comment about Abraham believing God in verse 6. Because of the righteousness imputed to Abraham, God blesses Abraham by guaranteeing that the divine promises regarding descendants and land will be fulfilled. (c) The terms of the covenant mention only descendants and possession of the land; there is no reference to blessing being mediated to others. This omission is significant and is one of the main ways in which the chapter 15 covenant differs from that outlined in chapter 17. The covenant in chapter 15 guarantees only some of the divine promises mentioned in 12:1-3. For the remainder we must look ahead to chapter 17.

4. The eternal covenant of circumcision

The introduction of a second covenant in chapter 17 is somewhat surprising. Why should God make another covenant with Abraham? To answer this, it is necessary to observe that the covenant in chapter 17 differs in a number of important

---

blessing for his descendants (and also for other nations), it is not immediately apparent that this thought is encapsulated in Genesis 15:6. To arrive at this conclusion Moberly relies entirely on the assumption that Genesis 15:6 parallels closely Ps. 106:31. Unfortunately, Moberly's approach is methodologically weak because it rests on a circular argument, a possibility which he himself partially recognises (p. 115, n. 43).

[17]See G.F. Hasel 'The Meaning of the Animal Rite in Genesis 15', *JSOT* 19 (1981) 69. Wenham, *Genesis 1-15*, 333, describes this covenant as a 'promissory oath'.

ways from that given in chapter 15. First, it is a conditional covenant. Whereas the promissory covenant of chapter 15 is unconditional, the establishment or ratification of the covenant of circumcision is dependent upon Abraham's continuing obedience to God. This is highlighted in the introduction to the covenant. After identifying himself as El Shaddai (God Almighty), the LORD says to Abraham, 'Walk before me and be blameless so that I may establish my covenant between me and you and increase you greatly' (17:1-2; my translation). Unfortunately, many English translations fail to appreciate the distinctive syntax of the Hebrew original and so miss the important link which exists between the initial imperatives, 'Walk before me and be blameless', and the fact that these must be obeyed before the covenant will be established.[18] The covenant will be ratified by the LORD only if Abraham walks before God and is blameless.[19] Significantly, for the actual establishment of the covenant we must look to the divine oath which concludes the account of the testing of Abraham in chapter 22.

Secondly, the covenant of circumcision differs from the promissory covenant of chapter 15 in that it is an eternal covenant. Whereas the covenant of chapter 15 is a divine guarantee to Abraham that his descendants will possess the land of Canaan, the covenant of circumcision entails a continuing special relationship between God and Abraham's 'seed'. Although the covenant may embrace those who are not Abraham's natural children - others within his household, including foreigners, may be circumcised (17:12) - God makes it clear that this covenant is intimately linked to the chosen family line; it will be established with the promised 'seed' Isaac and not Ishmael (17:19-21).

Thirdly, whereas the emphasis in chapter 15 is solely upon descendants and land, the covenant in chapter 17 focuses primarily on Abraham as the father of many nations. God states,

[18]T.D. Alexander, 'Genesis 22 and the Covenant of Circumcision', *JSOT* 25 (1983) 19; Turner, *op. cit.*, 76.

[19]According to N.M. Sarna, *Genesis* (Philadelphia, Jewish Publication Society 1989) 123, the expression 'walking before God' 'seems originally to have been a technical term for absolute loyalty to a king'.

As for me, this is my covenant with you: You will be the father of many nations. No longer will you be called Abram; your name will be Abraham, for I have made you a father of many nations. I will make you very fruitful; I will make nations of you, and kings will come from you' (17:4-6).

These words are echoed briefly regarding Sarah: 'I will bless her so that she will be the mother of nations; kings of peoples will come from her' (17:16). The mention of nations coming from Abraham and Sarah presents a problem if this is interpreted as referring only to those nations which are directly descended from both of them; strictly speaking, only the Israelites and Edomites come within this category.[20] However, it is likely that the concept of 'father' is not restricted here to actual physical descendants. Rather Abraham is the 'father' of all who are circumcised. Thus, God instructs Abraham to circumcise not merely his own family members but every male 'including those born in your household or bought with your money from a foreigner - those who are not your offspring (seed). Whether born in your household or bought with your money, they must be circumcised' (17:12-13).[21]

By changing Abram's name to Abraham, God underlines the importance of the fact that he will be the father of many nations. This occurs not because these nations are Abraham's natural descendants but because he is for them the channel of divine blessing. This understanding of 'father' is probably reflected in the unusual comment that Joseph 'was father to Pharaoh' (45:8). Furthermore, when God blesses Jacob in 35:11, echoing an earlier blessing by Isaac upon Jacob (28:3),

---

[20]The Israelites and Edomites are descended from Jacob and Esau respectively. The Ishmaelites and Midianites are probably not to be included here because they are not descended from Sarah. Sarna, *ibid.*, 124, observes that the phrase 'father of many nations' 'has a more universal application in that a large segment of humanity looks upon Abraham as its spiritual father.'

[21]Those who were circumcised enjoyed a special relationship with each other. We witness evidence of this in chapter 34 where the sons of Jacob promise Shechem and his father Hamor that if they are circumcised, 'Then we will give you our daughters and take your daughters for ourselves. We will settle among you and become one people with you' (34:16). Against this background the killing by Simeon and Levi of all those who have just been circumcised is exceptionally repulsive to their father Jacob (34:24-31).

a distinction is drawn between 'a nation' and 'a community of nations' coming from him. The implication would seem to be that whereas many nations will be closely associated with him, only one nation will be directly descended from him.[22]

In the light of the divine promises given in 12:1-3 it is clear that the covenants in chs. 15 and 17 complement each other. Whereas chapter 15 focuses on descendants and land, the emphasis in chapter 17 is upon Abraham as the one who imparts God's blessing to others; in this capacity he is the father of many nations. This understanding of the covenant of circumcision is later reflected in the divine oath of chapter 22 which establishes the covenant with Abraham.

5. The divine oath in 22:16-18

The divine speech in 22:16-18 forms a frame or inclusio with Abraham's call in 12:1-3 and so brings to a conclusion the main section of the Abraham narrative. All that was promised conditionally in 12:1-3 is now guaranteed by divine oath:

> I swear by myself, declares the LORD, that because you have done this and have not withheld your son, your only son, I will surely bless you and make your descendants (seed) as numerous as the stars in the sky and as the sand on the seashore. Your descendants (seed) will take possession of the cities (gate) of their (his) enemies, and through your offspring (seed) all nations on earth will be blessed, because you have obeyed me (22:16-18).

This oath not only signals the end of the main section of the Abraham narrative, but also establishes the covenant of circumcision promised in chapter 17. By demonstrating his obedience to God, even to the point of being willing to sacrifice his only son, Abraham fulfils the conditions laid down in 17:1; he shows beyond doubt his willingness to walk before God and be blameless.

Evidence that chapter 22 should be linked to the covenant of circumcision in chapter 17 may be deduced by considering the account of the covenant with Noah in chapters 6-9.[23] An analysis of this earlier covenant reveals that it has the following structure:

---

[22]The same idea may underlie Noah's comments regarding the relationship between Japheth and Shem: 'May God extend the territory of Japheth; may Japheth live in the tents of Shem,...' (9:27).
[23]T.D. Alexander, 'Genesis 22', 17-22.

(a) The promise of a covenant	6:18
(b) The obligations of the covenant	6:14-16,19-21; 7:1-3
(c) The fulfilment of the obligations	6:22; 7:5
(d) The sacrifice of a burnt-offering	8:20
(e) The establishment of the covenant	9:9-17

Remarkably, the same structure emerges if chapters 17 and 22 are taken together. Chapter 17 records the promise of a covenant with Abraham, accompanied by certain obligations: Abraham is to walk before God and be blameless. While these are more general than those given to Noah, God later tests Abraham's obedience in a specific way; he demands that Abraham should offer up his only son Isaac as a burnt-offering (22:2). In spite of the terrible consequences of killing his heir, Abraham displays his willingness to fulfil even the most testing of divine commands. After God's intervention and the deliverance of Isaac, Abraham offers up as a burnt-offering a ram which has been unexpectedly provided.[24] Finally, God establishes the covenant with Abraham by swearing an oath (22:16-18).

By linking chapters 17 and 22, new light may be shed on a number of issues. First, it is possible to account for the divine testing of Abraham. Through his obedience in chapter 22 Abraham demonstrates his willingness to keep the conditions of the covenant laid out in 17:1. Secondly, the fact that the events of chapter 22 are part of a conditional covenant explains why Abraham is considered in 22:16-18 and 26:2-5 to have merited by his obedience the divine guarantee of the promises concerning seed, land and the blessing of others. Thirdly, the oath in 22:16-18 forms a most fitting conclusion to the main section of the Abraham narrative. Although many scholars view verses 15-18 as a later addition to the original account of the testing of Abraham, the structure of the covenant requires the sacrifice of a burnt-offering before God could confirm with an oath the earlier promises. Verses 15-18 are not only an integral and essential part of chapter 22 but of the entire Abraham narrative.[25]

---

[24]It is noteworthy that in the whole of Genesis it is only here and in 8:20 that the term עֹלָה ('burnt-offering') is used to designate a sacrifice.

[25]R.W.L. Moberly, 'Earliest Commentary on the Akehah', 302-23 = *From Eden to Golgotha*, 55-73, argues that 22:15-18, as a secondary addition to the story of 22:1-14, 19, is 'an interpretation, or commentary, on the preceding

The divine oath in 22:16-18 not only embraces the contents of the earlier promissory covenant regarding many descendants and land but also includes the additional aspect that all nations will be blessed through Abraham's 'seed'. The mention of 'seed' is significant. Unfortunately, the identity of this 'seed' is not easy to determine. While the first mention of 'seed' denotes 'descendants' in the plural, the remaining references are ambiguous; they could refer either to many descendants or to a single descendant. This latter possibility deserves special consideration for three reasons. First, the book of Genesis as a whole devotes considerable attention to tracing a line of 'seed' which, beginning with Adam and ending with Judah, forms the early ancestry of the David dynasty.[26] Unfortunately, the importance of this single line of descendants is generally overlooked by scholars. Secondly, the Jacob and Joseph stories give prominence to the blessing which the patriarchs, as members of this family line, may bestow on others. Although Esau and Jacob are both the 'seed' of Isaac, it is clear that the brother who receives the father's blessing will be favoured more than the other. Thus it is Jacob who experiences God's blessing and is able to mediate it to others. Similarly, Joseph is undoubtedly favoured by his father Jacob who eventually imparts the blessing of the firstborn to Joseph's son Ephraim (48:1-22). Significantly, Genesis focuses on the blessing which others receive through Jacob and Joseph. They alone are presented as the ones who may impart blessing to

---

story' (p. 313, = p. 65). Central to his argument is the observation that whereas the divine promises elsewhere in Genesis 'always constitute a unilateral and unconditional offer on God's part' (p. 318, = p. 69), the promises in 22:15-18 are linked directly to Abraham's obedience. However, as we have suggested above, the fulfilment of the divine promises in 12:1-3 and 17:1-2 is conditional upon Abraham's obedience (*contra* Moberly). Consequently, since the divine oath in 22:15-18 is not fundamentally different from the divine promises found earlier in the Abraham narrative, there is no compelling reason to view them as a later addition. Moberly's basic understanding of 22:15-18 merely adds weight to the proposal presented here that these verses are an important part of the Abraham narrative.

[26]*Cf.* T.D. Alexander, 'From Adam to Judah: the Significance of the Family Tree in Genesis", *EvQ* 61 (1989) 5-19. The concluding chapters of Genesis draw an important distinction between Joseph and Judah. Although Joseph is reckoned as the firstborn, according to Jacob's blessing in 49:8-12, it is from the line of Judah that kings will descend.

others. Although other 'seed' exist, the Genesis narrative associates the power to bless with those who receive the first-born blessing. Thirdly, in announcing the covenant of circumcision to Abraham, God emphasises the unique role of Isaac; it is with Isaac that the covenant will be established and not with Ishmael (17:19, 21). Given the limited interest which Genesis displays in the descendants of Ishmael, it seems logical to conclude that the 'seed' of Abraham mentioned in 22:18 does not include Ishmael and his descendants. For these reasons, the possibility exists that the final reference to 'seed' in 22:18 denotes a single descendant.

Clearly, the covenants in chapters 15 and 17 differ markedly. Whereas chapter 15 records an unconditional promissory covenant which does not necessarily entail an ongoing relationship between God and the descendants of Abraham, the covenant of circumcision is both conditional and eternal. Furthermore, while it is implied in chapter 15 that Abraham's faith, credited as righteousness, is the catalyst for the making of the promissory covenant, the establishment of the covenant of circumcision rests on Abraham's obedience to God. As reflected in 26:2-5, Abraham's obedience is an important factor in the establishment of this eternal covenant.

Viewed as a whole, the Abraham narrative provides an interesting picture of the interplay between divine word and human faith and obedience. Initially, the LORD makes a series of promises, the fulfilment of which is conditional upon Abraham's obedience (12:1-3). As Abraham in faith obeys and journeys to Canaan, God declares that he shall have both land and descendants (12:7; 13:14-17). In time these statements are confirmed in a promissory covenant (15:18-21) which is linked to Abraham being credited as righteous on account of his faith (15:6). The narrative, however, does not conclude here, but goes on to highlight Abraham's continuing faith in and obedience to God, as revealed in the establishment of the eternal covenant of circumcision (17:1-27; 22:1-19), a covenant which focuses on the divine blessing that will come through Abraham and his 'seed' to all nations. Thus, from beginning to end, faith, expressed in obedience, is the hallmark of Abraham's relationship with the LORD.[27]

---

[27]This is not to say that the Genesis account portrays Abraham as perfect. Faults and weaknesses are also revealed. The emphasis is, however, that

Abraham's faith, however, is all the more remarkable when the following factors are also taken into account. Firstly, it is clear that the divine promises concerning nationhood (i.e., seed and land) and the blessing of all the families of the earth will never be fulfilled in Abraham's lifetime; at the very most Abraham will only experience the firstfruits of their fulfilment. Secondly, circumstances exist or develop which mitigate against the fulfilment of these promises. Sarah's barrenness is a major obstacle for much of the narrative, and even when all seems assured with the birth of Isaac, God himself places the future fulfilment of the promises in jeopardy by demanding that Abraham sacrifice Isaac. Yet, in spite of these factors Abraham displays a faith in God which in the book of Genesis is matched only by that of Noah.[28]

III. Abraham in the New Testament Epistles[29]

There is little doubt that within the New Testament Epistles the most noteworthy aspect of Abraham's life is his faith. We see this very clearly in Hebrews 11 which provides a detailed list of those 'ancients' who were commended for having faith. Significantly, approximately one-third of the chapter is devoted to Abraham (Heb. 11:8-19), making him by far the most

---

in spite of the shortcomings he displays, Abraham's faith secures his relationship with God.

[28]Turner (*op. cit.*, 113-14) arrives at a very negative assessment of Abraham's obedience to the divine imperatives given in 12:1-2. He does so on the understanding that the divine promises, whose fulfilment was conditional upon Abraham's obedience, were not fulfilled during his lifetime. Unfortunately, Turner fails to recognise that the fulfilment of the divine promises of necessity must occur in the distant future (e.g. Abraham's descendants will only take possession of the land after four hundred years have elapsed; *cf.* 15:13-16). Abraham's response to his divine call must be judged rather on the basis of those developments which occur in his relationship with God. As the recipient of the promissory covenant in ch. 15 and the divine oath in 22:16-18 he was clearly viewed by God as fulfilling the obligations which had been placed upon him.

[29]It is not possible to review here all that has been written on the relevant NT passages. Our intention is merely to establish in general terms that the NT writers were influenced by a particular understanding of the Genesis account of Abraham.

important person listed.[30] Fittingly, the author of Hebrews highlights Abraham's faith as an example of 'being sure of what we hope for and certain of what we do not see' (Heb. 11:1).

As regards Paul's understanding of Abraham, in Romans 4 and Galatians 3 the emphasis is clearly on the fact that, according to Genesis 15:6, Abraham was justified or made righteous by his faith and not by being circumcised and keeping the law.[31] For Paul, the sequence of events in the Abraham story is all important. Since Abraham is credited as righteous prior to being circumcised, circumcision is not necessary in order for an individual to be reckoned righteous in God's eyes. He writes,

> We have been saying that Abraham's faith was credited to him as righteousness. Under what circumstances was it credited? Was it after he was circumcised, or before? It was not after, but before! And he received the sign of circumcision, a seal of the righteousness that he had by faith while he was still uncircumcised. So then, he is the father of all who believe but have not been circumcised, in order that righteousness might be credited to them. And he is also the father of the circumcised who not only are circumcised but who also walk in the footsteps of the faith that our father Abraham had before he was circumcised (Rom. 4:9-12).

Here Paul stresses that Abraham is the father of those who have faith, whether they are his natural descendants or not. Thus, he concludes that Jews and Gentiles can only be justified by faith.

A similar, but not identical, argument is advanced in Galatians 2:5-3:29 as Paul responds to those who emphasise the necessity of circumcision in order to be children of Abraham and hence recipients of the promises made to him. He writes,

> Consider Abraham: 'He believed God, and it was credited to him as righteousness.' Understand, then, that those who believe are children of Abraham (Gal. 3:6-7).

---

[30]Moses, who is next in importance, receives about half the space given to Abraham (*cf.* Heb. 11:23-28).

[31]Genesis 15:6 is quoted in Romans 4:3 and Galatians 3:6.

By stressing the importance of faith over against circumcision Paul concludes that it is not necessary for an individual to be circumcised in order to be a child of Abraham.[32]

Paul, however, does not conclude his argument in Galatians at this point. He focuses on three further aspects of the Abraham narrative in order to drive home his case that the Gentiles are now the recipients of God's blessing. First, he sees in the justification of the Gentiles the fulfilment of the divine promise to Abraham that all nations would be blessed through him.

The Scripture foresaw that God would justify the Gentiles by faith, and announced the gospel in advance to Abraham: 'All nations will be blessed through you.' So those who have faith are blessed along with Abraham, the man of faith (Gal. 3:9).

By highlighting the importance which the Genesis narrative places on all nations being blessed through Abraham, Paul challenges the view of his opponents that God's blessing was only intended for the actual descendants of Abraham.[33]

Secondly, Paul argues that the divine promises made to Abraham find their ultimate fulfilment in Jesus Christ. To arrive at this conclusion Paul focuses on the concept of 'seed'. He argues that the promises were given to Abraham and to his 'seed', implying one person, and that this 'seed' is Jesus Christ. Some biblical scholars conclude that while Paul adopts here a form of rabbinic exegesis which might have been practised by his Jewish contemporaries, his approach is clearly not in keeping with modern critical methods of exegesis.

---

[32]F.F. Bruce, *The Epistle of Paul to the Galatians: A Commentary on the Greek Text* (Exeter, Paternoster 1982) 155, comments: 'The Galatians were being urged to become children of Abraham by adoption (since they were not his children by natural birth), and this, they were told, involved circumcision, just as it did for proselytes from paganism to Judaism. Paul maintains that, having believed the gospel and received God's gift of righteousness, they are Abraham's children already, and in the only sense that matters in God's sight. Abraham's heritage is the heritage of faith, and those who share this heritage are thereby manifested as sons of Abraham.'

[33]J.D.G. Dunn, *Jesus, Paul and the Law* (London, SPCK 1990) 251, concludes that Paul addresses in Galatians 'a covenantal nomism understood in narrowly nationalistic terms - 'works of the law' as maintaining Jewish identity, 'the curse of the law' as falling on the lawless so as to exclude Gentiles as such from the covenant promise...'

Unfortunately, these scholars have perhaps too readily dismissed Paul's interpretation without examining in detail how the term 'seed' in used in Genesis. The Hebrew word זֶרַע ('seed') is clearly a keyword in Genesis[34] and while it sometimes denotes a group it may also refer to a single individual (e.g. Gn. 4:25; 21:13). This latter possibility is significant, especially when we observe that the entire book of Genesis focuses on a particular line of seed which enjoyed a special relationship with God. This line, beginning with Adam and traced through his third son Seth, includes such famous individuals as Enoch, Methuselah, Noah, Abraham, Isaac and Jacob. Remarkably, Genesis devotes considerable attention, especially in the patriarchal stories, to identifying the seed of this special line. Furthermore, there are clear indications that this line of seed formed the early ancestry of the royal line of David. Apart from the reference to kings being descended from Abraham (17:6), Jacob's blessing of Judah in 49:8-12 indicates that royalty will come from the line of Judah. If Genesis as a whole focuses on a royal line of seed through which God will fulfil his promises to Abraham, then Paul's interpretation of the term זֶרַע as referring to Jesus Christ is in keeping with the common NT understanding of Jesus as the Davidic Messiah.[35] Thus, Paul affirms that it is only through faith in Jesus Christ, the 'seed' of Abraham, that Jews and Gentiles may now receive the blessing given to Abraham and become God's children.

Finally, Paul also argues in Galatians that the divine covenant made with Abraham takes precedence over the law given several centuries later at Mt. Sinai. Whereas his opponents were advocating that believers must keep the law in order to be righteous, Paul responds by noting that the law, given later to fulfil a temporary role until Christ came, could

---

[34]זֶרַע occurs 59 times in Genesis and 170 times in the rest of the OT. This latter statistic excludes the one occurrence of the Aramaic word זְרַע in Daniel 2:43. In Genesis זֶרַע comes in 1:11(x2), 12(x2), 29(x2); 3:15(x2); 4:25; 7:3; 8:22; 9:9; 12:7; 13:15, 16(x2); 15:3, 5, 13, 18; 16:10; 17:7(x2), 8, 9, 10, 12, 19; 19:32, 34; 21:12, 13; 22:17(x2), 18; 24:7, 60; 26:3, 4(x3); 28:4, 13, 14(x2); 32:12; 35:12; 38:8, 9(x2); 46:6, 7; 47:19, 23, 24; 48:4, 11, 19.

[35]The link between the 'seed' of Abraham and the 'seed' of David is explored more fully by M. Wilcox, 'The Promise of the 'Seed' in the New Testament and the Targumim', *JSNT* 5 (1979) 2-20. See also T.E. McComiskey, *The Covenants of Promise: A Theology of the Old Testament Covenants* (Grand Rapids, Baker Book House 1985) 19-35.

never make anyone righteous since it merely indicated the righteousness required by God, not the means of achieving such righteousness. As such it underlined the necessity of becoming righteous through faith.

Since Paul uses the Abraham narrative in four distinctive ways in Galatians to challenge the view of his opponents that Gentile believers must be circumcised and obey the law of Moses in order to know God's salvation, it is apparent that his understanding of the Gospel was heavily influenced by his reading of Genesis 12-25.[36]

Abraham's faith is also discussed in James 2:20-24. Here, however, the context differs from that found in Romans and Galatians. Whereas Paul seeks to demonstrate the priority of faith over circumcision, James is concerned to clarify the nature of saving faith: 'What good is it, my brothers, if a man claims to have faith but has no deeds? Can such faith save him' (Jas. 2:14)? At the heart of James's discussion is the desire to show that true faith in God will exhibit itself in righteous actions. Thus, he focuses on Abraham and in particular the offering of Isaac on the altar.

> Was not our ancestor Abraham considered righteous for what he did when he offered his son Isaac on the altar? You see that his faith and his actions were working together, and his faith was made complete by what he did. And the scripture was fulfilled that says, 'Abraham believed God, and it was credited to him as righteousness', and he was called God's friend. You see that a person is justified by what he does and not by faith alone (Jas. 2:21-24).

Here James reveals how faith in and obedience to God cannot be separated. While James accepts that Abraham was justified by faith, as stated in Genesis 15:6, he views the later actions of Abraham as visible expressions of this inner faith. Undoubtedly, he focuses on Genesis 22 because of the way in which Abraham is rewarded for his willingness to sacrifice Isaac. For James there can be no separation of faith and deeds. Thus, he views Abraham's actions in chapter 22 as the fulfilment or 'culmination' of what was stated in Genesis 15:6.

---

[36]For a much fuller treatment of the Galatian material, see G.W. Hansen, *Abraham in Galatians: Epistolary and Rhetorical Contexts*, (JSNTS 29; Sheffield, Sheffield Academic Press 1989).

Although James writes, 'that a person is justified by what he does and not by faith alone' (Jas. 2:24), it is clear from the context that this does not actually contradict what Paul has to say in Romans and Galatians. Both men were addressing different situations and therefore highlighted different aspects of Abraham's faith. On the one hand, Paul concentrated on Genesis 15:6 because he was responding either directly or indirectly to those who wished to emphasise the necessity of circumcision for salvation. On the other hand, James was concerned to show that Abraham's faith, by which he was justified, produced righteous actions. Thus, he writes, 'faith without deeds is dead' (Jas. 2:26). Undoubtedly, Paul and James would have agreed wholeheartedly with what the other had to say, given the different problems that confronted them.[37]

The final New Testament passage to be considered briefly is Hebrews 6:13-18. It is included here not because it focuses on Abraham's faith, but because it draws a distinction between the promise which God made to Abraham and the oath.

> Because God wanted to make the unchanging nature of his purpose very clear to the heirs of what was promised, he confirmed it with an oath. God did this so that, by two unchangeable things in which it is impossible for God to lie, we who have fled to take hold of the hope offered to us may be greatly encouraged (Heb. 6:17-18).

The oath mentioned here clearly refers to Genesis 22:16-18. Although it is not possible to be completely certain, the promise may refer to the covenant in Genesis 15. If this is so, then the author of Hebrews brings together the two covenants mentioned in the Abraham narrative in order to highlight how they guaranteed beyond any doubt the fulfilment of the divine promises made to Abraham.

---

[37]For a fuller discussion of James 2:20-24 which complements the present approach see D.J. Moo, *The Letter of James* (Leicester, IVP 1985) 107-116. Significantly, Moo argues that James's use of δικαιόω in vv. 21 and 24 differs from that of Paul. Whereas Paul views justification as a 'sovereign, judicial act in which God apart from any human "work", declares the sinner to be innocent before him (Rom. 4:5)' (p. 108), James applies 'the word to God's ultimate declaration of a person's righteousness' (p. 109); that is, 'James uses "justify" where Paul speaks of the judgement' (p. 109).

Conclusion

Although parts of the preceding discussion have of necessity been brief, it is apparent that all the references to Abraham in the NT epistles reflect a common, and distinctively Christian, interpretation of the Genesis narrative. The main elements of this interpretation are as follows: (i) Abraham's faith in and obedience to God is exemplary; his inner faith demonstrated itself in on-going obedience to God. (ii) Abraham was reckoned righteous by God on account of his faith prior to being circumcised. (iii) All who exhibit similar faith are Abraham's children and share in the divine promises made to Abraham. (iv) The divine promises to Abraham anticipate the coming of a royal descendant who will impart God's blessing to all the families and nations of the earth. Although the Genesis narrative does not identify this future king, the NT writers share the belief that he is Jesus Christ, the son of David. Clearly, these basic ideas influenced significantly the soteriology of the early church and its view of the nature of Jesus Christ's mission to the world. Moreover, on the basis of our own study of the OT material in the first part of this essay, it is apparent that the NT understanding of the Abraham narrative is derived from a careful exegesis of the Genesis text.

2

'YOU ARE ABRAHAM'S OFFSPRING, MY FRIEND'

Abraham in Isaiah 41

John Goldingay

Summary

The figure of Abraham has an important place in Isaiah 41. In vv. 1-7 the unnamed conqueror from the east stands for him as well as for the Persian king Cyrus, as the prophecy utilises parallels between the two figures in inviting the audience to reflect on the nature of Yahweh's activity in its day. In vv. 8-16 he is explicitly the ancestor of Israel, which inherits the relationship of friendship which he enjoyed with Yahweh. In vv. 21-29 the parallels between Abraham and Cyrus facilitate reflection on the reality and depth of Yahweh's speaking about historical events in retrospect and prospect.

Introduction

Compared with his prominence in the New Testament, in the Old Testament the appearances of Abraham are rather few, outside Genesis. One of them is in Isaiah 41, where a key point involves an explicit allusion to Abraham; but he is walking in the shadows from the beginning of the chapter. Israel's great account of its life with Yahweh in Genesis to Kings, whatever the process of its earlier development, reached final form in the exile, and that in itself evidences the way people in the exile were reflecting on the story of Abraham after many of them returned to the Babylonia from which Yahweh had taken him. Whether given through Isaiah of Jerusalem in the 8th century or through another Isaiah who himself lived in the 6th, Isaiah 41 is a message for such exiles, designed to encourage such reflection.

I. Abraham and Cyrus and the pattern of Yahweh's activity (vv. 1-4)

Isaiah 41 opens with a challenge, an invitation to foreign shores and peoples to draw near both to listen and to speak in court. The court scene would be familiar enough from everyday life in a middle eastern community. The open area inside the main gate of a city was a communal meeting place where (among other activities) legal matters could be discussed under the supervision of senior members of the community. When this 'court' convened, each party would ensure the presence of its 'witnesses' to support its case. The elders then had the power to give judgement over questions raised, though they might refer them to a 'judge' (e.g. the king or a priest) in difficult cases.

Prophets had long used this court scene as a theological metaphor. The Book of Isaiah itself begins with Yahweh appearing as the plaintiff in court, summoning heaven and earth as witnesses in a case against Israel (1:2-9), and it goes on to summon the people to join in arguing out the rights and wrongs of demands placed upon it by Yahweh as judge (1:18-20; *cf.* also 3:13-15; 66:16 at the book's close). Abraham, too, was quite familiar with the theological metaphor and with the kind of theological argument that the prophet there initiates (see Gn. 18:17-33).

In general, in such court scenes in Isaiah and elsewhere, Israel plays the part of the accused; if other nations appear, it is as witnesses, or as Yahweh's means of executing judgement at the conclusion of a case. The opening of a court scene is therefore calculated to cause some disquiet among Israelite hearers. Here their anxiety is complicated by the discovery that in contrast the nations are under interrogation. The prominence of the divine first person in this chapter, greater than has been the case since chapter 1, is another link with judicial language. The book began with Yahweh speaking in the first person to bring a case against Israel, so that the reappearance of the first person language is further reason for disquiet among the hearers. It will emerge that it is designed - in contrast to chapter 1 - actually to encourage Israel. Whether it will do so depends in part on whether Israel is any more prepared than the other peoples to accept the answer to its question.

Isaiah 40 has already hinted that Israel is tempted to the view that the gods worshipped by the Babylonians have real power in events. This is the other side of the community's demoralised disillusion with their faith that Yahweh had real power in the world. Two sets of people say their god is God: the question is who (if either) is right.

The passage needs to be read at two levels. At one level Isaiah 41:1-7 is a discussion between Yahweh and the nations regarding the powers active in certain historical events. The nations are challenged to offer some theological account of their meaning - or rather to accept the plaintiff's case that only one theological account is possible. The questioning invites the nations to insight but drives them deeper into self-deceit; as is the case with Israel itself, the word of God renders those who could not see even more blind (*cf.* 6:9-10).

Although the nations are thus the overt participants in this drama, at another level exiled Israel is its real audience. The question is how Israel reacts to political events. Verses 8-16 will invite Israel into a trust which contrasts with the other peoples' fear, but that depends on Israel's being willing to accept the prophet's understanding of current events. On the surface there would seem no problem here; in fact later sections will make explicit what is here implicit, that there is a deep problem. Prophet and people look at political events in quite different ways. The prophet seeks to utilise the Abraham story from their distant past as a means of changing their attitude to their urgent present.

The court scene involves or refers to four characters, all to one degree or another of veiled identity. The overt audience is named as 'foreign shores' and 'peoples' (v. 1); the reference of these terms is not explicit, and indeed we miss the point if we seek to give the terms specific narrow geographical reference. The first-person speaker is unidentified until verse 4, though the reference of the 'I' to Yahweh would be uncontroversial. In verse 2 this 'I' asks questions about a 'who' and a 'he': 'Who aroused from the east one whom right calls to its heel, gives up nations before him and makes him subjugate kings?' The 'who' is by definition unidentified until Yahweh provides the identification in verse 4 - though again the implied audience would know the right answer to the question. The 'he' remains unidentified; ancient and modern interpreters usually assume his identity is also obvious, but they disagree over who he is. The speaker's words contain an overt question to which the 'correct' answer is clear (in other words, it is practically a rhetorical question) and a covert one which is more complicated, concerning not the subject but the object of the sentence. It is here that Abraham walks in the shadows, though he is not alone. The Persian king Cyrus, about to conquer Babylon, is also there.

If I may let my readers into the secret that the prophet kept to himself at this point, Isaiah of Babylon sees certain parallels between the story of Cyrus and that of Abraham (and Israel as a whole), parallels in their origins, their actions, and their place in Yahweh's purpose. The rise of Cyrus is the most urgent topic for theological reflection in the exilic community, for Israelites as well as for Babylonians. How is God involved with it? The prophet takes the same scandalously positive stance in relation to this question as Jeremiah once took in relation to Nebuchadnezzar, and knows the community will take some convincing about this stance.

Now let me invite my readers to push the last paragraph to the edge of their minds and puzzle over the prophet's question along with the exiles. What is Isaiah talking about? The east is the direction (among others) from which God promises to bring back exiles (43:5) and from which a 'bird of prey' (presumably Cyrus) was called (46:11). The verb arise/arouse (עור in various stems) here denotes God's impelling an agent into activity (*cf.* 41:25; 45:13). A significant verb in Isaiah, it first appears in a chapter with many links with Isaiah 41, within a promise that Yahweh will 'arouse' scourges for Israel's Assyrian oppressors (10:26); Babylon was the promise's chief historical fulfilment. It is re-used in a passage capable of addressing the later situation of Babylonian domination in the promise in 13:17, 'I am arousing the Medes against them (the Babylonians)' (*cf.* Je. 51:11): 41:2 implies the assumption that the person referred to is Yahweh's means of fulfilling that commitment. One century's agent of Yahweh is another century's victim. In 45:13 the context makes clear that the object of the verb is the ruler of the Persian Empire, the part-Median Cyrus, who is indeed about to take control of Babylon. The verb is also significant in Jeremiah, and more equivocally so, though the historical relationship of some of these passages to Isaiah 40-55 is unclear. In Jeremiah 6:22 (Niphal) the verb refers to the unnamed northern invader who is about to 'arise' and attack Jerusalem, a warning of which Babylon was the historical fulfilment (*cf.* Ezk. 23:22). In Jeremiah 50:9 the image is turned against Babylon, against whom Yahweh is 'arousing' an unnamed northern invader (*cf.* 50:41; 51:1); in 25:32 the point is made with more general reference to the nations. In Jeremiah 51:11 it becomes explicit that Babylon's destroyer can be identified as the Medes. It implies that when aroused the person in question has huge force and power, like a weapon (2 Sa. 23:18) or a warrior (Joel 4:9 [3:9]), or like human love (e.g. Song 2:7) or divine wrath (Ps. 78:38), or like Yahweh in person (Ps. 80:3 [2]).

'Right' (צֶדֶק) and associated words are key expressions in Isaiah, especially in chapters 40-66. Applied to human beings, it appears in the company of words for fairness, faithfulness, honesty, commitment, and judgement, and is set in contrast to wickedness, perversity, and murder. It can also refer to the 'rights' of people such as Israel and the vindication of these in the form of their deliverance or salvation through the victory of those who strive in the case of the right. 'Right' is linked with salvation, renewal, healing, and glory; it suggests God doing the right thing in exercising sovereignty in the world (41:2, 10; 42:6; 45:8, 13; 51:5; 58:8; 62:1, 2). The question then asks who aroused the person through whom the divine order in the world or purpose for the world (no doubt as this especially involved Israel) is being put into effect. Abraham at least stands in the shadows.

Within verses 2-3, the subject changes, from the 'who' to the 'he' himself: 'His sword makes them like dust, his bow like driven chaff. As he pursues them, he travels in peace a path that with his feet he does not walk'. So he is one who 'pursues': the verb occurs initially in Scripture to refer to Abraham's victorious pursuit of the kings of Shinar, Ellasar, Elam and Goiim (Gn. 14:14, 15), but then (for instance) to denote the pursuit or persecution of Jerusalem by attackers such as the Babylonians (La. 1:3, 6; 4:19; 5:5; *cf.* also 2 Ki. 25:5; and the warnings of Dt. 28:22, 45; Is. 30:16; contrast the promises of Lv. 26:7, 8). When Abraham completes his victorious pursuit he meets the king of Salem - Shalem, to be more accurate (Gn. 14:18); Scripture's first actual reference to שָׁלוֹם comes shortly after in a promise to Abraham (15:15). Here in verse 3 the conqueror travels in שָׁלוֹם, 'peace', in the sense that he meets no effective resistance. He moves so fast that his feet scarcely touch the ground. He is practically flying, as we put it: compare Cyrus as a bird of prey (from the east) in 46:13 and Abraham's lightning pursuit of the four kings in Genesis 14:14-16.

We have noted that verses 2-3 draw attention to one question, 'who aroused. . .', and thereby draw attention away from another question: who is aroused? The Targum simply assumes it is Abraham. As we have seen, he was indeed aroused from the east, was a spectacularly victorious pursuer of foreign kings (see Gn. 14), was greeted in the name of *Shalem* by one whose own name Melchizedek declared that 'Right is my king', and was himself called to the service of right (see Gn. 15:6, but especially 18:19 and the verses that follow in which Abraham serves the cause of people in the right). Admittedly military victory is not the characteristic feature of the Abraham story, and some of this description better fits Israel as Abraham's progeny. In verses 9-16 it is Israel, Abraham's offspring, which is Yahweh's chosen servant, taken from earth's furthest bounds, called, supported by the right, and victorious over enemies. Its destiny is guaranteed by its being the offspring of this figure from the east. Although Abraham's calling has sometimes seemed irrelevant to the audience overtly summoned in verse 1,[1] theologically it is not at all so to the Israelite audience whom the prophecy actually addresses.

In contrast Theodorus of Heraclea in the 4th century and later the medieval rabbinic commentator Ibn Ezra suggested that the person was the Persian king Cyrus, and modern exegetes with their historical instinct usually assume this identification; the Good News Bible adds Cyrus' name here as the Targum once added Abraham's. We have noted the significance of passages such as 13:17-19; 44:28-45:13; 46:11 with their vision of Median conquest of Babylon and of Cyrus as a bird of prey from the east aroused in the service of the right and as a notable victor over nations and kings. To the east of Babylon Cyrus was crowned King of Persia in 558, and in the 540s won a series of spectacular victories over Persia's Median overlords north of Babylon (*cf.* 41:25) and then over Croesus of Lydia in Turkey, Babylon's most powerful ally (see the description in Herodotus 1.78-79).

The diversity of these opinions reflects an ambiguity in the passage, which requires its hearers to hold together at least Abraham, Israel, and Cyrus. To suggest that its theological presupposition is a typological relationship between Abraham and Cyrus is too precise;[2] as the example of the new exodus illustrates, typology properly involves the antitype being both a figurative and an enhanced version of the type, and neither of these applies to Cyrus in relationship to Abraham. All the passage requires is a limited parallel between the two in the context of Yahweh's purpose, which enables the passage to tease its hearers. It invites them to perceive parallels in the stories of Abraham, of Israel, and of Cyrus, and thus to be open to the possibility of seeing Yahweh as involved in a parallel way in all three. It is this desire to play on the parallels that determines the aspects of their stories to which it appeals (notably the military exploits of Abraham). Its failure overtly to identify any of these referents leaves its hearers free to decline this invitation without at this point turning their backs on the prophetic message as a whole. For the notion of seeing Cyrus in this way may seem scandalous, as chapter 45 will imply. The book's earlier assertions regarding such imperial powers (see

---

[1]See the comments of C.R. North, *The Second Isaiah* (2nd ed; London/New York, OUP 1967) on the passage.

[2]G.H. Jones, 'Abraham and Cyrus', *VT* 22(1972) 304-19.

10:5) might seem a preparation for this view of Cyrus, but perhaps the Israelite exiles have learned only too well the lesson urged by Jeremiah 29 which encouraged them to settle down in Babylon and identify its destiny with their own.

So (the plaintiff goes on to ask) 'Who acted effectively, calling the generations from the very first?' (v.4). The first half-line restates the question raised by verses 2-3; the subordinate participial phrase then significantly qualifies or clarifies its nature. The one who has acted so effectively is the one who has always been involved thus in events. If the hearers have understood verses 2-3 to refer to Abraham or to Israel in its early years, verse 4 restates the question about them; if they have understood verses 2-3 to refer to Cyrus, verse 4 sets Cyrus in the context of a much broader canvas of events and declares that the one behind the single event is also artist of that wider canvas. Verse 4a as a whole constitutes the beginning of the answer to the question in verses 2-3.

The summoning of the generations is a generalised form of that summoning which receives specific expression in Yahweh's summons to the victor in verse 2, which it underlies. The phrase 'the very first' refers to the beginnings of Yahweh's activity with Israel, here presumably the call of Abraham rather than the exodus. Isaiah is concerned with history from end to end as well as with geography from end to end. The prophecies in chapters 40-55 continue the affirmation which runs through the earlier part of the book: the triumphs of Assyria (22:11; 31:2) and its downfall (14:24-27; 37:26) illustrate how individual political events on a world canvas reflect purposes which Yahweh has formulated and which confute both gentile and Israelite wisdom (29:14; and see 28:23-29). Babylon's triumph and fall manifest the same pattern.

At last comes the plaintiff's own explicit answer to the questions pressed on foreign shores and peoples: 'I Yahweh am the first and I myself am with the last' (v.4). The expression 'I Yahweh' is formally a self-introduction asserting the mighty active presence of Yahweh; it thus promises good news to those who are looking for Yahweh but threatens discomfort to Yahweh's opponents. The phrase often occurs in free-standing form meaning 'I am Yahweh', not least at the point when Yahweh appears to Moses in Exodus 6, 'a statement laden with final significance and basically self-contained' in which 'we hear the ultimate statement Yahweh can make about himself'.[3] The phrase rendered 'I myself [am]' (אֲנִי־הוּא) which closes the bicolon in a balancing way, is literally 'I he'. It suggests that Yahweh always is, but it does so meaning that Yahweh is always there, is always present, and is always active. As the intervening phrase 'the first and with the last' hints, such a statement about how God always is presupposes that this being of God's is always in relationship and activity, consistent but dynamic and changing.

Within the chiasm formed by אֲנִי יהוה and אֲנִי־הוּא appears the affirmation that this God is 'the first and with the last'. The phrase explicitly refers not merely to Yahweh's person but to Yahweh's relationship with the people, as their ancient and recent history has unfolded. If the declaration 'I am Yahweh' recalls Yahweh's self-introduction at Sinai, 'calling the generations from the very first' suggests especially ancestors such as Abraham.

Further, it is striking that Isaiah 40-55 never amplifies Yahweh's self-introduction with an explicit reference to the exodus.[4] This is perhaps a sign of the prophet's desire to turn Israel away from the 'former things' to the 'new things'. Isaiah of Babylon wants the community to take the past seriously but also to see that past as the beginning and the paradigm for the present. Thus here in addition to being the first, Yahweh is '*with* the last (plural)'. Yahweh is not merely a God who acted at the first (for instance, in calling Abraham and forming Israel) but one who is now active in events involving the generation of the speaker and hearer's day (for instance, in calling Cyrus and restoring Israel).

II. Abraham and Israel, and the pattern of Yahweh's commitment (vv. 8-16)

The foreign shores might have responded to the challenge of verses 1-4 by opening their eyes to the facts, but they prefer to keep them tight shut and hold onto their fear of the imminent political future (see vv. 5-7). The prophecy's Israelite audience might be subject to the same temptation. The 'but' which opens

---

[3]W. Zimmerli, *I am Yahweh* (ET of 1933 German original; Atlanta, Eisenbrauns 1982) 19-20.

[4]Zimmerli, *I am Yahweh*, 21.

verse 8 draws attention to the very different position Israel occupies: 'But you as Israel are my servant...'. The encouragement of Israel contrasts with the fear of the foreign shores. It has its basis in an expansive description of Israel's status in verses 8-9, which has as one high point the declaration 'as Abraham's offspring you are my friend'.

The Hebrew consists in a collection of noun clauses and phrases, and there are various ways of construing them. LXX takes verses 8-9 as a series of vocative phrases which accumulate until a verb appears in verse 10 (*cf.* RSV). But an audience would be so familiar with noun clauses of the form וְאַתָּה יִשְׂרָאֵל עַבְדִּי that it would more likely hear the words as meaning 'You are Israel, my servant...' or 'You, Israel, are my servant...' (AV). 'Servant' (עֶבֶד) is a term of wide-ranging background. In secular usage it can denote slaves of a master, subjects or civil servants of a king, vassals of an emperor, soldiers undertaking military service, or ordinary people expressing voluntary or informal or polite subordination (as when Jacob addresses Esau as his servant; e.g. Gn. 33:5). The term clearly indicates an obligation to accept the authority of the superior party and to serve the latter's interests, and it can suggest servitude rather than merely the subordination of a subject. Paradoxically it can also contain a hint of power and/or privilege: the servant of a king may be an important person by virtue of that virtue of that position, and a certain security can come to a weak person through 'belonging' to a stronger one. The former has a claim on the latter. This aspect of servanthood is important in the present context.

In Isaiah Yahweh uses the term 'my servant' first as a description of the prophet himself (20:3), then of Eliakim to whom Yahweh intends to transfer Shebna's authority (22:20), then of David (37:35). That status is elsewhere reaffirmed for David in the context of exile (Je. 33:21, 22, 26; Ezk. 34:23, 24; 37:24, 25), and subsequently for the Davidic prince Zerubbabel (Hg. 2:23; and *cf.* Zc. 3:8). It is here declared to belong to Israel as a whole (*cf.* 22:1, 2, 21; 45:4; 48:20; 49:3). The motif is democratised.

A feature of Isaiah 40-55 is a reworking of motifs from the story of Israel's exodus from Egypt, and theologically the phenomenon of democratisation may be allied with this. An important aspect of exodus faith was an understanding of Israel 'as a liberated community of egalitarianism'; this understanding is compromised by the monarchy but reaffirmed in Isaiah 40-55.[5] It is the whole community which has the privileged position of being servant of Yahweh (though the community can turn that conviction into an ideological one as easily as can the individual - as chapter 42 will demonstrate). Further, a feature of that exodus faith is that 'Israel is founded precisely by those who reject and are rejected by the nonslippage of the world of the Egyptian (and Canaanite) totalitarianism. Israel, in contrast to those political forms, is a social movement of the failures and rejects who de-legitimate both the rationality of the empire and the coherence of the gods who legitimate those structures'.[6] 'Nonslippage' denotes allowance for the possibility of graciousness, forgiveness, and a move towards newness which may be initiated 'from below' and out of pain (e.g. the pain of Egypt) in a way which questions the established order. End-of-exile faith has parallel features to exodus faith. Once again the people is a community of failures and rejects, now promised a possibility of grace and newness out of the pain of Babylon. In verses 1-7 (and behind that in 40:12-26) once again its prophecy has de-legitimated the rationality of the empire and the coherence of its gods (neither of which can handle the arrival of the conqueror). At the moment the community itself, however, remains in 'Egypt' and its prophets struggle like Moses for its conscientisation.

The first person in the Old Testament to be described as 'my servant' is Abraham, and that in a 'fear not' oracle like the present passage (Gn. 26:24; *cf.* also Gn. 15:2; Ps. 105:6, 42). The term is also applied to the individual Jacob (Ezk. 28:25; 37:25), to Moses (e.g. Nu. 12:7, 8; Jos. 1:2, 7), Job (e.g. Jb. 42:7, 8), Nebuchadnezzar (e.g. Je. 25:9; 27:6), and many others. Outside Isaiah 20:3 it is uncommon with regard to individual prophets. In lament Psalms 'Your servant' is a common self-designation designed to convey humility and subservience.[7] Isaianic usage

[5]As another aspect of exodus faith was compromised by the building of the temple and the development of Israel's worship system with its priesthood, but is implicitly reaffirmed in some passages in Isaiah 56-66 such as 61:6; 66:1.

[6]Brueggemann, 'A shape for Old Testament Theology, I', *CBQ* 47 (1985) 28-46 [44] summarising the work of Gottwald.

[7]A. Schoors, *I am God Your Saviour* (Leiden, Brill 1973) 49.

presupposes that there is no tension between being a servant and a friend (see v. 8b), even the former being a position of honour and privilege (contrast John 15:15).

The prophet adds, 'as Jacob, you are the one I chose'. The 'fixed term' parallelism of Jacob-Israel from 40:27 reappears, but the term which is less familiar (when the reference is corporate) here comes in the second colon and already advertises that this three-colon line is an unusual one. As in 40:27, these are terms with which Yahweh addresses the people, terms with resonances from Israel's tradition which remind the audience of its special relationship with Yahweh going back into Genesis. In 40:27 there was an edge to their use as they introduced an offended response to Jacob-Israel's querying of Yahweh's involvement with its destiny. In 41:8 as the terms are taken up again their use is almost unequivocally affirming in the reminder it gives of the people's long-standing relationship with Yahweh. The fact that they are Jacob-Israel, which they might be tempted to think now counts for nothing, remains a powerful basis for Yahweh's commitment to them.[8] The use of the terms to address a small group of exiles from southern Judah is noteworthy.

In verses 8-9 the movement of choice is from God to humanity. Smart notes that such divine choice does not exclude the place of a responsive human choice (*cf.* Jos. 24:22) and also that the sin of Jacob is shown up the more sharply by the wonder of the gracious divine choice; this draws attention to the fact that the text here makes no allusion to such human choice or human failure.[9]

The notion of choice is implicit in the Abraham story: Yahweh had chosen Israel's ancestors, and in them their descendants. Yet this is not the terminology of Genesis itself and it is thus unlikely that Isaiah 40-55 derives its theology of divine choice from there. The theological language of choice is most prominent in Deuteronomy, where it applies in particular to the place where Yahweh wills to be worshipped (see chapters 12-18). Elsewhere it is commonly applied specifically to Jerusalem/Zion, but also (e.g.) to Levi, to Israel, and also to

---

[8]W.A.M. Beuken, 'The First Servant Song and its Context', *VT* 22 (1972) 1-30 [16].

[9]J.D. Smart, *History and Theology in Second Isaiah* (Philadelphia, Fortress 1965) on the passage.

David (e.g. 2 Sa. 6:21; 1 Ki. 8:16), specifically to David as God's servant (1 Ki. 11:34; Ps. 78:70). This seems particularly significant in the light of the description of Israel as God's servant here, which pointed to the theme of the democratisation of God's commitment to David. Democratisation appears also in the reference to choice. It is not merely the king who is Yahweh's chosen, but the (kingless) people. Whether the image of Yahweh's choice was applied first to people or king, in pre-exilic Judah the temptation would be for the latter to overlay the former; that tendency is here firmly put in reverse. 'After the cessation of the monarchy, the Prophet's message can revert to the truth that God elects Israel when he elects his Messiah'.[10] If the pre-exilic prophets had to avoid dangerous talk about the people being chosen, Isaiah of Babylon is now prepared to follow Deuteronomy and risk it.[11]

The people are not only Israel and Yahweh's servant, Jacob and Yahweh's chosen. In addition, Isaiah of Babylon declares, 'You are Abraham's offspring, my friend'. This further address with its first naming of Abraham (*cf.* 51:1-2) heightens the stress on gracious choice, in keeping with the assumption which is implicit if not explicit in Genesis and is taken up from there in Romans 4. In the New Testament the significance of being Abraham's offspring also reappears in Hebrews 2:16, where it accounts in part for Jesus' taking human nature in the implementing of a purpose of mercy and faithfulness. We have noted that Abraham and Jacob-Israel are among the figures the hearers will think about when they hear verse 2; as the offspring of Abraham (Yahweh's original servant - see above) the Jacob-Israel of the present is the heir to or embodiment of what was described there. The reference to Jacob-Israel is quite expected; these are the terms the people would use of themselves. The reference to Abraham in this unexpected third colon of verse 9 may bring the hearers up short in giving them a new, less familiar way of looking at themselves. They are Abraham's offspring, and therefore the heirs of promises that go behind the existence of Jacob-Israel (let alone that of David) and provide new foundations for their self-understanding.

---

[10]U.E. Simon, *A Theology of Salvation: a Commentary on Isaiah 40-55* (London, SPCK 1953) on the passage.

[11]K. Koch, 'Zur Geschichte der Erwählungsvorstellung in Israel', *ZAW* 67 (1955) 205-26.

The colon literally reads 'the offspring of Abraham my friend' and is ambiguous over whether 'friend' applies to the offspring or to Abraham. Versions and allusions usually assume it refers to the nearer noun (*cf.* 2 Ch. 20:7; Jas. 2:23). Rhetorically, however, it makes best sense to take each of the cola in verse 8 as coming to a climax with a novel affirmation regarding the people themselves, as servant, chosen, and now as friend.[12] By its very existence as a third colon verse 8b has special emphasis. This is augmented by its addition of Abraham to the more familiar pairing of Israel and Jacob; it is brought to a climax by the movement from 'servant' to 'chosen' to 'friend'.[13] Perhaps, after all, verse 8 assumes in advance of John 15 that it is better to be a friend than a servant.

A further question is raised by the form of the word 'friend', a noun formed from the active participle of the verb 'love' and thus implying 'the one who loves me'.[14] Deuteronomic usage (e.g. 4:37; 7:13) and the word's application to Cyrus in 48:14 draw attention to the fact that 'love' and 'friendship' are not matters of emotion so much as commitment.

The basis for describing Abraham as Yahweh's friend presumably lies in the special relationship Yahweh initiated with him, expressed classically as a 'covenant' in Genesis 17:7-10, which also significantly promises that this special relationship will extend to Abraham's 'offspring' (זֶרַע, as here). In other words 'as Abraham's offspring you are my friend' means 'I promised a special relationship to Abraham's descendants as well as to Abraham himself, and you are the beneficiaries of that promise'. In this moment of political peril you are not on your own.

---

[12]*cf.* R.L. Merendino, *Der Erste und der Letzte* (Leiden, Brill 1981) on the passage.

[13]Y. Gitay, *Prophecy and Persuasion: a Study of Isaiah 40-48* (FThL 14; Bonn, Linguistica Biblica 1981) on the passage.

[14]LXX and Aquila render 'whom I loved' and 'my beloved', making better sense in the light of the prophecies' usual emphasis and the particular stress of verses 8-9. They might imply a different pointing of the Hebrew (so M. Lambert, *Revue des études juives* 70 [1920] 209-15 [211]), but more likely the difficulty results from Hebrew's not having any word other than the morphologically one-sided אֹהֵב to signify reciprocal 'friendship', for which אֹהֵב is used in e.g. Jeremiah 20:6; Esther 5:10 (the Vulgate and Symmachus assume this meaning here).

As Israel/Jacob/Abraham's offspring 'you are one I took hold of from earth's furthest bounds and called from its corners, and said to you "You are my servant", I chose you and did not spurn you' (v.9). Verses 8-9 are chiastic in content, so that verse 9a relates to verse 8b and draws attention to one of the implications of the audience's being an Abrahamic people. It shares Abraham's position as a people taken from far away; the audience is spoken of as Israel in its land, for this is its theological position, whether or not it is geographically there now. The effect of describing the audience in the terms of verse 9a is indirectly to make a strong affirmation that the exiles will certainly return to that land. It is not merely to Abraham but to Abraham's descendants that the phrases in verse 9a apply. As Abraham's offspring the audience's being is that of a people taken to Palestine from earth's furthest bounds and corners, and this is therefore inevitably its destiny. Although the exiles are presently located in those far away regions from which Abraham came, theologically their location is in the land to which Abraham was taken, and fact must be expected soon to catch up with theology. The factor which is crucial to their destiny is not their human strength or lack of it but the divine strength which took hold of Abraham and which has hold of them in Abraham. It was Yahweh who created earth's furthest bounds (40:28), it was Yahweh who unmasked them (41:5), and now the audience is reminded that it was from these bounds that Yahweh had taken them.[15]

Whereas verse 8 is dominated by nouns, verse 9 is dominated by verbs. The former thereby emphasised the reality of the relationship between Yahweh and Israel and expanded on Israel's status, on what it meant to Yahweh. The latter complements that by drawing attention to the reality of Yahweh's activity on Israel's behalf which established their mutual commitment. It emphasises the dynamic and active as opposed to the relational side of Yahweh. Almost every word in the verse is taken up from previous verses. The most significant exception is the new statement that God 'did not spurn' Israel. In content the denial of rejection adds nothing,[16] but effective communication involves rhetoric and repetition or

---

[15]Beuken, *VT* 22, p. 15.

[16]B. Duhm, *Das Buch Jesaia* (Göttingen: Vandenhoeck & Ruprecht, 1922) on the passage.

restatement as well as rational content, and the appropriateness of the denial is underlined by its appearing also in Ishtar's words to Esarhaddon, '"Fear not, O king", I said to you, "I have not abandoned you"'.[17] The denial implicitly speaks to the sense of rejection expressed in 40:27 and more explicitly in 49:14; this particular verb will reappear in such a connection as part of the portrayal of the spurned wife in 54:6. The people are, after all, a community of failures and rejects.[18] The repetition of the verb 'called' points to a more general parallel and contrast with verses 2-4.

Although the address in vv. 8-9 is so important, the heart of the message of vv. 8-16 lies in the exhortation or invitation to which it leads: 'Do not be afraid, because I am with you . Do not be alarmed, because I am your God' (v. 10). It, too, has its links with Abraham. Such 'fear not' oracles are designed to stiffen resolve when someone might hesitate over a worrying situation or task. It has been customary to see them as 'salvation oracles' adapting the form of messages such as would be given to a needy person in the context of the worship of the temple, in a way presupposed by the lament Psalms.[19] This understanding has prima facie plausibility but suffers from several difficulties. On the one hand the argument regarding the background of the 'fear not' oracle seems to be circular; worse, the Psalms (and Jeremiah) give some indications regarding the nature of oracles responding to a lament Psalm, and these do not seem to correspond to these 'fear not' oracles (see e.g. Ps. 12:6 [5]; 60:8-10 [6-8]). On the other hand, there are many parallel 'fear not' oracles outside Isaiah 40-55 (e.g. war oracles) and these do not have the social contexts or specific functions presupposed by the theory.

Within the Old Testament, the first person urged and encouraged not to be afraid is Abraham, directly after the victory over the kings referred to above (Gn. 15:1). It follows

---

[17]J.B. Pritchard (ed.) *Ancient and Near Eastern Texts* (revised ed; Princeton, Princeton UP 1969) 450.

[18]LXX is surely right to keep to an aorist translation for the verb in the present context. The verse as a whole is a unity in referring throughout to the beginnings of Israel's story, when God took, called, addressed, chose - and did not spurn. The reference here is not to a rejection after an initial acceptance (as in 31:7; 54:6) but to an original refusal to accept (*cf.* the parallelism of 'choose' and 'spurn' in 7:15-16; also 5:24; 30:12; 33:15).

[19]C. Westermann, *Isaiah 40-66* (ET; London, SCM 1969) 11-13.

Abraham's risky refusal to be financially profited by that venture; it leads into his epoch-making declaration of trust and Yahweh's counting this as rightness. In Genesis, succeeding invitations not to be afraid are given to Hagar (!), Isaac, and Jacob (Gn. 21:17-18; 26:24; 46:2-4); these, too, presuppose a context of conflict, danger, or insecurity. Such promises to the ancestors have further parallels to the oracles in Isaiah 40-55 in addition to those shared with the war oracles. They are more inclined to encourage the hearers on the basis of noun clauses which describe Yahweh's relationship with them and to make promises such as 'I am with you', and their 'fear not' is more general. It is also noteworthy that 41:8-16 bases its appeal to its audience on the link between contemporary Israel and Abraham and Jacob to whom those oracles were given.

The link with crises such as battles gives the 'fear not' oracle a special link with people such as king. It may be doubted whether the ancestral 'fear not' stories involve a 'democratisation' of the war oracles,[20] but this is a feature of Isaiah of Babylon's prophecies, and insofar as the 'fear not' oracles originally belonged to people such as leaders, their application here to the people as a whole seems to be an instance of this process.[21] In chapters of Isaiah which particularly link with the present one, Ahaz has been urged not to be afraid (7:4) and that exhortation has been extended to the people as a whole (10:24); then Hezekiah has been urged not to be afraid (37:6) and here that exhortation is extended to the people as a whole.[22] Isaiah 41 thus links with each of these earlier chapters; the background of the exhortation to 'fear not' is at least as much earlier texts, in Isaiah, Genesis, and elsewhere, as the memory of experience in the First Temple period or the actual experiences of the exile (Babylonian or Israelite).

Specifically the 'I' of Yahweh affirms 'I am with you'. Like the name Yahweh with its explanation in terms of God

---

[20]Against H.M. Dion, 'The patriarchal traditions and the literary form of the "Oracle of Salvation"', *CBQ* 29 (1967) 198-206 [206].

[21]P.B. Harner, 'The salvation oracle in Second Isaiah', *JBL* 88 (1969) 418-34 [434].

[22]P.R. Ackroyd, *Studies in the Religious Tradition of the Old Testament* (London, SCM 1987) 116-9; E.W. Conrad, *Reading Isaiah* (Minneapolis, Fortress 1991) 34-51.

being there, present and active, the declaration 'I am with you' implies taking someone's side in a way which brings protection, support, deliverance, and success.

This application to the community reaffirms a significance of the motif going back to the exodus. When Yahweh says to Moses, 'I will be with you', this is for Israel's sake, and Israel is thus to be assured that 'I will be' is also their God acting on their behalf (Ex. 3:12, 14; *cf.* Dt. 20:3-4; 31:8). Jeremiah, too, speaks both of Yahweh being with him and of his being told not to be afraid, and of these statements applying to the people to whom he speaks (1:8; 30:10-11; 42:11; 46:27-28). Indeed, it is noteworthy that the motif of Yahweh being 'with *us*' is of great important in Isaiah 7:14; 8:8, 10. It is also noteworthy that Matthew's Gospel begins with a declaration that God is 'with you' to an individual, incorporates such a declaration regarding two or three, and closes with its application to the whole community (1:21; 18:20; 28:20).

Describing Yahweh's right hand as 'just' (v. 10) takes up the term from verse 2 (there rendered 'right'). If the audience identified the one summoned to the service of right as Abraham, the present promise makes explicit that the activity of right or justice was not confined to the moment of Israel's beginnings. The people might be inclined to think that such activity belonged to the distant past. Once again Yahweh stands forth as the God who is with the last and not merely the one who is the first, concerned for the people's rights now as was the case all those centuries ago. Yahweh's right hand concerns itself with order in the world and thus with what is right for Israel because of its key place in the divine purpose for the world. 'God has the order of the world in his hand, indeed he is himself this ordering'.[23] This is a characteristic of Yahweh to which Israel appeals in its prayer, as are Yahweh's strength, support, and upholding.[24]

---

[23]A. Jepsen, 'צֶדֶק und צְדָקָה im Alten Testament' in (ed.) H.G. Reventlow, *Gottes Wort und Gottes Land* (H.W. Hertzberg Festschrift; Göttingen, Vandenhoeck & Ruprecht 1965) 78-89 [86].

[24]'Yahwe thus speaks to Israel as if to a suppliant who appeals to his צֶדֶק in order to obtain his help against his enemies. When Yahwe warrants his צֶדֶק, this means that in the present circumstances he acts in accordance with his world order... His צֶדֶק... is at once his justice and his salvific will, which are specified for Israel in his election. The hand of his righteousness

III. Abraham and Cyrus, and the pattern of God's speaking (vv. 21-29)

As verses 1-20 continue to unfold we move some way from the starting-point when Yahweh challenged adherents of other religions to join in an argument regarding the identity of the heavenly power that stands behind key events in the middle east, and move some way from Yahweh's dealings with Abraham. The renewed legal language of verse 21 announces that there we return to a court scene like that of verses 1-7 with a new challenge regarding the same events.

Yahweh is once again spoiling for a legal battle, but the topic for discussion has changed. It is the verb 'announce' (נגד Hiphil) which sets the agenda for verses 21-29 (see vv. 22a, 22b, 23, 26a, 26b). The first occurrence covers events in general ('what happens'). The verb (קרה) suggests what takes place by chance, without pre-arrangement, in surprising fashion. The root appears only here in the Prophets. The question is raises is, who can explain the inexplicable or foretell the unplanned? Two parallel tricola break the announced events into ones which have already taken place (v. 22b) and ones yet to come (v. 23; also vv. 26a, 26b).

In explicating 'what happens', verse 22b begins by directing us to 'the first events' (הָרִאשֹׁנוֹת). Advertising the theme of the tricolon which follows, the term opens the line as a hanging nominative, resumed in the question 'what were they?' Once again the text's openness is capable of embracing at least the call of the ancestor Abraham and the initial stages of the career of Cyrus anticipated earlier in the Book of Isaiah and acclaimed in verses 2-3. Indeed there are other possibilities (e.g. creation or the exodus or the fall of Jerusalem). The truth is that at this stage we cannot know 'what' the first events are, let alone know what they 'are'. We can no more identify them than interpret them. Perhaps the text is tantalising us with the first question when it asks us the second in order to underline the significance of the latter by inculcating in us a double helplessness.

Behaving as if we know what those 'first events' are, Yahweh challenges the opposition to make a statement about

---

is his hand which realises all this' (A. Schoors, *I am God Your Saviour*, 54-55).

their significance which will enable the members of the court and the audience to see where they were designed to lead. To take them that far is to begin to deconstruct the distinction between looking back and looking forward, between the interpretation of history and the announcement of future events, for those implications lie in the future as well as in the present. Tellingly 'outcome' is the last word in the backward-looking of the two tricola; by its nature it points to the future which is explicitly treated in the second tricolon.

The criterion for determining who is God is the ability to make pronouncements about historical events, in anticipation or even in retrospect. A rabbinic saying speaks of revelation as the way people gain access to truths not only about the world above and below and the world of the future, which are not empirically accessible, but also about the world of the past, despite its being 'before us', in front of us, before our very eyes.[25] In part this may be because the distant past (especially the creation) is as inaccessible as those other realms and even the empirical facts about it have to be a matter of revelation, but in part it is because access to empirical facts about events does not bring with it insight into their 'outcome'. When Jewish tradition speaks of the narrative from Joshua to Kings as 'the Former Prophets' (רִאשֹׁנִים once again!), one significance of this phrase is that it designates the story as prophetic history, history told in the light of the kind of insight into the purpose of God which the prophets express. If we retitle it 'the Deuteronomistic History' we draw attention to the contribution of the Deuteronomists to the development of the conviction that history can be told in such a way as to indicate the way God is at work (and at work by speaking). Other middle eastern peoples as much as Israel believed that their gods were at work in their history, but to judge from the nature of their literature this conviction was not as central to their religion and convictions as was the case in Israel. At a moment of political crisis the question who can give a reliable account of the meaning of events would become a pressing one. In the world to which Isaiah 41 speaks, the rivals for recognition as interpreters of history were the gods of Babylon and the God of Israel. In the modern world the chapter's challenge is to a

[25]See C. Rowland, *The Open Heaven: a Study of Apocalyptic in Judaism and Early Christianity* (London/New York, SPCK 1982), 75.

discussion over whether there is any other contemporary theological or philosophical perspective (such as that of Marx) which offers a better account of the span of history.

At the end of verse 22 the case somersaults into what is a pickwickian concern for a court: 'Or inform us what is to come'. The term points to historical events about to be experienced by the community. It forms a pair with 'former events' in the sense of historical events in the community's recent or further past such as were referred to in verses 1-4. The gods are challenged to 'announce' them: outside Isaiah 40-48 'announce' normally denotes the reporting of an existent event or a fact. By nature it refers to already actual circumstances. The paradox of its usage here thus lies in its reference to the 'reporting' of an event before it actually happens.

The argument from prophecy in Isaiah is of a different kind from the apologetic argument from prophecy as it has often been used over the Christian centuries. When speaking of predictions and their fulfilment, Isaiah of Babylon is not referring to some individual, isolated objective words and events distant from the community's own world but important to them in some rationalistic way, but speaking of the life-and-death involvement of God in the community's destiny. Further, the link between the word which God speaks and the event which vindicates that word is not so much between prediction and fulfilment as between declaration of intent or command and fulfilment. The word is the means of God's acting and thus incidentally but intrinsically the means of its being clear that God has acted.

At the same time the generality of the statements in Isaiah 41 deserves to be noted. It implies the conviction that the lordship of Yahweh was effective not merely in recent events in the area around Babylon. We have suggested that the openness of the language about the conqueror requires that it should not be limited to Abraham (or the origins of Israel) or Cyrus but allowed to refer to all these as parallel events within the purpose of God. In verses 22-23 Westermann makes much of the generality of the participial expressions 'what is to come' and 'what is to arrive', calling the latter 'a bold experiment in the use of words, an attempt to express what we call "the future" in conceptual terms'.[26] The prophet is interested in the

[26]*Isaiah 40-66*, 84.

'historical continuum' between word and act; the proof of the reality of God lies not in having some religious experience but in 'the operational arc connecting his word and its effects at a far remove... God's deity is shown to be such by the continuity of his action in history'. The real point in Isaiah 41 is not the general fact of foretelling the future but the content of the alleged divine words. Beyond that, its real point is that over a century and more Yahweh had not only been speaking about judgement on Israel and then effecting it; Yahweh had also spoken even ahead of this judgement concerning events beyond which would lead to this people's new life, and Yahweh is now effecting them. It is this that Babylonian gods would find hard to match. The implicit claim of Isaiah 41, then, is that Old Testament prophecy and history offer a coherent account of the broad significance of the events of middle eastern history over the centuries, beginning with Abraham and ending with Cyrus, whereas no other religion does so or even purports to.

A scathing final challenge brings this first part of verses 21-29 to a conclusion whose force develops through verse 24 from the deprecatory 'you' with which it begins to the one with which it closes: 'There: you are a mere nothing. Your activity is a mere sigh. It is an abomination that one chooses in you'. The dismissal as 'nothings' of entities that seemed to the exilic community to be significant 'somethings' has already featured in 40:17, 23; 41:11-12. There the terms applied to nations in general and their rulers, and to the people who attack and arraign the community. For the first time this dismissal is explicitly extended to their gods in a threefold judgement.

Such a dismissal would make a perfectly feasible end to the case between Yahweh and the gods. They, their worshippers, and the Israelites tempted to join them, may be surprised and appalled to discover Yahweh restarting in verse 25. In truth, however, only a negative point has been established by verses 21-24; the gods are incapable of explaining the first events or unveiling how the future will unfold, this being - by implication - because they are not involved in shaping events at all. So is anyone shaping events and thus in a position to interpret and announce them? The answer comes in the form of a recurrence of the important verb which opened the plaintiff's first speech in verse 2. There it introduced a question, 'Who aroused...'. Here it claims, 'I aroused...'. Whereas verses 22-23 spoke about events in general terms, the text has likely always been concerned with the concrete; these poems characteristically move gradually towards revealing the specific concern they have from the beginning. Yahweh is proceeding from a superficially more general question about the announcing of past and future to the more specific question which always lay behind the general.

In the first colon, before we are again told that the conqueror's origin was from the east, we are kept on our toes by its being 'from the north'. Geographically it was from the east via the north that Abraham came to Palestine and that Cyrus cast his net around Babylon. Admittedly, if geography was in the forefront of the prophet's mind we might have expected 'I called him from the east and he arrived from the north'. But in any case talk of the north at least as much recalls the familiar motif of the north as the origin of the invader bringing judgement at the hand of Yahweh (no doubt because this was geographically the direction from which invaders came).[27]

I have scanned the line 2-2-2 with the Peshitta (and 1QIs^{a}) as giving a more straightforward construction than the metrically more usual 3-3 of MT which implies 'I aroused one from the north and he came, from the east one who would...'. The tricolon gives some emphasis to the last clause, where MT has 'he is to call on my name' (יִקְרָא בִשְׁמִי). 'On my name' is the new expression in this colon. Unfortunately the text is controverted.

Generally to call someone *by* name (the name they already have) suggests acknowledging them and/or summoning them in their individuality. In relation to Yahweh (e.g. 12:4) it appears with this meaning in the story of Elijah's contest with the Baal prophets (e.g. 1 Ki. 18:24), suggesting its specificity both to a context where many gods are acknowledged (*cf.* Je. 10:25; Zp. 3:29) and to one where the one named is being called on to act (*cf.* 2 Ki. 5:11; La. 3:55). It is used

---

[27]It has already appeared in Isaiah 14:31 following on the promise of judgement on Babylon, which is ironically the chief embodiment of the threatening force from the north in Jeremiah. Indeed the combination of Isaiah 14:13, 31 and 24:15 might give some support to Skinner's suggestion that north and east point to mystery (or even darkness) and light.

similarly with a human object to denote summons to activity; it suggests subordination, but at the same time potentially privilege (e.g. 40:26; 43:1; 45:4). As well as thus being used of human beings naming God and of God naming human beings, in Ex. 33:19 the phrase is used of God naming God ('I will call on/in the name of Yahweh'; *cf.* 34:5).

The idea that the conqueror would call on Yahweh's name is again applicable to Abraham, to Israel, or to Cyrus. Abraham did so on arrival in Palestine: see Genesis 12:8, 13:4; 21:33; 26:25 (each time וַיִּקְרָא בְּשֵׁם יהוה, the last in the context of a 'fear not for I am with you' oracle'). Israel did the same in its history. Regarding Cyrus, the idea that he would call on Yahweh's name has troubled interpreters, but unnecessarily. In a formal sense Cyrus did so according to 2 Ch. 36:23; Ezr. 1:2, but the Cyrus Cylinder indicates that he also firmly acknowledged Marduk, so that any politically correct statements he made must be seen as what they were. The prophet's vision of Cyrus truly recognising Yahweh was unrealised. But then so were the related prospects spoken of in passages such as 40:5; 41:5, 20. The acknowledgement of Yahweh by Cyrus would have a natural and appropriate place in any expectation of the world acknowledging Yahweh. In this sense the prophet is here saying nothing that implies that special significance attaches to Cyrus or the Persian empire. The same language about 'arousing' was used of the Assyrians and the Babylonians in their day, and Yahweh's working through Cyrus is in line with such earlier divine words and deeds (see on v. 2) - except that Yahweh is using this foreign agent within the context of Israel's restoration rather than its judgement.[28] The fact that neither the world's nor Cyrus's acknowledgement took place does not raise questions about text or translation here. It is no more exotic a statement than those in 44:28-45:5. Its language facilitates the continuation of the parallel of Abraham and Cyrus; the use of this precise expression of Abraham is important.

In verse 26 Yahweh comes to the central challenge of the speech to the court: 'Who announced it from the very first so that we might recognise him, announced it from beforehand so that we might say "He is in the right"?' The words have all appeared in verses 2-4, 21-24, and here they sum up sharply the

---

[28]So Westermann, *Isaiah 40-66*, on the passage.

question raised by these verses. Once more the reference of a phrase such as 'from the very first' is tied up with the reference of the events described. While 'from beforehand' means simply that, 'from the very first' suggests something more specific, the beginning of some particular moment or stage in God's activity. With Abraham, it relates to the beginning of Yahweh's activity with Israel announced in Genesis 12. With Cyrus, it relates to the very beginning of that story, which might be seen as lying in the prophecy concerning the Medes' defeat of Babylon in 13:17-22; 21:2-10.

'He is in the right' is simply 'right' and the word is usually rendered 'He is right' in the sense that 'He has got it right'. The significance of the word 'right' in this chapter and elsewhere, not least in Abraham's story, makes it unlikely that it is being used in a purely prosaic sense here. It will carry something of the connotation of 'He is the right' - in the context of a court speech, in the sense of winning the case; in the context of an assertion of Yahweh's purpose for Israel, in the sense of being involved in the rightful pursuit of its freedom; Yahweh has a claim to destiny.[29] It is this phrase which forms the novel element in the second colon and which brings it to its climax.

It transpires that the negative answer to the rhetorical question is not the speech's last word. Yahweh's own claim, which we have expected, at last arrives in verses 27-29. Whereas the idol-worshippers heard nothing from their gods to prepare them for the conqueror's appearance, Sion/Jerusalem had someone to tell of it beforehand (v. 27a) and also has someone to proclaim it as good news as it happens (v. 27b).

Yahweh has claimed to be open to investigation. It is possible to look back to long past announcements of Median conquest of Babylon for the sake of Israel's restoration, and to listen to present such announcements that this is the significance of current political events. Yahweh now adds the correlative point that it is not possible for the gods to make any similar claim. If they were to be asked about these events, there is among them no 'consultant' who could give any response to the question. The 'consultant' is a new figure at this point in the section; the language takes up 40:13-14 and behind that an

---

[29]C.F. Whitley, 'Deutero-Isaiah's interpretation of ṣedeq', *VT* 22 (1972) 460-75 [474].

important theme in Isaiah 1-39. Yet it is only the language which is novel. It presupposes an idea which has been central to verses 21-27, the idea that there is planning, policy-shaping, decision-making, and implementation involved in the occurring of historical events such as the advent of Abraham or Cyrus. The image of the consultant is new, but the framework of thinking is not.

He is not merely a person brought in to advise on a particular crisis. He is the strategist involved in the shaping of a plan which is then executed (*cf.* 9:6; 44:26).[30] The reality of such planning in heaven has already given an ironic twist to the Assyrian king's suggestion that Judah's planning does not take enough levels of fact into account (36:5). What Yahweh is referring to here is the idea of seeking to talk with the person responsible for the shaping of these events on the gods' behalf. From their company there is no answer because the plans were not formulated there. The point overlaps with that at the end of verse 26: the test is, has anyone heard anything? The judgement that emerges from the gods' inability to announce events before they take place or to account for them afterwards is that they, their deeds, and their images are a bane, nothingness, breath, and emptiness. It is crucial that Israel comes to accept or continues to accept this judgement.

Donald Wiseman has long been interested in Abraham not merely because of historical curiosity but because Abraham is a key figure for our understanding of our lives with God. Isaiah 41 is interested in Abraham because it anticipates that conviction. It invites us to view historical events as taking place under the sovereignty of Yahweh, who acted in bringing Abraham from the east at the beginning and according to their pattern. It invites us to see ourselves as the people of Yahweh called into the same friendship with Yahweh as Abraham enjoyed: like him we have no reason for fear. It invites us to rejoice in the evidence we have that Yahweh is the great interpreter of events past and announcer of events future, evidence which includes the story of Yahweh and Abraham.

---

[30]Conrad, *Reading Isaiah*, 151.

3

THE SLAUGHTER OF THE ANIMALS IN GENESIS 15

Genesis 15:8-21 and its Ancient Near Eastern Context

Richard S. Hess

Summary

A cuneiform text discovered in Northern Syria and dated to the early 2nd millennium BC describes the act of cutting the neck of a lamb while taking an oath. Comparisons with the slaughter of animals in the covenant-making ceremony of Genesis 15 have been criticised on the basis of closer similarities between the latter and Jeremiah 34, as well as other 1st millennium BC ceremonies. Examination of the original texts reveals problems with these later comparisons and provides new insights into the significance of the original proposal.

I. Introduction

It is a pleasure to dedicate this essay to Professor Donald J. Wiseman, whose own primary publication of the Alalakh texts, along with his later comparative studies, provided students of the Bible with greater awareness and appreciation of the world in which the patriarchs of Genesis 12-50 are described as living.[1]

In the fifteenth chapter of Genesis Abram requests from God assurance that the divine promise will be fulfilled. This is the promise that God will give the land of Canaan to Abram and to his descendants. He is commanded to bring a heifer, a goat, a ram, a dove and a young pigeon. The heifer, goat and ram are each to be three years old. All these animals are presented to God. Abram divides the bodies of the heifer, goat and ram. At night God speaks to Abram with the promise of the acquisition of the land by his descendants. A smoking pot of fire (תַנּוּר עָשָׁן) and a blazing torch (וְלַפִּיד אֵשׁ) pass between the animal carcasses. A covenant is made between God and Abram in which God promises the land to Abram. This is made explicit in v. 18, where the customary expression for making or 'cutting' a covenant appears:

> כָּרַת יְהוָה אֶת־אַבְרָם בְּרִית
>
> the Lord cut a covenant with Abram.

---

[1]D.J. Wiseman, *The Alalakh Tablets* (Occasional Publications of the British Institute of Archaeology at Ankara 2; London, British Institute of Archaeology at Ankara 1953); *idem*, 'Supplementary Copies of Alalakh Tablets', *JCS* 8 (1954) 1-30; *idem*, 'Abban and Alalaḫ', *JCS* 12 (1958) 124-9; *idem*, 'Ration Lists from Alalakh VII', *JCS* 13 (1959) 19-33; *idem*, 'Ration Lists from Alalakh IV', *JCS* 13 (1959) 50-62. For other publications of the cuneiform texts from Alalakh, *cf.* R.S. Hess, 'A Preliminary List of the Published Alalakh Texts', *Ugarit Forschungen* 20 (1988) 69-87; *idem*, 'Observations on Some Unpublished Alalakh Texts, Probably from Level IV', *Ugarit Forschungen* 24, forthcoming. For examples of his application of relevant material from Alalakh to the Old Testament, *cf.* D.J. Wiseman, 'Alalakh', 118-35 in D.W. Thomas (ed.) *Archaeology and Old Testament Study. Jubilee Volume of the Society for Old Testament Study 1917-1967* (Oxford, Clarendon 1967); *idem*, 'Alalakh Texts', 16-7 in K. Crim *et al.* (eds.) *The Interpreter's Dictionary of the Bible. Supplementary Volume* (Nashville, Abingdon 1976); *idem*, 'Alalah', 23-4 in J.D. Douglas *et al.* (eds.) *The New Bible Dictionary* (2nd ed; Leicester, IVP 1982).

II. The Evidence From Alalakh

The Alalakh texts represent archives of cuneiform tablets from two periods, the first half of the 2nd millennium BC and a period from the 14th or 13th century BC. The earlier tablets were discovered in level seven of the stratigraphy of Tell Atchana, the site identified with Alalakh. This site is located east of modern Antakya (Classical Antioch) near the border between Syria and Turkey. The texts found there were written in the Old Babylonian script. One of these tablets describes the swearing of an oath and involves a ritual not unlike that of Genesis 15. Wiseman's publication of this text, AT 456, led to the view that it preserves evidence for a covenant-making ceremony in the early 2nd millennium BC West Semitic culture of Alalakh.[2] Of particular interest are lines 39b-42:

> *ᵐab-ba*-AN
> *a-na ia-ri-im-li-im ni-iš* DINGIR.MEŠ
> *za-ki-ir ù ki-ša-ad* 1 SILÁ *iṭ-bu-uḫ*
> *šum-ma ša ad-di-nu-ku-um-mi e-li-iq-qú-[ú]*

> Abba-AN
> swore an oath of the gods to Yarimlim
> and he cut the neck of one lamb (saying):
> (May I be cursed) if I take what I have given to you.

Weinfeld identified both the content of Genesis 15 and the Alalakh text as land grants.[3] He noted several aspects of this literary form which are found in both texts. First, the grant constitutes an obligation of the master to the servant, not one on the part of the servant. Second, the giver takes an oath. In AT 456, line 42, there appears the oath from the mouth of the giver, *šum-ma ša ad-di-nu-ku-um-mi e-le-eq-qú-ú*('If I take that which I have given to you'). Third, the sacrifice of animals and the dividing of their carcasses forms a part of the property

---

[2]D.J. Wiseman, 'Abban and Alalaḫ'; *cf.* also A. Draffkorn, 'Was King Abba-AN of Yamḫad a Vizier for the King of Ḫattuša?', *JCS* 13 (1959) 94-7.

[3]M. Weinfeld, 'The Covenant of Grant in the Old Testament and in the Ancient Near East', *JAOS* 90 (1970) 184-203; *idem, Deuteronomy and the Deuteronomic School* (Oxford, Clarendon 1972) 74-5, 102.

grant. In Genesis 15 several animals are mentioned. In AT 456 the neck of a lamb (*ki-ša-ad* 1 SILA$_4$)[4] is cut.

The sacrificial aspect is demonstrated by another property exchange text from Alalakh level seven in which the neck of the lamb is also cut. This text, AT 54, contains a description of the 'lamb' (SILA$_4$) as *asakku*, i.e., 'set apart', in lines 16-18:

> GÚ SILÁ *a-sa-ki*
> IGI *ni-iq-mi-e-pu-uḫ* UGULA.UKU.UŠ
> *ṭa-bi-iḫ*
>
> The neck of the sacrificial lamb
> in the presence of Niqmepuḫ
> was cut.[5]

McCarthy does not agree that AT 456 is a grant which expects no responsibilities on the part of the recipient.[6] He argues that the stipulations of the text require responses of loyalty on the part of Yarimlim, the recipient. McCarthy likens the text to the treaty structure of the Hittites. However, he observes that the cutting of the lamb's throat has no Hittite treaty parallel. This is a West Semitic practice, found as early as at Mari, where an ass is slaughtered at the conclusion of a covenant. McCarthy identifies in this action the background for the Hebrew expression, 'to cut (כרת) a covenant'. At Alalakh the oath and the ritual of slaughter are syntactically co-ordinated but not equated.

III. Critical Evaluation of the Evidence

Van Seters has criticised the attempt to associate the events of Genesis 15 with any of the texts from Alalakh.[7] However, in order to do so he has limited himself to one particular

---

[4]For this reading, *cf.* B. Kienast, 'Die altbabylonischen Kaufurkunden aus Alalaḫ', *Welt des Orients* 11 (1980) 35-63 [53].

[5]*Cf.* Draffkorn, 'King Abba-AN of Yamḫad', 95.

[6]D.J. McCarthy, *Treaty and Covenant* (Analecta Biblica 21A; Rome, Pontifical Biblical Institute 1978) 86-97.

[7]J. Van Seters, *Abraham in History and Tradition* (New Haven and London, Yale 1974) 100-3. The relevant section of his more recent study does not address this comparison: see J. Van Seters, *Prologue to History: The Yahwist as Historian in Genesis* (Louisville, Westminster/John Knox 1992) 248-51.

association which Weinfeld has drawn between AT 1 and AT 456. Specifically, Van Seters wishes to disassociate any idea of sacrifice from the events described by these Alalakh texts. He argues four points: (1) the relevant Alalakh passage contains no mention of animals; (2) 'the house of Ishtar' may merely be 'the name of Ishtar' since restoration of the text is required; (3) no terms or indications of sacrifice are to be found in the Alalakh text; and (4) the practice of halving the animals and passing between their parts is not found at Alalakh. It occurs in Sefire I and especially in Jeremiah 34:18-20, which is to be reckoned as contemporary with the Genesis 15 text. These arguments have convinced some scholars, so that they stress the dependence of Genesis 15 upon Jeremiah 34.[8]

These conclusions need to be examined in the light of the relevant Alalakh texts and their study. Before that it is helpful to draw a distinction between AT 1 and AT 456. This distinction is not clear in Van Seters' work for three reasons: (1) He never identifies AT 1 but simply refers to it as a text linked by Weinfeld to AT 456. (2) He does identify AT 456 in the first paragraph on p. 102, but he does so in such a way that the four points which he makes in the following paragraphs seem to refer to this text, rather than to AT 1. (3) His reference in footnote 133 of the same page is to the wrong text. The note directs the reader to p. 126 of volume 12 of the *Journal of Cuneiform Studies.* This is the publication of AT 456. Instead, the note should refer to p. 26 of Wiseman's volume of published texts, where AT 1 is discussed.[9] When these distinctions are observed the importance of AT 456 as a source for comparisons remains.

I will now consider the four arguments which Van Seters uses to separate Genesis 15 from similar descriptions in the Alalakh texts. First, although no animal is mentioned in AT 1, it seems that an animal is mentioned in AT 456 in the relevant line (41). Wiseman's copy records what appears to be a ŠU sign, but this makes no sense of the line.[10] He follows a suggestion of J. Nougayrol in transliterating it as UDU,

---

[8]J. Ha, *Genesis 15, A Theological Compendium of Pentateuchal History* (BZAW 181; Berlin, Walter de Gruyter 1989) 71-8.

[9]Wiseman, *The Alalakh Tablets*, 26.

[10]'Abban and Alalaḫ', 127.

Akkadian *immeru*, 'sheep'.[11] Kienast reads SILA$_4$, Akkadian *puḫādu*, 'lamb'.[12] Whichever of the two options is accepted, the resulting translation specifies an animal which is slaughtered. Van Seters' observation, 'The argument about Yarimlim's sacrifice rests on a broken passage in which there is no mention of animals whatsoever',[13] addresses AT 1, not AT 456. Although some sections of AT 456 are marred, the major part of it is readable. The key lines about the oath and the slaughter of the animal (lines 39-42) are read and translated in their entirety and without any reconstruction by Wiseman and by others who have studied the text.[14] AT 456 provides a clear witness to the slaughter of either a sheep or lamb while taking an oath.

A second observation, that the restoration 'the name of Ishtar' is to be preferred to 'the house of Ishtar', also addresses AT 1, line 10. The expression 'the house of Ishtar' would refer to a temple devoted to the deity. Van Seters seems to prefer 'the name of Ishtar' because it removes further cultic significance from the text. In fact, my collation of AT 1 provided no indication as to which restoration should be preferred.[15] The broken text could allow for either. While the mention of a temple might demonstrate religious associations with the text, it is important to observe that this is not relevant to a comparison with Genesis 15. There as well, no temple is described in the covenant ritual between God and Abram, nor does any appear in AT 456.

Third, it is true that the interpretation of AT 456 alone does not require the reader to interpret it as a description of a sacrifice. Neither AT 1 nor AT 456 specify a sacrificial ritual. However, AT 456 has close parallels with a text which does seem to describe a sacrifice, AT 54. As already noted, the description of the sacrificial animal as *asakku*, 'set apart,' is found in AT 54 in a parallel clause which also describes the

---

[11]'Abban and Alalaḫ', 125.

[12]B. Kienast, 'Die altbabylonischen Kaufurkunden aus Alalaḫ', 53.

[13]Van Seters, *Abraham in History and Tradition*, 102.

[14]Kienast, 'Die altbabylonischen Kaufurkunden aus Alalaḫ', 53; McCarthy, *Treaty and Covenant*, 307-8.

[15]This collation was done in 1989. I thank Mr. T.C. Mitchell, then Keeper of the Western Asiatic Antiquities Collection at the British Museum, for permission to examine the tablet.

slaughter of the same type of animal, SILA$_4$, using the same verb for slaughtering, *ṭabāḫu*. As with AT 456 this text is concerned with a property transaction which is detailed in the lines preceding the description of the animal's slaughter. In both texts, this description is followed by stipulations or conditions regarding the keeping and breaking of the agreement. Both texts conclude with a list of witnesses. These close parallels suggest that the texts are describing the same ceremony at the point of killing the animal.

If one text includes *asakku* and the other does not, it probably does not imply that the animal in AT 456 was intended to be different from that in AT 54. It may simply be a difference in scribal style. The concept of an animal which is set apart resembles the biblical concept as expressed by the Hebrew root קדשׁ, 'to be holy, set apart'. In some usages of the Akkadian *asakku*, this separation may be a separation to a person rather than to a deity. However, it is also used of that which is set apart unto the divine sphere. In AT 456, the line preceding the description refers to the oath as *ni-iš* DINGIR.MEŠ, 'an oath of the gods'. This suggests a religious context. Farther than this the evidence from Alalakh cannot take us. However, it is enough to allow for the possibility of a sacrifice, and more than enough to require the slaughtering of the animal to be understood as part of a religious ritual, as seems to be the case also in Genesis 15. There Westermann finds ritual and sacrificial elements intended by the threefold repetition of 'three year old'(מְשֻׁלֶּשֶׁת/מְשֻׁלָּשׁ) and by the list of animals. These are used elsewhere for sacrificial ceremonies in the Old Testament.[16]

The fourth main objection, that Genesis 15 is better compared with an Aramaic Sefire treaty and with Jeremiah 34, is subject to dispute. As McCarthy observes, the Jeremiah text describes a rite of substitution in which the divided animal is used as a vivid illustration of what may happen to those who are disobedient.[17] The same is true of the comparison in Sefire I, where it is written:

[w'yk zy] ygzr 'gl' znh kn ygzr mt'l wygzrn rbwh

---

[16]C. Westermann, *Genesis 12-36. A Commentary* (ET; London, SPCK 1986) 225.

[17]McCarthy, *Treaty and Covenant*, 94.

> [Just as] this calf is cut in two, so may the wives of Matî'el be cut in two, and may his nobles be cut in two![18]

Another comparison may be made with the Neo-Assyrian treaty of Aššur-nerari V with Mati'-ilu, king of Arpad, lines 21-28:[19]

> SAG.DU *an-ni-u la* SAG.DU *ša* UDU.NIM [*šu-tú*]
> SAG.DU *šá* ^m^*ma-ti-i'*-DINGIR [*šu-u-tú*]
> SAG.DU *šá* DUMU.MEŠ-*šú* GAL.MEŠ-*šú* UN.MEŠ K[UR-*šú* *šu-tú*]
> *š*[*úm-m*]*u* ^m^KI.MIN *ina a-de-e an-nu-t*[*i i-ḫa-ṭu-ni*]
> *ki-i šá* SAG.DU *šá* UDU.NIM *an-ni-u qa-*[*ti-pu-u-ni*]
> [*ku*]*r-sin-nu-šu ina* KA-*šú šak-na-tu-n*[*i x x x*]
> S[AG.D]U *ša* ^m^KI.MIN *lu qa-ti-ip* DUMU.[MEŠ-*šú* GAL.MEŠ-*šu*]
> *ina* É? *lu ka-*[*ar-ru*]
>
> This head is not the head of a spring lamb, it is the head of Mati'-ilu, it is the head of his sons, his magnates and the people of [his la]nd. If Mati'-ilu [should sin] against this treaty, so may, just as the head of this spring lamb is c[ut] off, and its knuckle placed in its mouth, [...] the head of Mati'-ilu be cut off, and his sons [and magnates] be th[rown] into [...]

The text goes on to apply the same words and actions to the lamb's shoulder.

The Aramaic example is part of a list of curses which describes a number of unpleasant things.[20] The tearing apart of an animal is one destructive action among a variety of curses, given force by some sort of sympathetic, substitutionary ritual. The Neo-Assyrian treaty example is also concerned with curses, but the preserved examples both involve the progressive dismemberment of the same animal. Here as well, the substitutionary principle is at work. Jeremiah 34:18-20 uses a substitutionary image to warn the leaders of Israel. It is not clear that Genesis 15 intends to imply a substitutionary

[18] IA.39-40. *Cf.* J.A. Fitzmyer, *The Aramaic Inscriptions of Sefire* (Biblica et Orientalia 19; Rome, Pontifical Biblical Institute 1967) 94.
[19] S. Parpola and K. Watanabe, *Neo-Assyrian Treaties and Loyalty Oaths* (State Archives of Assyria 2; Helsinki, Helsinki UP, 1988) 9.
[20] *Cf.* also the Akkadian examples of Parpola and Watanabe, *Neo-Assyrian Treaties and Loyalty Oaths*, 58.

element. Nowhere is there the implication that God accepts the possibility of being torn in two if the promise to Abram is not kept. This is true despite the tendency of some commentators to assume that here is a self-imprecation oath performed by God.[21] In fact, not all of the animals are divided in two. Nor is it clear that there is a transformation of the rite which somehow results in the curse being applied to anyone who interferes with the divine promise.[22] Instead, the common element found in every case is that the life of each of the animals has been taken away. The implication of this is that God's own divine life forms the surety for the promise. The emphasis upon the life of the victim, rather than the dismemberment of the body, is also found in the examples from the Alalakh texts. There as well, animals are not divided into two pieces. They are slaughtered and so their life is taken away. The same is true of the act of covenant reconciliation between two warring parties as portrayed in the example from Mari.[23] However, this text is of greater interest for its reference to covenant making than for any similarity to Genesis 15. There is no concern with the promise or granting of land in the Mari example, unlike the Alalakh examples.

Understood as a personal commitment on the part of the divine giver of the promise, the sacrificial and symbolic significance of the animals may be that suggested by Wenham.[24] The slaughtered animals are Israel and the birds of prey which Abram drives off are the enemies of Israel. God's act of walking between the pieces signifies his presence with

---

[21]E.A. Speiser, *Genesis. Introduction, Translation and Notes* (Anchor Bible 1; Garden City, Doubleday 1961) 112-13; Westermann, *Genesis 12-36. A Commentary*, 228. *Cf.* further discussion in G.F. Hasel, 'The Meaning of the Animal Rite in Genesis 15', *JSOT* 19 (1981) 61-78.

[22]N.M. Sarna, *The JPS Torah Commentary. Genesis. The Traditional Hebrew Text with the New JPS Translation* (Philadelphia, Jewish Publication Society 1989) 115.

[23]M. Held, 'Philological Notes on the Mari Covenant Rituals', *BASOR* 200 (1970) 32-40 [33].

[24]G.J. Wenham, 'The Symbolism of the Animal Rite in Genesis 15: A Response to G.F. Hasel, *JSOT* 19 (1981) 61-78', *JSOT* 22 (1982) 134-37; *idem, Genesis 1-15* (Word Biblical Commentary 1; Word, Waco 1987) 332-33; V.P. Hamilton, *The Book of Genesis Chapters 1-17* (New International Commentary on the Old Testament; Grand Rapids, Eerdmans, 1990) 433-4.

his people. However, even here the symbolic identification of the life of the animals with God's own life reinforces the representation. His promise of the land is also a promise that his people will never perish entirely. God is with Israel. He guarantees by his life that he will bring them back to their land, no matter how unlikely or uncertain that may seem (vv. 13-16).

Thus it may be argued that Genesis 15 is closer to the Alalakh texts in its significance for the slaughtering of animals, while Jeremiah 34 is closer to the Aramaic and Neo-Assyrian treaties in its action of a dismemberment of animals which is involved in witnessing the covenant. The explicit statement of dismemberment and its equally explicit substitutionary significance occur together only in Akkadian texts of the first millennium BC and only in Jeremiah 34 in the Hebrew Bible.

IV. Conclusions

In conclusion, several observations might be made. First, the 2nd millennium remains a possible date for the custom of cutting the animals and the divine response as detailed in Genesis 15:8-21. Indeed, the fact of a closer similarity with the Alalakh custom and significance than with that of the 1st millennium practices implies that an earlier origin for this text is more likely, given the present state of the evidence.

The second observation has to do with the precarious nature of the archaeological evidence. It is indeed possible that the same custom might be found later or earlier than present evidence allows. This has been used to argue for a later date to the Patriarchal material. For this reason a single comparison is insufficient to establish a link to a particular time or culture. Much preferred is evidence which provides for many parallels and thus allows the evidence to find the place where it best fits in its context.

Third, it is significant to observe the history of a single comparison such as this one. It was first suggested with the publication of the Alalakh text. This was followed by modifications which took into account other similarities with biblical and extra-biblical material. In the case of Genesis 15 and AT 456, dispute focused on the question of form, whether the texts should be identified as land grants or as treaties. An alternative view studied the differences between the two texts and rejected any formal relationship between them. However, the rejection has not proven to be permanent. Indeed, it appears to rely upon interpretations of texts other than the key one, AT 456. When consideration is given to the context of AT 456 in light of other Alalakh texts (especially AT 54) and to the distinctive features of the ceremony in Genesis 15 in contrast to those found in other biblical texts (especially Jeremiah 34), the dismissal of the 2nd millennium comparison seems to rest on weak evidence. The possibility of a close relationship between the act of cutting up animals as described in Genesis 15 and that described in AT 456 remains.

4

GENESIS 12-50 IN THE NEAR EASTERN WORLD

Kenneth A. Kitchen

Summary

No valid assessment of the origins or date(s) of the 'patriarchal narratives' of Genesis 12-50 can now be made without setting them within their own overall Ancient Near Eastern context (inside a maximum span of c.3000-200 BC). Closely relevant first-hand data are here adduced from both Egypt and the Near East for comparison with various features found in Genesis 12-50. It emerges that the facts available indicate: (i) some features that can only have originated in the early 2nd millennium BC; (ii) other features valid both then and later; and (iii) some features of late 2nd/early 1st millennium date.

I. Introduction

In the last half-century, scholarly debate on the vivid narratives of Genesis 12-50 has produced a rainbow-wide spectrum of opinions on their nature, dating and contents. A century ago it was still possible to study these narratives in isolation, when scholars first started to dismiss the patriarchs as little more than phantoms projected back in time by writers from much later ages. Such views have been revived in recent decades - but in the wake of the colossal amount of information now organised and available on the biblical Near East from Chalcolithic to Roman times, it is no longer a tenable stance to study these narratives in isolation, if such study is to be considered scholarly in its nature. The Hebrew Bible was not written before 2000 BC or after 200 BC; it came into existence in the Near East, essentially within those broad dates. As its traditions profess to refer back beyond the patriarchs (Gn. 1-11), a perspective reaching back before 2000 BC has to be borne in mind. Hence, that area and general time span is the actual context which cannot be ignored. In the present study, given the vast wealth of data available, only a representative sampling can be presented.

II. Abraham, Isaac & Jacob (Gn. 12-36,38)

(a) Abraham in Egypt

After settling into Canaan, Abraham's first major adventure recorded in tradition was a visit to Egypt, to save himself, family and livestock from a famine in Canaan (Gn. 12:10-20). There, his wife Sarah was briefly abstracted into a pharaoh's harim, before he, she and their property were sent packing.

Abraham's visit to Egypt was made from a seemingly independent Canaan of minor city-states (be they [Jeru]salem, Sodom or Shechem, for example) with scope for pastoral tribal groups like Abraham and Lot (*cf.* Gn. 13:6-9). No such Canaan existed from the Davidic monarchy onwards (*c.*1000 BC, ff.), and it was already complicated by the presence of early Israel and Sea-Peoples' groups such as the Philistines from broadly 1200 BC. And during *c.*1500-1170 BC, Canaan was not an independent region, but subject to the ebb and flow of Egyptian rule. The Canaan of Genesis 12-50 is more like that of the Egyptian 'Execration Texts' of *c.*1850-1800 BC, with their lists of towns in Palestine and of tribal groups in their hinterlands. The side-by-side existence of city-based dynasties and of rural lines of princes is also attested in early 2nd millennium Mesopotamia;[1] were it not for the clay-tablet archives from the city-mounds, we would never have heard of these tribal rulers in the hinterlands of Mesopotamia, any more than of some of those in Canaan but for the Execration Texts. These texts were written out so that Pharaoh's possible foes might be ritually cursed (hence their modern name).[2] They likewise include ('U)rusalim (Jerusalem) and Shechem (like Gn. 12-50), while Shechem was also the victim of an Egyptian defeat in the time of Sesostris III, *c.*1850 BC.[3] The Egyptian Sinuhe portrayed as fleeing to Canaan *c.*1930 BC is seen as a satellite local 'sheikh' with Ammu-inshi, a tribal ruler in 'Iaa' (or, better, Araru) just SE of the Sea of Galilee.[4]

Visits to Egypt are known from such a Canaan by others besides Abraham. Most familiar is the case of a chief Ab(u)-sharru,[5] heading 37 'Asiatics' on a trading visit, shown in bright colour in a tomb-chapel under Sesostris II, *c.*1860 BC.[6] The Story of Sinuhe, again, has the hero rescued outside the

---

[1]See W. Yuhong and S. Dalley, *Iraq* 52 (1990) 159-165.

[2]For a good outline and bibliography of the several collections of such texts, see G. Posener, *Cinq figures d'envoûtement* (Cairo, JFAO 1987) 1-6 (to which add Y. Koenig, *Revue d'Egyptologie* 41 [1990] 101-125). For a survey of places named in the main Berlin and Brussels series of these texts, see W. Helck, *Die Beziehungen Ägyptens zu Vorderasien im 3. und 2. Jahrtausend v. Chr.* (2nd ed; Wiesbaden, Harrassowitz 1971) 44-67. See further A.F. Rainey, 'The World of Sinuhe', in *Israel Oriental Studies* 2 (1972) 369-408.

[3]Campaign by Sesostris III, stela of Sebek-khu (Manchester); translated (e.g.) by J.A. Wilson in J.B. Pritchard (ed.) *Ancient Near Eastern Texts relating to the Old Testament* (Princeton, Princeton UP 1950/69; hereafter *ANET*) 230.

[4]Translations by (e.g.) Wilson, in Pritchard, *ANET* 19/20; W.K. Simpson (ed.) *The Literature of Ancient Egypt* (2nd ed; New Haven/London, Yale UP 1973) 62-65; M. Lichtheim, *Ancient Egyptian Literature*, I (Berkeley, University of California Press 1973) 226-228.

[5]So, and not Ibsha or Absha (as sometimes given); it is spelt in the same way as names in the Execration Texts, as noted long since (e.g.) by W.F. Albright, *The Vocalisation of the Egyptian Syllabic Orthography* (New Haven, American Oriental Society 1934) 8 and n. 17.

[6]References in Kitchen, *Tyndale Bulletin* 42 (1991) 114, n. 2.

Egyptian frontier (in N. Sinai) by a sheikh and his tribesfolk 'who had been in Egypt'.[7]

Intimate details of life in the harims of the pharaohs are, of course, not usually available to us; but the pharaohs were happy to include foreign girls (whether princesses or otherwise) in their harims. In the early Middle Kingdom, *c.*2000 BC, Mentuhotep II (Nebhepetre) included the burials of 6 young ladies of his harim in his memorial temple at Deir el-Bahri in Western Thebes. Of these, two (as evidenced by the dark skins in the tomb-paintings, and a skull) were of Nubian origin, not Egyptians.[8] In the imperial days of the New Kingdom, the pharaohs continued to acquire eligible young ladies as additional wives or even to be chief queens: we have the burial-treasure of three Syrian girls under Tuthmosis III (*c.*1479-1425 BC);[9] Amenophis III and IV married wives from the North-Syrian state of Mitanni, as well as Babylonian and other princesses (as later did Ramesses II).[10]

The fleeting nature of Abraham's Egyptian visit would not suggest that he is pictured as penetrating very far into Egypt - no further than Jacob two generations later, *i.e.* the East Delta at most. In the 12th Dynasty, its founder Amenemhat I (*c.*1963-1934 BC) established an East-Delta provincial residence and temple, where later he was worshipped (near modern Ezbet Rushdi), called 'Ro-waty', 'Junction [Mouth] of the Two Ways', where the North-Sinai and Wadi Tumilat routes converged.[11] Within a mile or so was

---

[7]Wilson in ANET 19a; Simpson *The Literature of Ancient Egypt*, 60; Lichtheim *Ancient Egyptian Literature*, 224.

[8]Original publication, coffins and fragments of chapels in E. Naville *et al.*, *The XIth Dynasty Temple at Deir el-Bahari*, I-II (London, Egypt Exploration Fund 1907-10), Vol. I, 53-56 esp. 55 end, pls. 20-23 (esp. 23 bottom right) and Vol. II, 6-9, pls. 12 (bottom right) 13, 20 (centre); *cf.* also H.E. Winlock, *The Rise and Fall of the Middle Kingdom in Thebes* (New York, Macmillan 1947) 25-27.

[9]H.E. Winlock, *The Treasure of Three Egyptian Princesses* (New York, Metropolitan Museum of Art 1948).

[10]*Cf.* letters EA 1-5, 17, 22 end, e.g. in W.L. Moran, *The Amarna Letters* (Baltimore, John Hopkins UP 1992) 1-11, 41-42, 57; for Ramesses II, see Kitchen, *Pharaoh Triumphant* (Warminster, Aris & Phillips 1982) 83-89, 92-95.

[11]For references, see M. Bietak, *Avaris and Piramesse* (London, OUP 1979; 2nd ed 1986) 228.

situated Avaris, which the Hyksos rulers of Egypt (*c.*1650-1540 BC) made their East-Delta base and court. So, both native and foreign pharaohs resided here seasonally during *c.*1950-1550 BC. But thereafter, during most of the 18th Dynasty, Delta and Asiatic affairs were governed from Memphis, almost 100 miles to the south-west. Only at its end, Haremhab (*c.*1323-1295 BC) renewed the temple of Seth at Avaris, shortly before Ramesses II (*c.*1279-1213 BC) established his Delta capital there, Pi-Ramesse, the Raamses of Exodus 1:11. Thus, West-Semitic visitors to the East Delta might well be involved with the pharaonic court in the 12th to Hyksos Dynasties, but not again until *c.*1300 BC. Finally, in Genesis 12:20, the pharaoh speeded Abraham's exit by appointing men to escort him out; a pendant in reverse to the men detailed by another king to escort the Egyptian exile Sinuhe back into Egypt and to the royal court, *c.*1900 BC.[12]

(b) The Real Background to Genesis 14

This racy narrative of alliances and wars of eastern kings has been discussed *ad nauseam* by biblical scholars, most of whom are unaware of its real background.[13] The narration itself is essentially plain and straightforward. An alliance of 4 kings from the north and east subdued a group of 5 local kings of the Dead Sea area. After the latter rebelled, the alliance returned to punish the 5 rulers, taking their property, along with Lot. Abraham was told, with his allies; he pursued the alliance, recovering Lot and goods in a surprise night-attack. In victory, he paid a tithe to the ruler of Salem, priest of El-Elyon (identified with his own deity), refusing any repayment from the defeated king of Sodom other than the expenses of his levies and allies. The entire story is sober in tone; no marvels occur, nor divine interventions, for example. Only the climax (tithes at Salem) is religious, because it was always so in the

---

[12]For translations, see Wilson, *ANET*, 21b; Simpson, *The Literature of Ancient Egypt*, 70-71; Lichtheim, *Ancient Egyptian Literature*, 231.

[13]Typical are: J.A. Emerton, *VT* 21 (1971) 24-47, 403-409; T.L. Thompson, *The Historicity of the Patriarchal Narratives* (Berlin, de Gruyter 1974) 187-195; J. Van Seters, *Abraham in History and Tradition* (Yale, Yale UP 1975) 296-308; W. Schatz, *Genesis 14. Eine Untersuchung* (Bern/Frankfurt, Lang 1972); *cf.* the review of Schatz by Van Seters, *BiOr* 33(1976) 220-221.

biblical Near East; verses 18-20 are thus integral to the whole, not an addition.[14] Night-attacks on foes, or night-marches to surprise them are part of known Near-Eastern military tactics.[15]

Alliances between groups of local rulers might have occurred in Palestine at any time before its full occupation by the Davidic monarchy and its successors (Judah and Israel) on the one hand and the Philistine pentapolis on the other, *i.e.* before about 1000 BC, to earliest times. But in Mesopotamia, whence the 4-king alliance largely came,[16] this is not so. In Mesopotamia, the dominance of alliances of kings (often in rival groups) belongs to only two historical periods. The earlier is that of the old Sumerian city-states of the 3rd millennium BC, before the empires of Akkad and Ur III; this is too early to be relevant. The only other such period is broadly 2000-1700 BC, *i.e.* between the fall of the 3rd Dynasty of Ur, and the supremacy of Shamshi-Adad I of Assyria and Hammurabi of Babylon. After their time, Mesopotamia proper was dominated by just these two kingdoms until Persia swallowed all. But within 2000-1700 BC, just such alliances proliferate.[17]

---

[14]As it was viewed (e.g.) by Van Seters, 302. In Egyptian war-reliefs, such as the great New-Kingdom sets of scenes (*c.*1300-1170 BC) at Karnak, Luxor, Medinet Habu, Abydos, Abu Simbel, etc., the scenes of battle, conquest and victory always culminate in presentation of booty to the gods; Neo-Assyrian kings would dictate a letter to their god Assur, reporting on their campaigning; in Syria; the stela of Zakkur king of Hamath, includes thanks to his god; and so on.

[15]Thus, tribal troops attacked Hittite forces by night under Tudkhalia III (Güterbock, *JCS* 10 [1956] 92, A.ii.1) while the Hittite king Mursil II repeatedly made night-marches to surprise his foes at dawn (Four examples in A. Götze, *Die Annalen des Mursilis* [Leipzig, Hinrichs 1933; reprinted Darmstadt, Wissenschaftliche Buchgesellschaft 1967]) 127/129 (lower half) 149:24ff.; 159:21ff.; 175:17ff.

[16]Bracketed by Elam under a Chedor-la'omer (=Kutir-*x*) in the south-east and by tribal groups under Tid'al (a Tudkhalia) in the north (SE Asia Minor) with a king of Shin'ar in between, which is Shankhara/Sangar, a term for Babylonia, in which the elusive Ellasar tends to be located by most.

[17]Half-a-dozen examples, commonly of four or five kings, are given in K.A. Kitchen, *Ancient Orient and Old Testament* (London, Tyndale 1966) 45-6, n. 50 with references). *Cf.* the slippery Yashub-Adad who moved from one alliance to another every few months (W.L. Moran, in *ANET*, 3rd ed. [1969] 628 = *Supplement*, 192).

Most famous is a letter in which Zimrilim king of Mari is told: 'There is no king strongest by himself - 10 or 15 kings follow Hammurabi of Babylon, and so for Rim-Sin of Larsa, and so for Ibalpiel of Eshnunna, and so for Amutpiel of Qatna; but 20 kings follow Yarimlim of Yamkhad.'[18] It is this political configuration for eastern powers which - alone - fits the situation in Genesis 14. And it is only in this period that the distant realm of Elam was ever involved in international politics anywhere west of Babylonia and Assyria proper.[19] Thus, we find an Elamite envoy accompanying his Syrian colleague all the way west to the latter's home city of Qatna in central Syria, but detained briefly en route by the beady-eyed Bahdi-lim, bureaucratic servant of the king of Mari - and again, when they returned via Mari eastward to Elam![20] Clearly, there were moments when Elamite influence penetrated westwards to within reach of the Mediterranean.

As for eastern kings intervening in the Levant before the time of the major empires of Assyria or Egypt, the point-of-view of just such a ruler is well given by Yahdunlim of Mari (*c.*1830 BC), who campaigned in the westlands to the shores of the Mediterranean, as detailed for us in his foundation-text (in 9 copies) for the temple he built thereafter to Shamash the sun-god.[21] More florid than Genesis 14, this text is only slightly longer than that passage. After praise of Shamash and the king, the narrative (like Genesis 14) proceeds in the 3rd person, telling how the god 'hastened to march with Yahdunlim', the first Mari king to conquer the mountains with their timber, and reach the sea; here, as climax, he made offerings to the personified 'Ocean' (as did Abraham to El-Elyon), and his troops bathed. On the region's peoples he imposed his rule and 'perpetual tribute', still paid to him when the text was written (*cf.* Gn. 14:1-4a). But 'that same year', elsewhere, three allied

---

[18]Often cited; e.g. Moran in *ANET*, 628/192.

[19]As the Mari archives well show. That Elam, even as *primus inter pares*, stands in Genesis 14 for the Persian empire (Van Seters, *Abraham in History and Tradition*, 305) is unlikely.

[20]J.R. Kupper, *Correspondance de Bahdi-Lim* (ARMT VI; Paris, Imprimerie Nationale 1954) 32/33, 36/37 (letters 19, 22); noted also by W. Hinz, in *CAH* (3rd ed; Cambridge, CUP 1973) II/1, 263.

[21]Published in full by G. Dossin, *Syria* 32 (1955) 1-28 (text and translation, 12-17); see also A.L. Oppenheim's translation in Pritchard, *ANET*, 3rd ed. [1969] 556-557.

kings rebelled (helped by a fourth) against Yahdunlim, who then attacked them, destroying their settlements (*cf.* Gn. 14:4b-11). Then the grateful victor passes on to the building of the temple for his patron Shamash, invoking curses on whoever might misuse it. So, here too, religious considerations form a climax to the whole. In each case - Yahdunlim and Genesis 14 - we have a self-contained narrative capsule, basically independent of any other known document. Despite spurious claims to the contrary,[22] there is no link here with the continuous chronicles of the 1st millennium BC, whose classic form is that of a series of quite staccato reports, regnal year by regnal year, through a whole series of reigns;[23] slightly fuller yearly records then followed through a tablet-series, reign by reign.[24] This has nothing in common with Genesis 14, other than the banality of presenting ostensibly historical narrative.

(c) The Patriarchs in Treaty and Covenant.

In Genesis 14:13, we are told that Abraham was in (treaty) alliance (בְּרִית) with Mamre, Eshcol and Aner at Hebron. This is of a piece with Genesis 21 when Abraham and Abimelech of Gerar made a treaty, as later did Isaac and Abimelech of Gerar (Gn. 26) and more family-wise, still later Jacob and Laban (Gn. 31). Thanks to quite recent discovery and publication (still in process) of early 2nd millennium treaties from Mari and Tell Leilan, we can view the patriarchal treaties in a fresh light.

From the early 2nd millennium BC, we now have some 10 or 11 'new' treaties or covenants, only 4 or 5 as yet fully

---

[22]As made by Van Seters, *Abraham in History and Tradition,* 300, and *BiOr* 33 (1976) 220. Contrary to his belief that Mesopotamian chronicles are all 'late' (*i.e.* 7th-2nd centuries BC), we have Assyrian fragments under Tiglath-pileser I (*c.*1100 BC), Babylonian fragments under Nebuchadrezzar I (*c.*1120 BC), Old-Hittite chronicles of mid-2nd millennium BC (E. Laroche, *Catalogue des textes hittites* [Paris, Klincksieck 1956] Nos. 8-9, 16-18); a very laconic Mari eponym-chronicle of *c.*1800 BC (M. Birot, *MARI* 4 [1985] 219-242) and the Sumerian Tummal chronicle of 18th century BC or earlier (E. Sollberger, *JCS* 16 [1962] 40-47).

[23]For typical examples, see A.K. Grayson, *Assyrian and Babylonian Chronicles* (New York, Augustin 1971) Nos. 1, 11, 14, 16, 19, 20, 21, 22, 24.

[24]Nos. 3, 4, 5 (gap) 6, in Grayson, *op. cit.*, show this procedure.

published.[25] At this epoch, one potentate would commonly request an agreement or alliance with another before the formal enactment of a treaty was entered into.[26] In the case of at least 3 or 4 treaties from Mari and one from Tell Leilan, we have a formal document, beginning in each case with a series of gods by whom it is sworn,[27] or enjoined to be sworn.[28] Then follow the stipulations and matters for agreement. One is an alliance against a common foe (Zimrilim & Hammurabi of Babylon, against Elam); in a second and third, the lesser partner promises friendly, non-hostile acts and attitudes to the senior (Zimrilim to Ibalpiel; Atamrum & Zimrilim). In a fourth, the theme of non-aggression combines with commercial ties (Assyria with Till-abnu). Such documents exhibit much the same concerns as are found in the reports of treaties in Genesis 21, 26 and 31. Here, in each case, Abimelech requires of Abraham, then of Isaac, as does Laban of Jacob, assurance of, and agreement to, non-hostile relationships. Likewise, a formal oath is a prominent feature in Genesis 21, 26, 31, as it is at Mari and Tell Leilan. We may tabulate:

[25]The 11th/5th is the fragment from Mari, M.7550, edited by F. Joannès, in D. Charpin, F. Joannès (eds.) *Marchands, Diplomates et Empereurs* (Paris, Éditions Recherches sur les Civilisations, A.D.P.F. 1991) 176-177. It appears to be the oath-section from the beginning of a treaty of [Zimrilim] of Mari with a ruler of Kurda (either Simahlane or Hammurabi of Kurda).

[26]*Cf.* J.-M. Durand, in L. De Meyer *et al.* (eds.) *Fragmenta Historiae Elamicae* (Paris, Éditions Recherches sur les Civilisations, A.D.P.F. 1986) 115-116.

[27]Zimrilim of Mari and Hammurabi of Babylon (Durand, in *Fragmenta Historiae Elamicae,* 111-128); Zimrilim and Atamrum of Andariq (Joannès, in *Marchands, Diplomates et Empereurs,* 167-178).

[28]Zimrilim and Ibalpiel of Eshnunna (D. Charpin, in *Fragmenta Historiae Elamicae,* 139-166); Till-abnu of Apum and Assyria (J. Eidem, in Marchands, *Diplomates et Empereurs,* 185-207); and probably [Zimrilim] and [X] of Kurda (see note 25 above).

Element	Gn. 21	Gn. 26	Gn. 31
Witnesses	-----	-----	vv. 44-52a
Oath - asked	v. 23	v. 28	-----
- given	v. 24	v. 31	v. 53b
Stipulations	v. 23 respect succession, territory	v. 29 non-hostility	v. 52 non-hostility
	v. 30 ownership well	v. 29 pact	v. 52 respect territory
Ceremony:	- (or v.33: tree?)	v.30 feast	v. 54 sacrifice, feast
Curse:	-----	-----	v.53 (implied)

In the initial propositions ('small tablets') for treaties at Mari, etc., curse-formulae do not appear; this is added only on the final ('large tablet') document.[29] In Genesis, we have only the narrative-reports of agreements, not verbatim final texts, hence curses do not explicitly appear; but Genesis 31:53 implies mutual acceptance by Laban and Jacob of a self-curse of the judgement of God (El) on either, if unfaithful to the agreement. The Mari records teem with narrative reports of the making of treaties, and (as in Genesis) the curse-formulae do not appear either, except as implied by symbolic rites such as killing a donkey-foal[30] (as it dies, so would a treaty-breaker die). When such treaties involved the parties meeting in person (as in Genesis 21, 26, 31), then the two parties might exchange gifts - so, Abraham gave livestock to Abimelech (Gn. 21:27) - or share in feasting, even sacrifice (Isaac with Abimelech, Gn. 26:30; Jacob and Laban, Gn. 31:54). So in the Mari sources: Atamrum of Andariq exchanged presents with his vassal Ashkur-Adad, and the two kings drank from the same cup.[31] As for formal witnesses, they are not quoted in the surviving Mari and allied documents, unless the gods of the oath are treated as such. And this occurs only with Laban and Jacob in Genesis 31 (vv. 44-52a), invoking the agreement itself with pillar and cairn as witnesses. This 'occasional' occurrence of witnesses is reflected in sources from before the 14th century BC. Thus, a witness-

[29]See D. Charpin, *Archives Royales de Mari,* XXVI/2 (Paris, Éditions Recherches sur les Civilisations, A.D.P.F. 1988) 144 and references.
[30]For instances, real and prospective, see Joannès in *Marchands, Diplomates et Empereurs,* 175, Sections 2 and 3.
[31]Joannès, *loc. cit.* (n. 27).

section heads the treaty of Naram-Sin of Akkad (Mesopotamia) with Elam (*c.*2300 BC) and then not again until the treaty of the Hittite king Arnuwandas I with Ishmerikka about 1400 BC. But after 1400 BC, during the next phase in the history of treaties, the picture changes completely: the witness-clause becomes regular, and falls in the latter part of the document. It returns to the head of such documents in the 1st millennium BC - but by then, the oath-section found in our early 2nd millennium BC treaties has disappeared from the formal text of treaties. So, the early treaties like Mari and Genesis 21, 26, 31, are distinct from those (i) of the later 2nd millennium and (ii) those of the 1st millennium BC. And they are entirely different from earlier treaties of the 3rd millennium BC. In short, so far as one may determine on the data we have, the treaty-reports of Abraham, Isaac and Jacob belong with the treaties of the first half of the 2nd millennium BC - and not with those of either earlier or later epochs.

In closing this topic, it should be said that the personal covenants between man and deity in Genesis are entirely distinct from the treaties with such as Abimelech or Laban. Instead, they consist (i) of a promise from deity to the man his client, and (ii) of a confirmatory sign (as witness). So, with Noah in Genesis 6:8, 9:9f. (sign: rainbow); Abraham, Genesis 15:9-21 (sign: furnace & lamp); Abraham, Genesis 17:2,4-9 (signs: new name, circumcision); implied for Isaac in Genesis 17:19/21 (*cf.* 26:24/25); and Jacob's vision in Genesis 28:12-19 (his pillar as witness of the vision). They form a consistent series in themselves. Later examples, from David onwards, are less distinctive in their features.

III. The Joseph Narrative (Gn. 37, 39-50)

(a) The Presence of Semites in Egypt

In Middle-Kingdom Egypt of the 12th to 13th Dynasties (*c.*1963-1786, 1786-1600 BC), and called by the Egyptians simply 'Asiatics', many West-Semitic-speaking individuals appear at various social levels. As the property of temples, they served, some as dancers, others as porters. As slaves, some might be handed-over as payment by the state to officials and private owners, and (as private property) could be passed on from one owner to another.[32] Such Semites occur on family monuments as domestic servants (*hery-per* in Egyptian), as cup bearers, as personal confidants, and even entrusted with the family cult (libating to the dead).[33] Papyrus Brooklyn 35.1446 of *c.*1740 BC[34] sheds vivid additional light on this situation. Of 77 people listed on its reverse as belonging to a large Egyptian household, 48 were 'Asiatics', engaged in quite varied occupations,[35] bearing good West-Semitic names that find an echo in Hebrew names. Such are a Menahem, a Shipra (*cf.* Ex. 1:15), Sakar (*cf.* Issachar), an Asher, an Aqob (related to Jacob).[36] What is noteworthy is that this household with over two thirds of its minions being Asiatics lived not in the Delta close to the Levant but at Thebes, over 300 miles south of the Delta, some 500 miles away from south Canaan. So, the numbers of such people in the north would have been all the greater. Archaeological illustration of this situation comes from Tell el-Dab'a in the East Delta, with its extensive cemeteries of Middle-Bronze-Age Canaanites, Canaanite temples and pottery, etc.[37]

How did these people come to be in Egypt? For the Middle Kingdom there was very little evidence until recently - by contrast with the following New Kingdom (*c.*1550-1070 BC) when conquering pharaohs (16th to early 12th centuries BC) brought many captives from Canaan into Egypt, to be employed in state and temple servitude, some passing into private hands as slaves; Canaanite merchants also visited

---

[32]*Cf.* G. Posener, *Syria* 34 (1957) 151-152, citing the Illahun papyri of *c.*1800 BC.

[33]References in Posener, *op. cit.*, 154, 155, citing various stelae.

[34]W.C. Hayes, *A Papyrus of the Late Middle Kingdom* (New York, The Brooklyn Museum 1955); for a discussion of its foreign personal names, see W.F. Albright, *JAOS* 74 (1954) 222-233; see also Posener, *Syria* 34 (1957) 147-163; and for a brief note on the possible relevance of the papyrus for OT studies, see K.A. Kitchen, *Tyndale Bulletin* 2 (1957) 1-2.

[35]E.g. domestic servants (*hery-per*) (*cf.* Gn. 39:2); brewers, cooks, tutors/guardians; women as cloth-makers, hairdressers and storekeepers; *cf.* Hayes, *op. cit.* , 103-108 and table.

[36]Details, see Albright, *op. cit.* , and Posener, *op. cit.* , 148-150.

[37]For a convenient brief account, see M. Bietak, *Avaris and Piramesse*, esp. 236-263, 283-288, 291-295. On subsequent work there, *cf.* M. Bietak, *Ägypten und Levante* 2 (1991) 47-75.

Egypt then. For the Middle Kingdom, we now at last have some specific data, from blocks from Memphis whose text offers us parts of two years from the annals of Amenemhat II (within *c.*1901-1866 BC).[38] In this record, Asiatics enter Egypt under several circumstances. In line 8, an Egyptian force is sent into the Levant to make havoc, and (line 16) duly returns with booty including 1,554 Asiatics as prisoners. Others arrive as tribute, proffered by Semitic chiefs and rulers (line 13), so 1,002 Asiatics. Another expedition sent in two ships to Lebanon returned with a massive argosy of exotic products, and also 65 Asiatics (line 21) - most probably by trade and purchase, not by war or tribute, in this case. Thus, many a young Semite (like a Joseph) might enter Egypt as a bought slave, as a slave sent as tribute, or as a prisoner-of-war (as in later times).

(b) A Question of Cost

In Genesis 37:28, we read that his brothers sold Joseph for 20 shekels of silver. The price of slaves through successive epochs of antiquity is a matter of some interest. Away back in the late 3rd millennium BC, a decent slave fetched (on average) from 10 to 15 shekels of silver. A rate of 10 shekels was the commonest during the 3rd Dynasty of Ur (21st century BC).[39] In the first half of the 2nd millennium BC (esp. *c.*1800-1700), 20 shekels - as for Joseph - is the basic average price. This figure (expressed as 1/3 mina) is given as the mean in the laws of Hammurabi,[40] §§116, 214, 252. Precisely this figure of 20 shekels recurs in real-life documents at this same period. So, at Mari

---

[38]H. Altenmüller and A. Moussa, *Studien zur Altägyptischen Kultur* 18 (1991) 1-48 and plate at end; supplemented by J. Malek and S. Quirke, *Journal of Egyptian Archaeology* 78 (1992) 13-18.

[39]See the list of prices (from extremes of 2/3 shekel up to 55 shekels) in A. Falkenstein, *Die neusumerische Gerichtsurkunden*, I (Munich, Beck 1956) 88-90; here two-thirds of the examples are of 8 to 10 shekels. Similarly for the earlier empire of Akkad, *cf.* I. Mendelsohn, *Slavery in the Ancient Near East*, (New York, OUP 1949) 117 and n. 164.; for an examination of particular classes, 10 cases of 9-15 shekels, 4 of 20 shekels, 2 in between, plus a few very cheap or very dear, *cf.* D.O. Edzard, *Sumerische Rechtsurkunden des III. Jahrtausends*, (Munich, Beck 1968) 87, Table 5 and the references there.

[40]Translations, e.g. in *ANET* 170, 175, 176.

in a legal document,[41]and in other Old-Babylonian legal records of this period as the basic and common price-tag (varying in special circumstances).[42] In the later 2nd millennium BC, the basic price of slaves crept upwards, to 30 shekels (and more) as at later 15th-Century Nuzi,[43] and 14th-13th century Ugarit,[44] compare the replacement-price quoted in Exodus 21:32 (30 shekels). Thereafter, in the 1st millennium BC, price-inflation continued. Male slaves in Assyria fetched 50/60 shekels,[45] compare for the 8th century BC, the ransom-price of 50 shekels exacted by Menahem of Israel from his notables to pay Assyrian tribute (2 Kings 15:20). In the post-exilic Persian Empire period, slave-prices simply took off, running up to 90 or even 120 shekels, for example.[46] Thus, Joseph at 20 shekels fits the early 2nd millennium BC, Exodus at 30 shekels fits the later 2nd millennium BC, Menahem at 50 shekels fits the early 1st millennium BC, and none of these fit the altogether higher prices of the later exilic and post-exilic periods.

(c) What's in a Name?

On his appointment to office as the pharaoh's chief minister, Joseph was given an Egyptian name, Zaphenath-pa'aneah (in English form) and an Egyptian wife Asenath, daughter of a Potiphera, (high) priest of On (*i.e.*, Heliopolis) - Genesis 41:45 - the latter's name being reminiscent of his former employer's

---

[41]G. Boyer, *Archives Royales de Mari,* VIII (Paris, Imprimerie Nationale 1958) 23, No. 10:1-4.

[42]See, e.g. M. Van De Mieroop, *Archiv für Orientforschung* 34 (1987) 10, 11. References for Old-Babylonian slave-prices within a 15-30 shekel span (averaging just over 22 shekels) may be found in Falkenstein, *op. cit.*, 88, n. 5 end; *cf.* the earlier study of B. Meissner, *Warenpreise in Babylonien* (Berlin, de Gruyter 1936) 34 and the references there.

[43]*Cf.* B.L. Eichler, *Indenture at Nuzi,* (New Haven, Yale UP 1973) 16 and n. 35, and the texts listed, 17-18.

[44]Briefly dealt with by Mendelsohn, *op. cit.*, 118 and n. 181.

[45]*Cf.* the list in C.H.W. Johns, *Assyrian Deeds and Documents,* III (Cambridge, CUP 1924) 542-546. For the Neo-Babylonian period see also B. Meissner, *Babylonien und Assyrien,* I (Heidelberg, Winter 1920) 365-366 and the references there; also *Warenpreise in Babylonien,* 35-36.

[46]Meissner, *Babylonien und Assyrien,* 366; Meissner, *Warenpreise in Babylonien,* 36; Mendelsohn, *Slavery in the Ancient Near East,* 117 and n. 174 (additional references).

(Potiphar, Gn. 39:1). Naturally, these outlandish names have attracted much comment. Regarding Zaphenath-pa'aneah, the suggestion of G. Steindorff, a century ago, has enjoyed wide, not to say dogmatic acceptance.[47] He understood it as Egyptian *Dje(d) pa Nute(r) (e)f-'ankh*, to be translated 'The God has said: "he will live!"'[48] This particular type of name (*Djed* DEITY *ef-'ankh*) is very well attested from the late 20th Dynasty down to the 26th Dynasty and after, say *c.*1100-500 BC.[49] But this particular form of the name, with 'God' instead of a named deity, is still purely theoretical,[50] and may be purely imaginary.[51] Its theoretical status is not the only problem. It is, by meaning, a birth-name, the kind given to a child at birth (as various scholars have pointed out) and hence eminently unsuitable for Joseph at 30 years old.[52]

---

[47]G. Steindorff, *Zeitschrift für Aegyptische Sprache* 27 (1889) 41-2; 30 (1892) 50-52.

[48]So, with H. Ranke, *Ägyptische Personennamen*, I (Hamburg, Augustin 1935) 409-412, *passim* for the related names; Steindorff had translated 'the god spoke and he lives'.

[49]For examples with various deities, see Ranke, *loc. cit.* and K.A. Kitchen, *Third Intermediate Period in Egypt 1100-650 BC* (2nd ed; Warminster, Aris & Phillips 1986) index, 501-502. There is no warrant whatsoever for referring such names only or mainly to the 26th Dynasty.

[50]Alan Rowe's claim that this name had been found in a text at Bubastis, reported by W.F. Albright (*The Biblical Period* [Oxford, Blackwell 1949/1952] 56, n. 15) has never been substantiated; all mention of it disappeared in Albright's later works (*The Biblical Period from Abraham to Ezra* [New York, Harper & Row 1963] 98, n. 27, and *BASOR* 140 [1955] 31); hence it must be disregarded unless definite evidence be produced.

[51]A.R. Schulman remarked of this reconstructed name, 'I do not think that an exact original prototype [of *Djed-pa-nuter-ef-ankh*] ... will ever be found in the Egyptian documents, for I doubt that it ever existed.' He considered it a Hebrew construct of Egyptian type, not origin; see *Studien zur Altägyptischen Kultur* 2 (1975) 241.

[52]For a list of some objectors, see Schulman, *op. cit.*, 240, n. 26. Schulman's suggestion (241) that Joseph's appointment marked 'the beginning of a new life for him', and that hence a birth-name would not come amiss, seems implausible. A Hebrew narrator looking for an Egyptian name had plenty to choose from other than this kind.

Thus, we are fully entitled to present a better solution to Zaphenath-pa'aneah if it exists.[53] Quite some time ago, this writer presented precisely such a solution, but only in brief;[54] hence, a slightly fuller treatment is in order here. The Hebrew 'name' is rather long and falls into two parts. The second half clearly contains the Egyptian word *'ankh*, 'life/to live', as is almost universally conceded; before it is some element containing *p* or *f*. The first half, conversely, seems much more 'Semitic' at first sight: *Zaphenath* is directly reminiscent of the common Semitic root *zaphan*,[55] and of very little in Egyptian.[56] However, if a simple metathesis of the *p* and *t* be conceded, giving *Zat(h)nap(h)* for *Zap(h)nat(h)*, then the situation is radically different. *Zatnap* corresponds precisely to Egyptian *djad(u)-naf*, 'who is called...', introducing a second name after the first - for example, 'Ankhu *djad(u)-naf* Hedjeri' means 'Ankhu called Hedjeri'. In its masculine and feminine forms, this construction appears in the Middle Kingdom (from *c.*2000 BC), and stayed in use into the New Kingdom to at least the 18th Dynasty.[57] The verbal variant of this construction, *djad.tu-naf* (and feminine equivalent) was current mainly from

---

[53]We may safely lay aside both the philologically brilliant but onomatologically improbable solution offered by J. Vergote, *Joseph en Egypte* (Louvain, Publications Universitaires 1959) 142-146, based on a conflation of the LXX and Masoretic forms, and the weird and wonderful equivalents produced by some early investigators (for a sampling, see Vergote, *op. cit.*, 151-152).

[54]In J.D. Douglas *et al.*, *The New Bible Dictionary* (London, IVP 1962) 1353; and in its successor, *The Illustrated Bible Dictionary*, III (Leicester, IVP 1980) 1673.

[55]For Hebrew, see F. Brown, S.R. Driver, C.A. Briggs, *Hebrew and English Lexicon* (Oxford, OUP 1907) 860-861; for Aramaic and Phoenician, see C.-F. Jean, J. Hoftijzer, *Dictionnaire des inscriptions sémitiques de l'ouest* (Leiden, Brill 1965) 246; for Amarna Canaanite, see *Chicago Assyrian Dictionary*, 16/S (Chicago, Oriental Institute 1962) 96b; for Ugaritic, see C.H. Gordon, *Ugaritic Textbook* (Rome, Pontifical Biblical Institute 1965) III, 475:2185. Here and in what follows, I use a simplified transcription of Egyptian and Semitic names, for technical reasons.

[56]In Erman and Grapow, *Wörterbuch der Aegyptischen Sprache* (Leipzig, Hinrichs 1931) V, 568, 571-572, there is no root *dj-p-n*, and only four items under *dj-f-n* (three of Graeco-Roman date).

[57]See the references given by Erman and Grapow, *op. cit.* (n. 56 above), *Belegstellen*, V, 92, to p. 623:1.

the 18th Dynasty (*c.*1550-1300 BC) onwards, into the Later Period.[58] Thus the construction is superabundantly attested in Egyptian, in two closely-similar forms, covering between them the period of *c.*2000-600 BC.[59] But is the assumption of metathesis justified? The answer is 'yes'. It is a common feature when names and words transfer from one language into another. Compare the *k/s* and *s/k* sounds in Greek *(Al)eksandros* and Arabic *Iskander*; or the Hurro-Hittite *Ini-Tesub* becoming in Egyptian *Ini-Tebus*. Or in the Bible itself, Egyptian *Taharqa* becoming in Hebrew *Tirhaqah*. And not least with our name itself. Hebrew ***Zapnat*** becomes in the Greek of the LXX ***Psonth***... The reason in our case (*Djat-naf* to *Zapnat*) is very simple. The consonantal succession was totally foreign to a Semitic speaker and writer, so it was switched to a sequence that was very familiar, *z-p-n(-t)*. Hence, there is no problem in accepting *Zapnat* from Egyptian *Djad(u)-naf*.[60]

The second half of the name (*'pa'aneah'*) is very straightforward. As Engelbach long ago foresaw, names of the type Pa(i)ankh are very rare and unsatisfactory. But at least two other better solutions exist. One is to understand *(E)f-ankh*, as in the birth-name solution, but as an independent name. Such a name is attested from Middle-Kingdom times to the Greek period.[61] The other, far better-based solution is to

---

[58]Erman and Grapow and *Belegstellen, locc. citt.* In Papyrus Brooklyn 35.1446, a variant *iw djad.tu-naf* occurs, taking this construction back to *c.*1800 BC; see Hayes, *A Papyrus of the Late Middle Kingdom*, pl. I:5, 6, 10, etc.

[59]This solution was partly foreseen by R. Engelbach (*Journal of Egyptian Archaeology* 10 [1924] 204-206), but he did not work out the philological details, nor provide a solution to the *pa'aneah* segment.

[60]In *Djad*, 'say/call', the *d* would normally become a *t*, and by the Late Period (1100 BC onwards) dropped away completely; but in this construction, the *d* > *t* would be protected by the following *na.f* in *status pronominalis*, as in feminine nouns with suffixes (*cf.* Gardiner, *Egyptian Grammar* [Oxford, OUP 1957] §78, obs., and p. 432 end). The verbal suffix *.t(u)* would coalesce with (or even replace) the *d* > *t* of the *djad* to which it was affixed. Either way, the result is a *djad/t-naf*, from the Middle Kingdom to at least the New Kingdom and probably later. For another metathesis from Egyptian into Semitic (*r* and *n*), *cf.* Eg. *Bakenranef* (as **Bukun-rinip*) appearing in Assyrian as *Bukur-ninip* in Ranke, *Keilschriftliche Materialien zur altägyptischen Vokalisation* (Berlin, Reimer 1910) 27.

[61]For references, see Ranke, *Ägyptische Personennamen*, I, 14:5.

understand *Pa'aneah* as Egyptian *(I)p-ankh* or *(I)pi-ankh* or *(I)pu-ankh,* closely-related variants of each other.[62] These are very common in the Middle Kingdom, but not any later. So, at court, the pharaoh is to be envisaged as calling his new minister *Yosep djad-naf (I)pi-ankh,* 'Joseph called (I)pi-ankh'. In Hebrew the link-word *djad-naf* and name proper *(I)p-'ankh* were simply taken over as one epithet of Joseph. The case of a foreigner in Egypt being given an Egyptian name introduced by *djad-naf* is now known to be a very common one, from the Middle Kingdom, as Papyrus Brooklyn 35.1446 of the 18th century BC makes very clear.[63]

Joseph's wife Asenath also bears an Egyptian name. But which? The classic explanation owed to Sethe[64] was to derive it from Egyptian *Nes-neit* ('she belongs to (the goddess) Neit', with elision of initial *n,* giving *Es-neit.* For this, we have cuneiform and Greek transcriptional evidence during the 1st millennium BC. However, this name is not attested, it is theoretical, although there are plenty of other such names compounded with those of other deities - (N)es-Amun, (N)es-Hor, etc.[65] And, as Spiegelberg objected,[66] the *a*-vowel in Hebrew Asenath and LXX Greek Asen(n)eth did not agree with the *e*-vocalisation of the (N)es-names. He therefore suggested a name *Iu.s-en-Neit* (pronounced *As-en-Neit*) instead. This, too, is unattested; it has a parallel with one other deity - Mut is attested.[67] The *iu.es-,* pronounced *As-en-,* is certainly preferable to Sethe's *(N)es.* But the ancient goddess Neith is rather rare in personal names - she belonged mainly in Sais in the West Delta, whence we have almost no data on personal names. In the East Delta, at Heliopolis, she would not be expected to occur in names. Is there an alternative? Again, yes. We have men called *Iuf-ni,* 'he belongs to me' (spoken by a parent), and commonly women called *Ius-ni,* 'she belongs to me' (ditto), well-attested in the Middle Kingdom.[68] We have

---

[62]References to the three forms in Ranke, *op. cit.,* 21:30; 22:16; 23:18.

[63]See Hayes, *op. cit.,* 99-102, with relevant plates.

[64]K. Sethe, *Das ägyptische Verbum,* I (Leipzig, Hinrichs 1899) §223,1.

[65]*Cf.* Ranke, *Ägyptische Personennamen* I, 173-180, *passim.*

[66]W. Spiegelberg, *Aegyptologische Randglossen zum Alten Testament* (Strasburg, Schlesier & Schweikhardt 1904) 18-19.

[67]Ranke, *Personennamen,* I, 15:3, of New-Kingdom date. Slightly modified, this is accepted by J. Vergote, *Joseph en Egypte,* 149-150.

[68]See Ranke, *Personennamen,* I, 14:7 and 15:4, respectively.

women called *Ius-n-ites* and *Ius-en-mutes*, meaning 'she belongs to her father' and 'she belongs to her mother'.[69] We have a man called *Iuf-en-at*, probably 'he belongs to you' (fem.), *i.e.* to his mother.[70] From this, it is a very short step indeed to suggest that our Asenat(h) is simply a *Ius-en-at*, 'she belongs to you' (fem.), in exactly the same way, and pronounced *As-en-at*.. This explanation for Asenath eliminates the unrealistic link with Neith, fits the vocalic pattern in Hebrew and Egyptian, and derives from an attested name (even if in the masculine only at present).

There remain Potiphar and Potiphera. The universally acceptable interpretation of Potiphera is that it is from the Egyptian *Pa-di-Pre*, 'the gift of the (god) Re', a well-known type of name (*Pa-di*-DEITY), and in fact attested just once on a stela in Cairo Museum, attributed to the 21st Dynasty (=*c.*1070-945 BC), but quite possibly later.[71] It is also usually conceded that Potiphar is simply the same as Potiphera with the final *'ayin* consonant omitted. This is possible, but leaves one very sceptical - but I have no good alternative to this suggestion at present.[72] Pre is merely a variant of Re (the sun-god), with the definite article prefixed; it is attested from the 19th Dynasty (Sethos I/Ramesses II), 13th century BC. The name *Pa-di-Re* (without *P* of *Pre*) was reported on funerary cones from Thebes, attributed to the 18th Dynasty, and the first examples of the similar name *Pa-di-Khons* to the New Kingdom.[73] However this may be, we certainly have the name *Pa-di-su-er-nehah* in the time of Sethos I, *c.*1290 BC.[74] Thus,

---

[69]Ranke, *Personennamen,* I, 15:1, 7 respectively; of Middle-Kingdom date.

[70]*Ibid.*, I, 14:12, of the 1st Intermediate Period/early Middle Kingdom.

[71]Published by A. Hamada, *Annales du Service des Antiquités de l'Egypte* 39 (1939) 273-276, pl. 39.

[72]The name Potiphar (no *'ayin*) is incised in Hebrew or Aramaic script (mid-1st millennium BC?) on an Egyptian sacred-eye amulet (Michailides Collection); see J. Leibovitch, *Annales du Service des Antiquités de l'Egypte* 43 (1943) 87-90, fig. 25. The amulet may be genuine; but has the Semitic epigraph been scratched on in more recent times?

[73]References in Ranke, *Personennamen,* I, 124:16 (after Daressy) for *Pa-di-Re;* I, 125:21 for *Pa-di-Khons.*

[74]W. Spiegelberg, *Rechnungen aus der Zeit Setis I* (Strasburg, Trübner 1896) 23, pl. X.a: Verso II.1.a; K.A. Kitchen, *Ramesside Inscriptions*, I

the Egyptian original of Potiphera (and possibly of Potiphar) would not date before the 19th Dynasty (13th century BC) and could be current long after. The name-form *Pa-di*-DEITY (and in the feminine, *Ta-di(t)*-DEITY) is simply a modernised Late-Egyptian form of an earlier type of name: *Dd(w)*-DEITY, feminine *Ddt*-DEITY, 'gift of (DEITY)'.[75] In the early 18th Dynasty, in the 16th-15th centuries BC, we have a transitional form of name in this category, attested (so far) only in the feminine version: *Ta-didi(t)-es*, 'The one that she [=goddess] has given', *lit.* 'the gift of her' [=goddess].[76] The masculine would be: **Pa-didi*-(DEITY or pronoun-suffix). Given the clear existence of the sequence of types of name with the same meaning: *Didi*-X, then **Pa-didi*-X, *Ta-didi(t)*-X, then *Pa-di*-X, it is possible to suggest that in fact Joseph's father-in-law was originally called **Didi-Re*, a name which became later (if not **Pa-didi-(P)Re*) the present *Pa-di-Pre.*

To sum up, Zaphenath-pa'aneah (Joseph) could either derive from a purely theoretical name of a known type, but of unsuitable application (12th-5th centuries BC) or from a commonly and solidly attested link-word and name having no problems (link-word, Middle/New Kingdoms, and one variant still later; name, overwhelmingly Middle Kingdom). The best suggestion for Asenath has a very close relative in the Middle Kingdom, the second best (type, *As-en-Neit*) would occur in the Middle and New Kingdoms in principle; the Late-Period equivalent, **(N)es-Neit*, is in every way inferior (unattested; wrong vocalisation, etc.) Potiphera is of a form that began in the New Kingdom, going on through the Late Period; it is simply the modernised form of an older type of name with the same meaning (going back massively to the Middle Kingdom).

(d) Other News in Brief

(i) Semites in high office in Egypt: Not all Levantines in Egypt remained on the bottom rungs of its society. With particular skills, some climbed into broadly 'middle-class' niches. Such

---

(Oxford, Blackwell 1975) 269; in English, Kitchen, *Ramesside Inscriptions, Translations,* I (Oxford, Blackwell Publishers 1993) 223 (end).

[75]For these names, which abound in the Middle Kingdom, *cf.* Ranke, *Personennamen,* I, 401-404, *passim.*

[76]In tombs of Paheri and Qenamun; Ranke, *Personennamen,* I, 375:3, 4.

were an 'Asiatic and Chief Craftsman, Tawti (='David') and his colleague 'the Chief Craftsman 'Epir' (*cf.* Ephron) from a 19th/18th century BC stela in Rio de Janeiro.[77] Half a millennium later, *c.*1280 BC, we have a family of 7 generations of Chief Draughtsmen of (the Temple of) Amun, whose founder Pada-Baal ('Baal has redeemed') entered Egypt *c.*1450 BC. He married a lady with a Hurrian name (Ibri-kul), his male descendants married girls sometimes of Semitic background, sometimes Egyptian, down to Didia whose own mother and mother-in-law were each called Tal, 'Dewdrop', in good West-Semitic.[78] In the New Kingdom, at the highest levels, we find such people as (*e.g.*) Urhiya (Hurrian for 'True one'), a general under Sethos I, and his son Yupa (Canaanite, 'fine/handsome').[79] Going back to the late Middle Kingdom, still higher, we have the Superintendent of the (Royal) Seal or 'Chancellor', Hur, well-known from numerous scarab-seals *c.*17th/16th centuries BC.[80] Joseph's appointment would be at this level, as a supremo, personally responsible to the pharaoh, or as a vizier. In New-Kingdom times, we have scenes of presentations of the royal seal to the highest dignitaries, or their mention of this - so, Huy, Viceroy of Nubia (under Tutankhamun), and Nebwenenef, High Priest of Amun (under Ramesses II).[81] And from early times (3rd millennium BC

---

[77]Full publication, K.A. Kitchen and M. de C. Beltrão, *Catalogue of the Egyptian Collection in the National Museum, Rio de Janeiro* (Warminster/Rio, Aris & Phillips and UFRJ-MNRJ 1991) I, 64/65-66/67; II, pl. 45; on the foreigners, *cf.* Kitchen, in S.I. Groll (ed.) *Studies in Egyptology presented to Miriam Lichtheim* (Jerusalem, Magnes 1990) I, 635-638; and in S. Quirke (ed.) *Middle Kingdom Studies* (New Malden, Sia Publishing 1991) 88-89 with fig., p. 90.

[78]The family of Didia, especially on Louvre C.50; see D.A. Lowle, *Oriens Antiquus* 15 (1976) 91-106, figs. 1-2, pls. I-II; also Kitchen, *Ramesside Inscriptions, Translations* I, 265-269, and VII (forthcoming) 19-21; for notes, *idem, Ramesside Inscriptions, Notes and Comments* (Oxford, Blackwell Publishers 1993/4) I, 222-226, and VII, *ad loc.* (in preparation).

[79]For this family, see J. Ruffle and K.A. Kitchen, in J. Ruffle, G.A. Gaballa, K.A. Kitchen (eds.) *Glimpses of Ancient Egypt, Studies in honour of H.W. Fairman,* (Warminster, Aris & Phillips 1979) 55-74.

[80]There are many examples in G.T. Martin, *Egyptian Administrative and Private-Name Seals* (Oxford, Griffith Institute 1971) 78-85:984-1088a, pls. 28-42A, *passim.* For the name, *cf.* Hebrew Hur (Brown, Driver and Briggs, *Hebrew Lexicon.* 301a).

onward), many royal officials bore the title 'Seal-bearer of the King'.[82] And some Semites even ascended the throne briefly in the 18th century BC before the Hyksos kings took over. Such were 'Ameny the Asiatic' and the kings Khandjer (name, Semitic *hanzir*, 'boar').

(ii) 'Death comes as the End': Both Jacob (Gn. 50:2-3) and Joseph (Gn. 50:26) were reportedly embalmed at their deaths in Egypt. But the old man requested that he be buried in the ancestral family tomb, back in Canaan - in effect, to be gathered to his fathers, like so many people there in the Middle Bronze Age,[83] in the Late Bronze Age,[84] and into the Iron Age under the Hebrew kingdoms.[85] However, of Joseph it is stated that 'he was put in a coffin in Egypt' (with a deferred hope of being reburied in Canaan). He and his family thus appear as being more assimilated to Egyptian cultural usages than old Jacob. Other Semites, too, ended up 'in a coffin in Egypt' - from the Late Middle Kingdom/Hyksos epoch, one thinks of the coffin of that indubitable Semite 'Abdu, of the 17th/16th centuries BC, containing also a handsome dagger of one Nahman (another good West-Semitic name) bearing the cartouche of the Hyksos king Apopi.[86] In later periods, most especially the New Kingdom, other foreigners entered even

---

[81]For the former, see N. de Garis Davies and A.H. Gardiner, *The Tomb of Huy (No. 40)* (London, Egypt Exploration Society 1926) 10f., pls. V, VI, left (before the king, pl. IV); for the latter, Kitchen, *Pharaoh Triumphant, Life and Times of Ramesses II*, 47.

[82]Examples, Middle Kingdom, W.A. Ward, *Index of Egyptian Administrative and Religious Titles of The Middle Kingdom* (Beirut, American University of Beirut 1982) 170:1472; H.G. Fischer, *Egyptian Titles. A Supplement* (New York, Metropolitan Museum of Art 1985) 86:1472.

[83]As (e.g.) at Jericho, *cf.* K.M. Kenyon, *Jericho* I and II (London, British School of Archaeology in Jerusalem 1960/1965) *passim*.

[84]In brief, *cf.* (e.g.) R. Gonen in A. Ben-Tor, *The Archaeology of Ancient Israel* (New Haven, Yale UP 1992) 240-241, when single-pit burial also came into use.

[85]*Cf.* E. Bloch-Smith, *Judahite Burial Practices and Beliefs about the Dead* (JSOTS 123; Sheffield, Sheffield Academic Press 1992).

[86]*Cf.* G. Daressy, *Annales du Service de l'Antiquités de l'Egypte* 7 (1906) 118-119 and pl. (dagger); P. Lacau, *Sarcophages antérieurs au Nouvel Empire* (Cairo, Service des Antiquités 1906) II, 86-87 [28108], pl. 19:1,2 (typical Middle-Kingdom box-coffin).

more fully into Egyptian ways, and had completely Egyptian tombs; one thinks again (at random) of general Urhiya mentioned above.[87] And, of course, much later - witness Carian tombstones in Saite and Persian-period Egypt.[88]

IV. Concluding Perspective

From this brief conspectus of part of the content of Genesis 12-50 and its background, we must turn to nature and date in concluding. In terms of dating, several levels of reference need to be distinguished, as follows.

(1) Certain specific 'early' indicators should first be noted. (a) The Canaan of the patriarchs is much more that of the Middle Bronze Age and of the Execration Texts than it is of later times, *e.g.* the Egyptian-dominated land of the Late Bronze Age, and still less of the Iron Age regimes of monarchic Israel and the neighbouring Philistines. (b) A pharaoh at least seasonally resident in the east Delta (*cf.* Abraham, Joseph) well suits the Middle Kingdom and Hyksos period (early 2nd millennium BC), but not the succeeding 18th Dynasty (ruling from Thebes (briefly) then Memphis). Under the 19th and early 20th Dynasties, kings again had an east-Delta residence, but this (Raamses of the Exodus) is too late to be relevant to the patriarchs; and the 1st-Millennium residence of Tanis is conspicuous by its total absence from Genesis. (c) The geo-political setting of alliances in Mesopotamia is exclusively a phenomenon of the period within *c.*2000-1700 BC, neither earlier (except for the early Sumerian city-states, too early) nor later (when the twin powers of Assyria and Babylon dominated). (d) The treaty-type used by the patriarchs is that of the early 2nd millennium BC, neither earlier nor later (on the combined evidence of over 90 such documents now known). (e) The scale of rising basic slave-prices through the centuries clearly indicates the earlier half of the 2nd millennium for Joseph (going at 20 shekels) - wholly different from the inflated prices of (*e.g.*) the Exilic period and after (90 to 120 shekels). (f) The social customs of the patriarchs clearly correspond to those demonstrably current in the earlier half of the 2nd

[87]References, J. Malek, *Topographical Bibliography*^{2}, III/2:2 (Oxford, Griffith Institute 1979) 661 ('Iurokhy').

[88]See J. Boardman, *The Greeks Overseas* (3rd ed; London, Thames & Hudson 1980) 137/8, and figs. 158-9.

millennium BC, and generally not later.[89] (g) The personal names of the patriarchs and their families largely correspond to the usage mainly found in the early 2nd millennium BC, especially the so-called 'Amorite Imperfective' names (type: Jacob, Isaac, Joseph, Ishmael) in the light of a recent total analysis of the data.[90] (h) Of the Egyptian personal names, the best equivalents for Zaphenath-pa'aneah and Asenath belong overwhelmingly to the Middle Kingdom (early 2nd millennium BC), rarely later; Potipher(a) is a modernised form (late 2nd millennium BC onwards) of an early-2nd-Millennium form (Didire).

(2) Then we have features that are fully consistent with the early 2nd millennium BC, but are not exclusive to it - they continue later also. They therefore are consistent with items under (1) but do not constitute independent evidence. (a) Semites visit Egypt independently for succour or for trade in both the Middle Kingdom and the New Kingdom, and no doubt (if less obviously) in the Late Period also. (b) The interest of the pharaohs in acquiring foreign wives is attested for the Middle and New Kingdoms; it is less clear (but probable) later. (c) Semites in varying roles (high or low) in Egyptian society are very evident in Middle and New Kingdom times, but are much less visible later on. (d) Of the Egyptian personal names, Potipher(a) dates itself (as a modernised form at best) to the late 2nd millennium BC. (e) Burials of Semites and others resident in Egypt are well-attested in the Middle Kingdom ('Abdu at Saqqara; Canaanite cemeteries at Tell el-Dab'a), and this continued in the New Kingdom (Urhiya and others); we find Carians and Greeks likewise in the Late Period.

(3) Features which are clearly (or probably) later than the early 2nd millennium BC in Genesis 12-50. (a) The 'land of Rameses' of Genesis 47:11 in the terminology of the narrator puts that narrator in the early 13th to early 12th centuries BC,

---

[89]See for essential details, Kitchen, *Bible in its World* (Exeter, Paternoster 1977) 58-61, 68-74 and notes thereto. Assertions to the contrary by Van Seters (e.g. in *Abraham in History and Tradition*, 68-71 on dialogue-documents, an Egyptian adoption-papyrus and one anomalous Neo-Assyrian tablet) are wholly spurious, *cf. ibid.*, 70-71 and references.

[90]See Kitchen, 'New Directions in Biblical Archaeology' in J. Amittai (ed.) *Acts, IInd International Congress of Biblical Archaeology 1990* (Jerusalem, Israel Exploration Society in press) for the full data.

the *floruit* of Egyptian (Pi-)Ramesse in the east Delta (after Ramesses VI, it fell into desuetude), *i.e.* at the latest (and likeliest) date for the Exodus (13th century BC). (b) The place-name Dan in Genesis 14:14 is surely a substitution for the earlier Laish, subsequent to the events of Judges 18; hence it would be a scribal revision from that date onward. (c) In Genesis 36:31, the heading to an Edomite king-list sets them in Edom 'before an Israelite king reigned.' While this could be construed as an abstract reference to the non-existence of such people as 'Israelite kings', it is more easily understood as reflecting the period of the Hebrew monarchy, perhaps the united monarchy. It would either be a gloss of that date (to clarify the date of the Edomite rulers) or evidence of a version of our text at that date.

The net result of the foregoing review may properly be summarised as follows. (1) There are sufficient features in Genesis 12-50 to show clearly that a variety of aspects of this text have indubitable roots in the early 2nd millennium BC. The best solution to that situation is to infer, accordingly, that we do have definite patriarchal traditions from that time, despite fashionable protestations to the contrary. There is not the slightest possibility of some of these features being dreamed up arbitrarily in the exilic and post-exilic period. (2) There are, equally, some indicators that would place a narrator of this part of Genesis in the later 2nd millennium BC: Rameses belongs to the 13th/early 12th centuries BC, which would indicate the general date of this stage of transmission of the traditions. (3) The allusion to Dan and to Edomite rulers before any Israelite kings would suit a third stage in transmission of the data at most likely the time of the united monarchy (David/Solomon). There is not a scintilla of objective evidence for anything substantive later.

As for the nature of the narratives in Genesis 12-50, for brevity's sake, readers must be referred to a factually indispensable treatment given previously.[91] From that survey it is clear that the patriarchal narratives come closest to historical writing, not to fictional writing; they should be treated as serious sources of data from the early 2nd

---

[91]See Kitchen, *The Bible in its World* (Exeter, Paternoster 1977) 61-68, where the actual phenomena of narrative in the biblical Near East are clearly set out on a strictly factual basis.

millennium BC, but pulled together later in that millennium with final formatting in the early 1st millennium BC.

5

ABRAHAM AND MELCHIZEDEK

Horizons in Genesis 14

J. Gordon McConville

Summary

This essay considers the meaning of the Melchizedek incident in its context in Genesis 14, and in relation to other parts of the Bible, especially Hebrews. The chapter as a whole is intelligible broadly within the early history of Israel, and in terms of the themes of Genesis: it presents the figure of Abraham in a 'public' aspect found elsewhere in Genesis; and, especially in the encounter with Melchizedek, it relates to the promise of land and posterity. Abram's confrontation with the King of Salem affects the outcome of his meeting with the King of Sodom, making a contrast between the acceptance of the land by promise, and the belief that land is held by might. The author of Hebrews makes a specific application of the incident which, while it cannot be deduced entirely from the plain sense of the text, is yet based on its central themes of promise and faith.

Introduction

'In Abram became flesh that which had previously been celestial; he based on the divine, he supported himself upon it, when he victoriously scattered the robbers from beyond the Euphrates.' (Thomas Mann, *Joseph and His Brothers*)

Melchizedek, the priest-king of Salem, makes his one brief and tantalising appearance in the biblical narrative in the story of Abram's defeat of the alliance of eastern kings who had attacked a coalition of city-states, including Sodom, in the region of the Dead Sea (Gn. 14). In that story, the eastern kings subdue and plunder the Sodomite alliance, and subsequently put down a rebellion (vv. 1-11). Abram is drawn into the events because, in the course of the second encounter, the invaders also carry off his nephew Lot, a resident of Sodom (v. 12; *cf.* 13:12). Adopting the role of a warrior on the stage of world events, Abram pursues and defeats the aggressors, obtains the freedom of Lot and other captives, and brings back the stolen loot (vv. 13-16). The goods are in due course returned to their rightful owners, represented in the narrative only by the King of Sodom (vv. 17, 21-24). And so the story reaches its satisfying conclusion.

Yet the whole story has not thus been told. For in the middle of its climax (vv. 18-20) occurs the unheralded entrance of Melchizedek, the priest-king of Salem, who blesses Abram by 'God Most High', and to whom Abram gives 'a tenth of everything' (vv. 18-20). The effect of this encounter spills over into the last scene between Abram and the King of Sodom, for Abram takes up from Melchizedek the name of 'God Most High', whom he now identifies as Yahweh (v. 22). Here therefore a major theological issue is broached, and it is clear that the Melchizedek episode cannot be detached cleanly from its context.

These initial observations raise immediately the question in what sense, if any, are vv. 18-20 integral to the form and meaning of Genesis 14? This seems to be the prior question in any study of the passage. It leads on to a second, however, namely, what theological echoes does the incident have in other parts of the Old Testament, and the New? This question has a literary- and historical-critical dimension, and also biblical-theological ramifications. For the incident gives birth to the idea of Melchizedek as a 'priest for ever' (Ps. 110:4), which becomes so important in the argument of the Letter to the Hebrews (Heb. 6:13-7:22).

My immediate purpose in the following is to consider the meaning of the Melchizedek incident in its context. This involves the question of the unity of the chapter, and in turn the possible settings and purposes of its parts. My aim in pursuing these questions is to try to understand how the Melchizedek incident was intended to function in the passage, whether or not it was originally integral to it. Beyond this stage of the study, however, I also want to ask whether links of a biblical-theological nature can be made between the Genesis passage and the other biblical passages which interpret the incident (Ps. 110; Heb.).

Genesis 14: a Unity?

One treatment of the chapter in question is entitled 'The Riddle of Genesis 14',[1] and this we may take as fair warning of trouble ahead as we begin. The chapter has always been regarded as problematical, posing an insoluble problem to source-criticism which could not find a home for it in any of the four source-documents, JEDP.[2] The problems which critics have raised concerning the chapter are the following. First, there is an alleged disjunction between the subject-matter of vv. 1-11 and that of vv. 12ff. The former section consists of an account of a war between two groups of allied powers, in which the only named protagonists are kings. The issues are international and political. Abram is only introduced at v. 12, along with Lot, and thus into what Westermann sees as a different world, '..the small world of the Canaanite city-states which emerges so clearly from the Amarna letters', a world of individual heroisms and kinship bonds. Westermann supports this thesis with literary-critical arguments.[3] Verse 12 is said to follow clumsily on v. 11, which seems to have already rounded off the account of the eastern alliance's depredations. The same verse also anticipates, clumsily again, the introduction of Abram in v. 13, which seems to be new (because of the designation 'Abram the Hebrew'). Finally, vv. 18-20 are almost

---

[1]J.A. Emerton, 'The Riddle of Genesis xiv', *VT* 21 (1971) 403-439.
[2]See Emerton, 'Riddle', 404-407.
[3]C. Westermann, (*Genesis 12-36*, London, SPCK 1985) 198-9.

universally regarded as an intrusion into vv. 17, 21-24.[4] The appearance of Melchizedek interrupts the logic of Abram's return with the recovered booty. The King of Sodom, having come out to meet Abram (v. 17) is unceremoniously set aside for the latter's unexpected interview with this priest-king of Salem, who has not been involved in any of the action hitherto (vv. 18-20). That exchange complete, the conversation between Abram and the King of Sodom resumes, apparently as if nothing has happened. A contradiction is sometimes pointed out between Abram's gift of part of the booty to Melchizedek, in the form of a tithe, and his return of the goods to the King of Sodom, qualified only by a share kept for his allies, but not by the tithe to the King of Salem.[5]

The pointed connection between Melchizedek's apostrophe of 'God Most High' (v. 20) and Abram's allusion to 'the LORD, God Most High, maker of heaven and earth' (v. 22), is editorial and cannot hide the secondariness of the intrusion.[6] To the literary-critical argument is added the observation that these verses take us into yet another 'different world', this time that of a settled cult, priests and tithes.[7]

These are the main features of the chapter which, alongside a number of more minor points,[8] have shaped the criticism of it. After arguments for the composite nature of the chapter comes the need to account for it. This has been done in a number of ways. Westermann (echoing Emerton's interpretation at a number of points) thinks that the three sections of the narrative identified above derive originally from separate times and settings in Israel's history. Verses 1-11(12) consist of the report of a campaign, together with lists incorporated into it. The campaign narrative has analogues in the ancient world, in the chronicles of kings describing their

---

[4]*Ibid.; cf.* Emerton, 'Riddle', 407.

[5]Emerton, *ibid.*, 408.

[6]Westermann, *Genesis 12-36*, 202.

[7]*Ibid.*, 203-4.

[8]These include repetitions within the war-account in vv. 1-11, the secondariness of the explanatory notes (e.g. in v. 2: 'that is, Zoar'); the secondariness of Aner, Mamre and Eshcol; the reappearance of the King of Sodom after he has apparently died in the bitumen-pits, v. 10; but see Emerton, 'False Clues in the Study of Genesis xiv', *VT* 21 (1971) 24-47, esp. 27-8.

military successes.[9] The second section (vv. 12-17, 21-24) is a narrative of liberation, which corresponds to the stories in the Book of Judges, in which a hero-figure delivers the people from foreign oppression ('Replace Abraham with Gideon and the story could take its place unaltered in the book of Judges.').[10] The Melchizedek episode forms the third and final section, coming from a period close to that of the liberation narrative, and intended to justify aetiologically a current practice. Westermann finds the setting for the episode in the first temple, in the context of Zion-theology. The name Salem occurs for Jerusalem also in Psalm 76:3, a Psalm of Zion. The name Melchizedek recalls the priestly name Zadok, and as priest-king he represents the idea of sacral kingship.[11] The practice which is aetiologically justified by the story is the bringing of the tithe to Jerusalem. The whole chapter, finally, comes from the post-exilic period, because of the elevation of Abraham to the status of a world-figure, which Westermann (following Gunkel) thinks conforms to a pattern found also in Judith and Daniel.[12]

Westermann's view is similar in some respects to that of Emerton, though the latter's treatment is distinctive. Emerton is chiefly interested in vv. 18-20, and the relationship between these verses and their framework, by which he apparently means the bulk of the chapter (though like Westermann he does think that vv. 1-11 and vv. 12-24 had distinct origins).[13] He finds v. 12 itself awkward and thinks that Lot played no part in the original narrative.[14] That narrative, consequently, cannot be attributed to the source J. However, the narrative in vv. 18-20 is likely to have been inserted into a pre-existing framework, as it can hardly have had any prior independent existence of its own.[15] Like Westermann, he dates the Melchizedek episode to the first temple period, indeed to the time of David himself, and thinks it supports his claim to rule, not only over the Israelites, but also over the peoples of

[9]Westermann, *Genesis 12-36*, 190-1.
[10]*Ibid.*, 191; *cf.* Emerton, 'Riddle', 432-434.
[11]*Ibid.*, 191-2, 203-205.
[12]*Ibid.*, 192.
[13]Emerton, 'Riddle', 431.
[14]*Ibid.*, 406-7.
[15]*Ibid.*, 409.

Canaan, by virtue of the assimilation of the Jerusalem god Elyon to Yahweh. David thus actually becomes the successor to Melchizedek as priest-king in Jerusalem, and also benefits (paradoxically) from the association with Abram. Emerton differs from Westermann in rejecting the function of the tithe in the episode as aetiological, since this is not a regular cultic tithe, and in ruling out any echo of the Zadokite priesthood in the name of Melchizedek, or any hint of a claim that is thus entered on their behalf.[16] He also focuses more clearly than Westermann on the intention behind the probable fact that vv. 18-20 was inserted into an already existing story. His approach is therefore in a sense 'canonical', though he does not himself express his intention in those terms.

The treatment of the chapter by J. Van Seters is conceived as a response to that of Emerton. Van Seters argues that many of the features which Emerton regarded as secondary are integral to the narrative. Lot, for example, cannot be removed from v. 14, since this provides the motivation for Abram's actions; the finale of the episode (vv. 22f.) shows clearly that the motive can hardly have been the booty![17] Certain apparent evidences of secondariness, furthermore, such as the glosses, are intentional archaisms. The narrative of the campaign is shown to be a late development of the Chronicle form, because it reports on relations between the factions from a third party's point of view. That section of the chapter is in fact a carefully contrived introduction to the story of Abram and Lot that follows.[18] Finally, vv. 18-20 are an addition to this unified narrative, and therefore should not be used as a key to understand the whole story. That story is no more and no less than a celebration of the virtues of courage, loyalty and piety, of the sort which is also found in the post-exilic period in writings such as Judith.[19] The intrusive vv. 18-20 (the very last editorial addition to the Pentateuch in Van Seters' view) are an extension of the tendency in both J and P to assimilate the god El/Elyon to

---

[16]*Ibid.*, 418-425.

[17]J. Van Seters, *Abraham in History and Tradition* (New Haven/London, Yale UP 1975) 298.

[18]*Ibid.*, 297, 300-1.

[19]*Ibid.*, 304-5.

Yahweh, in the context of the claims of the Hasmonaean kings to be 'priests of the Most High God'.[20]

It is now in place to reconsider the main issues in the argument about the interpretation of the chapter. I am not concerned here with arguments about its unity for its own sake. My stated aim concerns the meaning of the chapter as a whole. Nevertheless I do think that its interpretation requires a consideration of the relationship among its various parts. The attempt to understand what the chapter means requires us to consider issues of dating, and dating questions may in turn (at least in principle) be decided by whether or not the parts may be thought to belong together. Initially, however, we may ask which of the arguments offered above in relation to the various parts of the chapter carry most weight.

The Interpretation of Genesis 14

1. The Campaign: vv. 1-11

We begin by considering the parts of the chapter in turn. The date of the narrative of the campaign is notoriously difficult to settle. No positive identifications of the kings is possible, nor can the events themselves be aligned with what is known from elsewhere about relations between eastern powers and the region of Palestine in question, though affirmations of the impossibility of a campaign of the kind claim too much.[21] The quest of the origin of the narrative itself has hardly been more fruitful. Emerton has shown the weakness of Astour's attempt to explain the account by comparison with the so-called Spartoli tablets, which contain accounts of four different attacks on Babylon.[22] The style of the narrative, furthermore, does not permit of ready analogy with Mesopotamian annals, since, in contrast to these, it is written in the third person. Van

---

[20]*Ibid.*, 306-308.

[21]Westermann, *Genesis 12-36*, 193-4; *cf.* G.J. Wenham, *Genesis 1-15* (Waco, Texas, Word Books 1987) 318-320, especially his stricture on de Vaux's claim that the five cities of the Plain could never have been vassals of Elam (R. de Vaux, *The Early History of Israel*, Vol. 1, [London, DLT 1978] 219); also K.A. Kitchen's essay in this volume.

[22]Emerton, 'False Clues', 39-46; M.C. Astour, 'Political and Cosmic Symbolism in Gen. 14 and in its Babylonian Sources', in A. Altman (ed.) *Biblical Motifs: Origins and Transformations* (Cambridge Mass., Harvard UP 1966) 65-112.

Seters believed that this represented a late development in the writing of annals.[23] It is not clear, however, that he has identified an essential distinction between annalistic accounts and what he sees as the late 'Chronicle form' which he thinks lies closest to Genesis 14:1-11.[24] Westermann, on the other hand, thought that a Babylonian account, undatable in itself, underlies the text, though in its present form this is late (post-exilic).[25] A decision about the date of this part of the chapter cannot be made, I think, on the basis of analogy alone (since there is not enough evidence). Where it is dated late (Van Seters and Westermann) it is not on such grounds alone, but as part of a view of the origin of the chapter as a whole.

ii) Abram's Victory: vv. 12-17

Are matters clearer in the case of the account of Abram's victory over the invading kings? The analogy with the hero-narratives of the Book of Judges is not as close as Emerton and Westermann thought. Van Seters, considering the comparison in form-critical terms, pointed to an absence from the Abram narrative of a 'scene of personal combat so typical of the *Heldensage*'.[26] Westermann's assertion that one could read Gideon for Abram in the account is at the least an overstatement, since the issues in our narrative are different from those in the Book of Judges: Abram is not the charismatic leader who arises 'from the ranks' to deliver people and land from an invading enemy; rather, as an acknowledged political leader, who has 'allies', he pursues a retreating raider in order to rescue his kinsman Lot. The themes of people and land are less fully developed here than they are in the deuteronomic

---

[23]Van Seters, *Abraham*, 299-300; *cf. idem*, 'The Conquest of Sihon's Kingdom: a Literary Examination', *JBL* 91 (1972) 187-189.

[24]A list of date-formulae for Hammurapi's reign records events in the third-person (*ANET*, 269-271); the first paragraph of the account of Adad-Nirari III's expedition to Palestine is written in a mixture of third and first person (*ANET*, 281-2, *cf.* 284). The unusualness of Genesis 14:1-11, and its integration into a narrative which has other characteristics than the merely annalistic, simply highlights the question about true analogies. Notice incidentally, K.L. Younger, *Ancient Conquest Accounts* (JSOTS 98; Sheffield, JSOT Press 1990) 263 on the essential continuity of these from *c.* 1300 - *c.* 600 BC.

[25]Westermann, *Genesis 12-36*, 192-3, *cf.* 207.

[26]Van Seters, *Abraham*, 304-5.

literature. For the same reason, there is no clear congruity between Gideon's rejection of kingship (Judg. 8:22f.) and Abram's resistance to the King of Sodom's overtures. Granted, the Old Testament's coolness towards Canaanite kingship probably lies behind both incidents, but it is construed in quite different ways.[27] Westermann, therefore, in his pursuit of the comparison with Gideon, has angled his reading of the narrative in a particular way. It is this perspective on the story which enables him to make the distinction we have noted between the public, political world of the campaign report (vv. 1-11) and the allegedly more private, family world of vv. 12ff. Here, therefore, as in the case of the campaign report, it is difficult to decide upon the character of the part without taking a view of the whole. Westermann's belief that the middle section of the narrative (vv. 12-17, 21-24) is essentially a hero-legend has led him to neglect an aspect of that section (Abram's recognition by other powerful figures as a major player in the political arena) which could make a link with the campaign report.

Are there better analogies for this part of the chapter? Emerton finds a similarity in spirit between the story of Abram and the King of Sodom and other stories where the hero shows nobility of character, a number of them told of David (e.g. 2 Sa. 24, where David refuses to give to God something that has cost him nothing, v. 24).[28] The account of David's rescue of the people of Ziklag (1 Sa. 30) has perhaps better claims to similarity with Genesis 14 than most others, because of the elements of recovery of captives, including David's wives Ahinoam and Abigail (*cf.* Abram's rescue of his kinsman Lot), and of the question of the disposal of the spoils of war.[29] Yet such comparisons can do little more than highlight typical elements in stories about the heroes of Israel's past; they cannot in themselves pinpoint specific dates or settings. The particular, unusual characteristics of a story are likely to be more telling in this regard.

---

[27] *Pace* Westermann, who describes Abram as 'the charismatic leader from an Israelite tribe', and sees the dialogue with the King of Sodom as exactly analogous to Gideon's rejection of kingship; *Genesis 12-36*, 202.

[28] Emerton, 'Riddle', 432-3.

[29] Westermann, *Genesis 12-36*, 191.

Before leaving this middle section of the chapter, it is worth asking whether it has affinities with other parts of Genesis itself. And here it seems to me that the contrast that is often said to exist between our chapter and the dominant tendency in the patriarchal narratives - namely the contrast between the major public figure and the nomadic clan-leader - is overdrawn. Other parts of the patriarchal narratives suppose that Abra(ha)m is a significant figure on the world stage. Both Pharaoh (ch. 12) and Abimelech (ch. 21) treat him with respect; the former, indeed, furnishes him liberally with wealth before letting him leave Egypt. The Hittites of Hebron, furthermore, regard him as a 'mighty prince' (23:6).[30] Interestingly, the latter passage, like ch. 14, places Abraham in the area of Mamre, in the vicinity of Hebron.[31] Abram's dominant role in Genesis 14 does not seem so incongruous in the light of these hints of his political *gravitas.* It may be, then, that Genesis itself supplies the most relevant comparative material, by way of a context for the narrative, if not in terms of analogies of theme and motif.

iii) Abram and Melchizedek: vv. 18-20

We come finally to vv. 18-20, that part of ch. 14 which is almost universally regarded as an addition to its immediate context. The belief that this is so has naturally led to the question about the original setting and purpose of these verses, probably within some earlier tradition from which it has been adopted for the purposes of the final editor of the chapter.[32] Most treatments agree that 'Salem' stands for Jerusalem (*cf.* Ps.

---

[30]Wenham, *Genesis 1-15,* 320; *cf.* D.J. Wiseman, 'Abraham Reassessed', in A.R. Millard and D.J. Wiseman (eds.) *Studies in the Patriarchal Narratives* (Leicester, IVP 1980) 139-156, esp. 144-149.

[31]See Emerton, 'Riddle', 404. Emerton thinks the understandings of Mamre in 14:13 and 23 are different, since the latter identifies Mamre and Hebron (v. 19), whereas Mamre appears as an individual in the former. The phrase 'oaks of Mamre', 13:18, however, which apparently forms part of the context of ch. 14, functions as a designation of a location, and Emerton's contrast may not be decisive. It is, furthermore, conceived in terms of contrasts between the documents P and J; the appropriateness of this for Genesis is a question in current criticism, to which the conclusions of the present study will be relevant.

[32]Emerton, 'Riddle', 409; *cf.* Westermann, *Genesis 12-36,* 203.

76:3; also the reference to the 'King's Valley', v. 17, *cf.* 2 Sa. 18:18), and that some link is being established between the priesthood of Melchizedek and later Israelite or Jewish worship in Jerusalem. The unit has been variously dated, however, to the time of David, the divided monarchy and the post-exilic period.[33]

The question is what circumstances provide the best setting for a story of a patriarch of Israel paying homage to a Canaanite priest-king, in the name of the God Elyon, at (probably) Jerusalem. A number of interpreters have favoured the post-exilic period, notably, in recent times, Van Seters. Van Seters saw echoes of the later Hasmonaeans, who aspired to be both kings and 'high priests of God Most High'.[34] He thinks it unlikely that the title originated with the Hasmonaeans, but that it should be traced to the late Persian or early Hellenistic periods, and that it was probably a fixed title by their time. Melchizedek therefore represents the priesthood of the second temple, with its implied royal claims.

Van Seters' view suffers from certain handicaps. It cannot be supposed, as he does, that the Jerusalem high priesthood aspired to royal status soon after the return from Babylon.[35] The relevant biblical texts imply separate aspirations for the priest and the scion of David, initially Zerubbabel (Zc. 3 and 6). De Vaux, whom Van Seters cites as an authority for his view, actually assumes a lapse of time before the two aspirations were fused in the figure of the High Priest in the manner of the Hasmonaeans.[36] There is an obvious question too as to how the interests of the Hasmonaeans might have been felt to be served by their identification with a priest-king of ancient Canaan. Van Seters thinks the passage legitimates a certain kind of syncretism, which fuses the deities 'Elyon and *'el qn 'rṣ*.[37] There is a double assumption here,

---

[33]See Westermann, *Genesis 12-36,* 189, for a brief history of interpretation.

[34]Van Seters, *Abraham* , 307-8.

[35]*Ibid.*, 308.

[36]It seems clear from these passages that two figures are in view, the 'Branch' being distinguished from the priest. Zechariah 6 is widely held to have suffered corruption, and lost the name Zerubbabel. See R. de Vaux, *Ancient Israel: Its Life and Institutions* (London, DLT 1965[2]) 400-1. *Cf.* Emerton, 'Riddle', 416-7.

[37]Van Seters, *Abraham,* 307.

namely that El and Elyon were originally separate deities, and that the present passage evidently intends to fuse them.

The former assumption is not fully substantiated by the evidence. Certain inscriptional evidence (Sefire 1) can indeed be read as implying that El and Elyon were at one time understood to be separate gods. F. M. Cross argues, however, on good grounds, that this need not be the case.[38] This gives rise to the possibility that Elyon is used in our text merely as an epithet, and here Cross, who leans to this view, is supported by Westermann, who thinks that '..Elyon, even though it was once an independent divine name, could be understood purely as a divine predicate', and that this indeed was characteristic of the Jerusalem cult.[39] Van Seters' belief, therefore, that Genesis 14:18-20 aims to fuse the two gods El and Elyon in the post-exilic period, cannot be demonstrated. The natural reading of the divine names is that both Elyon and *'el qn 'rṣ* are epithets.[40] The possible fusion of El/Elyon and Yahweh in v. 21, however, is another matter, which we shall return to.

For some of the reasons already advanced, the case for such a late date is regarded as weak by other writers. Emerton had considered it (before Van Seters wrote). In his view neither the divine names nor the name Melchizedek itself forced a post-exilic date, nor was there evidence for a post-exilic priest-king before the Maccabees. On the other hand, pre-exilic kings could take on priestly functions.[41] The likeliest time, in his opinion, is that of David, who will have chosen Jerusalem, which was already a centre of Canaanite worship, in order to unite the cults of Yahweh and El, and thus to establish his rule over Israelites and Canaanites alike. Paradoxically, David benefits from suggested associations with both Melchizedek (as the former king in Jerusalem) and Abram, the ancestor of Israel who is thus represented as having worshipped in David's city.[42]

---

[38]F.M. Cross, *Canaanite Myth and Hebrew Epic* (Cambridge, Harvard UP 1979) 51-2. See also R.E. Clements, *God and Temple* (Oxford, OUP 1965) 44-47 (whose argument Van Seters expressly rejects).

[39]Westermann, *Genesis 12-36*, 204.

[40]Cross, *Canaanite Myth*, 50-1.

[41]Emerton, 'Riddle', 414-419.

[42]*Ibid.*, 420-422.

Westermann too prefers a setting in the context of the pre-exilic Jerusalem cult. The names 'Salem' (Ps. 76:3), Elyon (Ps. 46:5) and even Melchizedek (*cf.* Zadok, David's priest) are at home in the Zion-theology. For him, the fragment is an aetiological justification of the practice of tithe-giving in Jerusalem.[43]

A Davidic or pre-exilic dating of the passage is free from some of the problems that beset the post-exilic theory. In the earlier time, the history of Jerusalem as a place of Canaanite worship is likelier to have been an issue that needed addressing. The transitions to both monarchy and temple-worship were controversial in early Israel, and were accompanied by the cadences of Canaan. It seems clear too that the use of the language for God that was found in Canaan required some digesting in Israel (*cf.* Ex. 3, 6). Emerton is right to point out that the passage (both in itself and as placed in its context) is remarkably open to Canaan. He is right too to oppose the view that some significant difference is intended between the cults of Salem and Sodom (the latter possibly standing for the cult of Molech, or religion in general 'outside the land').[44] If a contrast is intended between the Kings of Salem and Sodom it does not appear to be at the level of cultic legitimacy.

I question, however, whether the Davidic monarchy, or the Zion tradition, provide the home for the meeting of Abram and Melchizedek. It is not clear that Elyon is exclusively associated with Jerusalem (*cf.* Dt. 32:8). Nor does Melchizedek (the king in Jerusalem) fit the pattern of the warrior-king in the terms of that tradition; it is Abram who is the warrior here.[45] I question, furthermore, whether the rapprochement of El and Yahweh which is clearly intended by the author of v. 22 is best understood as an attempt by David to unite the cults of two Gods, hitherto deemed to be separate, and thus to establish his rule over Canaanites as well as Israelites. David's strategy in fixing on Jerusalem as his capital seems to have had its context

---

[43]Westermann, *Genesis 12-36*, 203-206.

[44]Emerton, 'Riddle', 423-425; he challenges in particular H.S. Nyberg, 'Studien zum Religionskampf im Alten Testament', *Archiv für Religionswissenschaft* xxxv (1938) 329-382, and J. W. Bowker, 'Psalm CX', *VT* 17 (1967) 31-41.

[45]Genesis 14 thus differs at this point from Psalm 110.

in the need for Israelite unity. Furthermore, the idea of a uniting of separate cults seems to me to be misconceived. The affirmation by Abram in v. 22 might as well be understood as entering a claim for Yahweh against other understandings of God[46] (In any case, for linguistic and contextual reasons, I think that the adoption of the term El in Old Testament texts, and its use for the God of Israel, is not necessarily a co-option of the Canaanite deity.[47])

The Melchizedek episode, therefore, should not be placed too specifically within early Israel's struggle to articulate its faith in the context of the Canaanite world of ideas. It cannot be traced confidently to David, nor have its terms sufficient force to locate it within a developed Zion-theology (*pace* Westermann). Rather, it fits comfortably in the world of Genesis, in which Abram moves with ease among the peoples of the land. His openness to a Canaanite king is hard to locate elsewhere in the Old Testament traditions (and the point applies also to his help for Sodom - despite the rebuff given to that king's offer of a reward) .

Genesis 14 and the Documentary Hypothesis

We have now reviewed arguments for the date and setting for the various parts of the chapter. Are there conclusions which can be drawn for the chapter as a whole? We noted at the beginning that it had resisted attempts to align it with the traditional Pentateuchal documents, JEDP. Recently, however, affinities have been observed with some of these, particularly D and P.

Astour's attempt to plead for a connection with D was idiosyncratic, and we noticed Emerton's response to it. Blenkinsopp, however, with a debt to Perlitt, has recently espoused the idea of a deuteronomic level of redaction of Genesis, recognisable in terms of a characteristic view of promise and covenant and a concern for the land. Genesis 15 is crucial in this reconstruction.[48] By the same token, the themes

---

[46]So W. Brueggemann, *Genesis*, (Interpretation; Atlanta, John Knox 1982) 136; *cf.* R.W.L. Moberly, *The Old Testament of the Old Testament* (Minneapolis, Fortress 1992) 86-7.

[47]I have argued this point at greater length in 'Yahweh and the Gods', *EJT* 2:2 (1993) forthcoming.

[48]J. Blenkinsopp, *The Pentateuch* (London, SCM 1992) 121-124, 129-130.

of kinship and land in ch. 14 might lead to the hypothesis of deuteronomic influence there too, and indeed some see thematic connections of this sort between it and the following chapter.[49] There are also affinities with deuteronomic conquest traditions in the striking resemblance of some of the names of people and places in Transjordan (Gn. 14:5f.) to names in Deuteronomy 2:10-12, 20. None of these affinities, however, is sufficiently strong to link Genesis 14 firmly with D. Our narrative does not exhibit a concern for the land in a specifically deuteronomic sense. Indeed, it permits debate whether the region of the 'Plain' lies within the land of Canaan or not (though it seems to be placed firmly outside it in Genesis 13:12).[50] On the assumption that Lot forms an integral part of the narrative,[51] the primary issue here seems to be kinship not land. This is not foreign to D, of course, but not peculiar to it either. Interestingly too, Lot's relationship to the father of Israel is more positively expressed here than Deuteronomy portrays the nation's relationship with his descendants, Ammon and Moab (Dt. 23:3f.; *cf.* Gn. 19:30-38).

The case for a link between the Lot story and Deuteronomy is stronger in respect of the conquest narrative, because the rights of Moab and Ammon to their respective territories are there upheld, and the connection with Lot expressly established (Dt. 2:8b-13, 16-20). The connection is the more impressive because the passages in Deuteronomy also contain the demographic details mentioned above. These affinities, however, may be explained by the availability of the Lot traditions to the author of Deuteronomy 2 (in keeping with the deuteronomic interest in the patriarchs).[52] A comparison of Deuteronomy 2 and 23, however, warns that the deuteronomic attitude to Lot is complex, and therefore not easily brought into connection with Genesis 14.

---

[49]L. A. Turner, *Announcements of Plot in Genesis* (JSOTS 96; Sheffield, JSOT Press 1990) 67-8.

[50]See L. R. Helyer, 'The Separation of Abram and Lot', *JSOT* 26 (1983) 77-88, esp. 79-80; Turner, *Announcements*, 67.

[51]Emerton disputes this, 'Riddle', 407; *cf.* Blenkinsopp, *Pentateuch*, 117. But see further below.

[52]See Emerton, *ibid.*, 405. Blenkinsopp rightly rejects Van Seters' view that the term 'the fathers' in Deuteronomy refers to the exodus generation; *Pentateuch*, 115; *cf.* Van Seters, 'Confessional Reformulation in the Exilic Period', *VT* 22 (1972) 448-459.

Finally, Abram's friendly relations with Canaanite kings cannot easily be squared with Deuteronomy's uncompromising attitude to Canaan. Abram's rebuff of the King of Sodom's offer of a reward is certainly a key moment in the story, to which we shall return. Yet it is not a rejection of Canaanite kingship in the explicit manner of Deuteronomy.

Modern study of the Pentateuch tends to lay increasing emphasis on the importance of P in its final production, and in general to look for exilic and post-exilic influence in its various parts. A number of writers look to this late stage of Pentateuchal composition for an explanation of the final form of Genesis 14. Westermann and Van Seters think that the concept of Abram as a world-figure is intelligible only in the late period, and compare Daniel and Judith because of their encounters with world-empires.[53] Blenkinsopp's reading of Genesis in general owes much to his belief that it enshrines a pattern of exile-return. The narrative's elimination of Lot, along with Esau and Ishmael, from the right to land-claims reflects a peculiarly post-exilic concern.[54] Inasmuch as Genesis 14 belongs to the story of Lot's exclusion from a claim to the land it could be aligned with P for this reason.

None of these reasons, however, is quite convincing. The analogy between Abram and Judith or Daniel is inapposite because Abram is not cast as the Jew living under Imperial rule. The enemies come from outside and make no attempt to conquer the land. Abram's fraternising with Canaanites, furthermore, hardly fits with the struggle for purity and identity of the post-exilic Jews. The perceived exile-return pattern does not force an exilic or post-exilic date either. The topic as such is too general in ancient literature to force such a dating. And specifically, our narrative does not quite fit the idea of the exclusion of non-Jews from land-claims after the exile. If Lot (as the progenitor of Moab and Ammon) represents foreign elements, then Abram's affirmation of his kinship with him in rescuing him becomes problematical.

Some recent studies have revived older attempts to assign the chapter to J largely on the grounds of the Lot

---

[53]Westermann, *Genesis 12-36*, 192; Van Seters, *Abraham*, 305. *Cf.* the idea that P marks a departure from D because of its 'universalistic' outlook (Blenkinsopp, *Pentateuch*, 238-9).

[54]Blenkinsopp, *Pentateuch*, 120.

traditions.[55] However, these attempts do not easily cope with some of the features of the narrative which we have noticed, namely the explanatory glosses, the problematical relationship between the parts of the chapter, and the fact that, in the terms of traditional theory, some of the vocabulary in the chapter is closer to P than to J (e.g. רְכֻשׁ, נֶפֶשׁ meaning person, v. 21). Furthermore, there are narratological connections with ch. 15:1-6 (the resumption of the term מָגֵן/מִגֵּן, shield, 14:20; 15:1; and see below on the motif of the heir), which is widely assigned to E.

Genesis 14 in Genesis

Indeed, it is plain that the narrative does make links with other material in Genesis, the Lot-Sodom motif being the most obvious. The narrative connections with the surrounding material are in fact quite subtle. The events of ch. 14 follow neatly from those of ch. 13, whose outcome is the separation of Abram from Lot, the former living at Hebron, the latter at Sodom. Lot's presence in Sodom is the spring of the action in the next 'scene' (ch. 14). The point is made explicit in 14:12. This verse is often regarded as a clumsy afterthought to the story of the raid on Sodom.[56] It can equally well be seen, however, to highlight the significance of the events of vv. 1-11 in the light of the preceding scene, and thus to pose a question about Abram's response. In the light of his separation from Lot in ch. 13 what is the nature of his relationship with him now? Does he owe him an obligation as kinsman? And indeed, now that Lot has placed himself outside the land of promise, does that kinship relationship have any bearing on the fulfilment of the promise of posterity (12:2)?[57] That issue is resumed in 15 (notice the link to the preceding in 15:1a) with Abram's lament about his lack of an heir.[58]

Links of this sort are not in themselves in dispute. The important question is what status they should have in trying to

---

[55]See the discussion in Wenham, *Genesis 1-15*, 306.
[56]Westermann, *Genesis 12-36*, 198-9.
[57]Helyer, 'Separation', 78-82, thinks that Lot, by placing himself outside the land, brings to an end the hope of posterity through him. Turner, in contrast, thinks Lot-as-heir must be brought back within the land, (*Announcements*, 67-8).
[58]Helyer, 'Separation', 83.

come to an understanding of the narrative? Westermann makes his methodological priorities clear. On the interpretation of ch. 14 according to its different parts he says: 'One must first study the constituent parts and the tradition-history of each; only then can one study the chapter as a whole and determine its type and age'.[59] Van Seters asserted the need to understand the 'basic story' before considering vv. 18-20.[60] Other value-judgements are associated with this kind of approach, for example, the view that the story of the campaign (vv. 1-11) is incompatible with the story of Abram's recovery of Lot because of a perceived contradiction between the public or political and the relatively 'private', family capacities in which he is portrayed in the two sections. Such judgements, I think, can divert attention from real connections that might exist in the wider context. Canonical criticism and other modern approaches to reading the Old Testament have taught us to look carefully for such connections before making decisions which orientate the discussion at the outset towards certain kinds of conclusions.

This point applies at the level of the parts of the chapter itself, but also at that of its setting within Genesis. Where the chapter has been thought intractable as regards its origins this has usually been because of the kind of question brought to it: how does this narrative relate to the previously identified 'documents'? The picture is different when affinities are sought for it on a broad canvas in Genesis in a less trammelled way. And we have had hints in our study so far that there are 'Genesis' issues, of a sort that set the book apart from the rest of the Pentateuch.[61] The matter of the 'public' and 'private' aspects of the portrayal of Abraham is a case in point. As we have seen, Genesis 14 is not unique in supposing that Abraham had considerable standing in the political world of

---

[59]Westermann, *Genesis 12-36*, 189.

[60]Van Seters, *Abraham*, 303.

[61]See R. Rendtorff's challenge to the traditional documentary approach to Pentateuchal criticism, in which he emphasised differences between Genesis and the other books, *The Problem of the Process of Transmission in the Pentateuch*, (ET of 1977 German original: JSOTS 89: Sheffield, JSOT Press 1990); see also G.J. Wenham, 'The Religion of the Patriarchs', in Millard and Wiseman (eds.) *Essays on the Patriarchal Narratives*, (Leicester, IVP 1980) 157-188; and now Moberly, *The Old Testament of the Old Testament*.

his day. (See above on Gn. 12; 21; 23:6). The assignment of the last named passage to the source P may have discouraged the recognition of a significant parallel between these two chapters. But the presence of this note in the traditions about Abraham should give pause to the confident polarisation between public and private portrayals within a narrowly circumscribed passage considered in isolation (such as Westermann's treatment of Genesis 14).

Abram and Melchizedek

My purpose in the foregoing has been to prepare the ground for an interpretation of Genesis 14:18-20 in its context. The background to the enquiry has been the widespread belief that the verses are unsuitable to their context, and the consequent uncertainty about how they should be evaluated in relation to it.[62] My contention has been that such a view requires an understanding of what properly constitutes that context. This led us to consider not only the interrelationship of the parts of the chapter, but also to think about the character of the portrayal of Abraham in the patriarchal narratives broadly conceived.

A number of issues emerged that our passage appeared to share with the patriarchal narratives at large. First, the relationship between Abram and his political environment plays a key role in the chapter. Abram's recognition as a powerful figure occurs at several points in the narratives, and his action in ch. 14 is not out of keeping with this picture. The relationships with both the Canaanite kings, Salem and Sodom, is intelligible in terms of the portrayal of Abram as a major player in international affairs. There is nothing 'accidental' about the intrusion of the Melchizedek incident in this sense. The double encounter in vv. 17-24 certainly poses questions of strict coherence, but the problem is not at the level of the role in which Abram is cast; this is in keeping with the portrayal of Abra(ha)m more broadly in the narratives.

---

[62]Van Seters' opinion that vv. 18-20 are secondary in literary-critical terms is hermeneutically decisive for him: '..the original *written* story did not have vv. 18-20, so one must deal first with the version that does not have it and then account for its addition. In no case should vv. 18-20, the addition, be used as a point of departure to explain the chapter as a whole'; *Abraham*, 299.

Second, his relationship with his kinsman Lot, the spring of the action in Genesis 14, has as background the wider motif of Lot and Sodom (Gn. 13; 18-19), which in turn is connected with Abram's occupation of the land (Gn. 13). The Abram-Lot relationship is thus set against the background of the promise (12:1-3). Its primary focus is apparently the promise of posterity, because of the absence at this point of an heir in Abram's direct line.[63] If Lot is presented as a possible heir to Abram in Genesis 13, ch. 14 shows how he ceases to be cast in that role. The element of land is also connected, however, because the unfolding of the posterity element in the narrative turns on Lot's unexpected choice of a location outside the land proper. The issue, then, in ch. 14, is essentially problematical. What is at stake when Abram rescues Lot? The motivation in terms of kinship is clear. But is Abram trying to preserve his stake in Lot as heir? If so, the attempt is flawed because of Lot's prior choice, and it has something in common with Abra(ha)m's later attempt to force the promise by means of Ishmael.

The rescue of Lot, therefore, takes its place naturally in the larger story of the hazardous progress of the promise. Indeed a pattern might even be discerned in the unfolding of the promise, in which this incident plays a part. This first section of the story of Abram and Lot (Gn. 13-14) is the first act, as it were, in the drama of the fulfilment of the promise of a son to Abram. When Lot is excluded the need for an heir in direct line is accentuated. The issue is raised again by Abram immediately after the events of Genesis 14 (in 15:1-6), whence the story unfolds by way of the births of Ishmael and finally Isaac. The drama reaches a new high point with the near-sacrifice of Isaac (Gn. 22), and is rounded off when he is spared. The story of the death and burial of Sarah (Gn. 23) may be seen as the laying to rest of the posterity aspect of the promise. The latter chapters, furthermore, have two important features which echo Genesis 14. First, ch. 22 involves Abra(ha)m worshipping on a mountain 'in the land of Moriah' (22:2), often seen as a cryptic allusion to Jerusalem - rather like Salem in ch. 14.[64] Second, in ch. 23 the element of

---

[63]Turner, Helyer; see above.

[64]See Moberly, *Old Testament*, 91-2 and n. 13, who also points to Moriah and Salem as allusions to Jerusalem.

posterity in the promise (rounded off in the death of Sarah) is connected with the element of land, because of the stake in the land symbolically claimed by Abra(ha)m in his purchase of the field at Machpelah. It is thus like ch. 14 in posing the question about the (still future) possession of the land. This resemblance to ch. 14, incidentally, is cemented by the location of Machpelah 'to the east of Mamre' (v. 17; *cf.* 14:13). And it is here too, as we recall, that Abra(ha)m appears in the role of a major figure, again as in ch. 14. These echoes of the one chapter in the other reinforce the view that they belong together within the unfolding story of the promise.

The third aspect of the patriarchal narratives which features in ch. 14 is that of religion. Who is Abram's God, and how does he relate to the worship of the peoples of the land? Abram's encounter with Melchizedek makes an obvious contribution to the airing of this issue. That the issue is not confined to vv. 18-20 within the chapter is clear from the resumption of Melchizedek's name for God by Abram, duly modified, in his subsequent dialogue with the King of Sodom (v. 22). Arguably too, that dialogue plays an important part in the patriarchal narratives' articulation of what it means to worship Yahweh in the midst of peoples who do not.

I think, indeed, that the 'interruption' in vv. 18-20 is explicable in terms of these themes, and in its context. There is no question that it is an interruption; the appearance of the King of Salem is quite unexpected. This is not to say, however, that it is a mere intrusion. There are signs, as G. J. Wenham has shown, that its relationship with the context has been carefully crafted. Melchizedek knows that Abram has won a victory (v. 20). Abram's refusal to be made rich by the King of Sodom (הֶעֱשַׁרְתִּי, v. 23) entails a play on the word for tithe (מַעֲשֵׂר, v. 20). Melchizedek's bringing out bread (הוֹצִיא לֶחֶם, v. 18) contrasts with the King of Sodom's going out to war (יָצָא, מִלְחָמָה, vv. 2, 8, 17). And finally, as already observed, Abram's ascription of praise to 'Yahweh, El-Elyon, creator of heaven and earth', v. 22, picks up the terms used by Melchizedek, v. 19, with the significant addition of the name Yahweh.[65] It is clear, therefore, that the Melchizedek episode has been carefully placed. But what does it mean?

---

[65]Wenham, *Genesis 1-15*, 305.

Its most obvious effect is to stall the narrative, postponing the final exchange between Abram and the King of Sodom. That exchange, which resolves the issue of the stolen goods and the captives, and sees them safely back in their rightful place, could be read aside from the intervening Melchizedek encounter. Nevertheless, it is also possible to read it as having been affected by the interruption. The main reason for thinking so is the absence of an express allusion to Lot in the final negotiations. Hitherto in the narrative the fate of Lot has been closely connected with that of the property (vv. 12, 16).[66] The connection is highlighted just before the King of Sodom comes forward to deal with Abram (v. 16). It is precisely this that will be at stake in the expected parley with the King of Sodom, introduced at v. 17. After Melchizedek intervenes, the King of Sodom's opening gambit takes up precisely the point of v. 16: 'Give me the persons (הַנֶּפֶשׁ), but take the goods for yourself' (v. 21). While Lot is not expressly mentioned here, he is clearly present in the conversation, in the term הַנֶּפֶשׁ.[67] The King of Sodom's highlighting of the issue of 'the persons' suggests a kind of claim on Lot. There is an issue here; where and to whom does this man belong? And significantly, Abram does not demur when the King of Sodom makes his claim. Lot who has chosen to live outside the land of promise is claimed in turn by the power that has authority there. The exchange between Abram and the King of Sodom is an eloquent laying to rest of that line of the story which might have ended in Lot as Abram's heir in the promised land. The reason for this lies, I believe, in the significance of Abram's encounter with the King of Salem.

I have argued that the encounters between Abram and the two kings are in keeping with the portrayal of Abram as a major political figure. The two meetings, however, contrast with each other, in such a way as to permit an evaluation of Abram's role on the world stage. If Abram is to be a participant in the large affairs of nations, in what way shall he bear his part? If he is to receive a land, by what right shall he hold it? The double-encounter sets forth two possibilities. The King of

---

[66]Note the chiasmus in v. 16, emphasising the close link between the two; see Wenham, *ibid.*, 303.

[67]This word is an interesting shift from הָעָם, v. 16, and an unusual use of the collective singular (see K-B 3/iii, 672). Perhaps it is chosen to hint particularly at Lot.

Sodom accepts that one may hold by right whatever can be gained by strength. Though he has suffered at their hand, he is firmly in the same world as the kings of the east, who came to plunder and subdue. His offer to Abram recognises the latter's right to possess by virtue of his prowess, and also seeks to enlist him as ally, or perhaps vassal. This route Abram repudiates along with the spiked gift.

The King of Salem, on the other hand, proclaims that Abram's victory has been a gift of God (v. 20). When Abram gives him 'a tenth of everything', he is not merely deferring to a superior; to say this merely poses anew the question why he should recognise the unheralded king in this way (and not another, such as the King of Sodom). Rather, he is assenting to what Melchizedek has said. Possession is by gift of God, and is marked by an appropriate attitude to what is given. To say that the gift to Melchizedek contradicts the subsequent returning of the goods to the King of Sodom is to miss this. The two gifts, to Salem and Sodom, are brought into conjunction: the gifts of God are marked by the giving of a portion in return; in contrast, a king's pretended power to give is resisted by a refusal of the gift. This contrast is precisely that which is effected by the word-play noted above (הֶעֱשַׁרְתִּי ,מַעֲשֵׂר).

In the gift and the polite refusal, therefore, Abram shows how he will possess the land; he will receive it as a gift. (It may be no accident that Abram is here designated הָעִבְרִי, with its implication of being an 'outsider'.[68] The fully developed theological correlative of the idea is found in Leviticus 25:23). Perhaps we can say that Abram learns this, or relearns it, in the encounter with Melchizedek, for this is implied in the suggestion that the one encounter bears upon the other. Yet he is not a bland receiver of the doctrine, for in assimilating it he re-expresses, now for the benefit of the King of Sodom (v. 22), his own faith in the God, Yahweh, who has promised him land and posterity. The priest-king of Salem knows that it is the Most High, the Maker of heaven and earth, who alone can give; but Abram knows that this is none other than Yahweh.

---

[68]K-B 3/iii, 739.

The Melchizedek incident, therefore, contributes to all three themes noted above as belonging both to the patriarchal narratives at large and to chapter 14 in particular. Abram's presence on the world-stage will be characterised by his understanding that all wealth and power is a gift of God; he will hold fast to the specific promises of the God whom he knows, rather than try to force them (in this case via Lot - a resolution in which he will falter again); he enters a claim that the God who is known in Canaan as Elyon is none other than the God whom he has met as Yahweh. Perhaps we can go further. In the proclamation of Yahweh as the Most High God, Abram puts the events narrated in a new light, for the promise which he has received involves a reading of history. Through Abram all the families of the earth will bless themselves (Gn. 12:3). The deliverance of Sodom may betoken this; and the confession in the ears of its king announces it.

This then is the rationale underlying Melchizedek's sudden appearance on the scene in this drama. Its very suddenness contributes to its power, representing, as it were, the breaking in of God on human affairs and human thought. Melchizedek needs no other justification for accosting Abram than that he represents God, no more than Elijah, that unknown from Tishbe, would need for appearing before Ahab (1 Ki. 17:1). This 'interruption' bespeaks an irruption, and is well suited to its purpose.

Melchizedek as 'Priest for Ever'

What then of Melchizedek as 'a priest for ever' (Ps. 110:4; Heb. 7:3)? The author of Hebrews takes the term 'priest for ever' from Psalm 110:4. That Psalm celebrates the kingship of David in the context of the Old Testament's theology of Zion. It seems to be the primary reference-point for him on the topic, for the passage is applied messianically to Christ in 5:6, according to his general understanding of the Psalms. The particular concerns of Psalm 110 do not seem to be taken up. Rather, when he explores the meaning of Melchizedek further, he bases his interpretation on the Genesis passage. There, he notes the priest-king's sudden appearance in and disappearance from the narrative (7:3), his blessing of Abram (7:7), and the latter's gift of a tithe (7:4). Thus far his reading of the passage is straightforward. Beyond that, however, he sees the significance of the incident in terms of his argument that Melchizedek represents a superior priesthood to that of Levi. Both Melchizedek's blessing of Abram and the latter's gift of a tithe imply the priest-king's superiority to him, the father of Levi (7:4-10). Melchizedek, therefore, has a priesthood aside from physical descent and the requirements of the law (7:16), which becomes a suitable type of the priesthood of Jesus - of the tribe of Judah (7:14) - whose eternal priesthood is superior to the established Levitical priesthood of the author's day (7:15-22).

Clearly, therefore, the author of Hebrews has applied Abram's encounter with Melchizedek to an issue which was paramount for him, namely the fact that Jesus transcended all previous institutions given to Israel. His special application of it does not emerge directly from the text of Genesis 14, which says nothing about Melchizedek's genealogical status, nor implies the 'eternity' of his priesthood. The idea of Melchizedek as being without genealogy is a shaping of the tradition to what was for him a burning issue, the strongly 'genealogical' claims of the Levitical priesthood. Perhaps too the interpretation of Salem as 'peace' (v. 2) subtly opposes the claim of Jerusalem to be the place where God dwelt, paramountly, in the temple. (Our author is clearly in control of the method he is using. The question whether he really thought that Melchizedek had no parents hardly arises.)

Yet the Hebrews interpretation should not therefore be dismissed as an arbitrary use of the text. We saw that the main concern of Genesis 14:18-20 was to show that the promise to Abram would be appropriated by faith on his part. Correspondingly, it would not be realised through identifying with a system that stood over against that promise (the religio-politics of Canaan). These points find echoes in the underlying concerns of the writer to the Hebrews. The issue is fundamentally one of promise, with its corollary, faith (Heb. 4:1-3). This, indeed, is the opening note struck by the passage which concerns Melchizedek (6:13-15). The priesthood of Christ, furthermore, is affirmed against the continuing claims of another system, which in the view of Hebrews is now obsolete, namely the Levitical priesthood. True faith accepts the way of salvation which God has given, and does not place its trust elsewhere. (In its manner of adopting Salem, incidentally, it has something in common with Genesis, which at most merely hints at Jerusalem through this name). The epistle, therefore, may be said to draw on the tradition of Melchizedek in order to promote its doctrine of the fulfilment of God's promises in Christ.

In pursuing its argument, the letter to the Hebrews has adopted a line of exegesis which in its specifics goes beyond the original passage. Yet I think it can be argued that it is in accord with it at a deeper level. Indeed, one can go further: the interpretation in Hebrews is suggestive for a re-reading of Genesis 14. The bold idea of a priest who is 'without father, without mother, without genealogy, having neither beginning of days nor end of life, but resembling the Son of God' (7:3) puts the sudden appearance of Melchizedek in a new light. It suggests precisely the idea of a novel intervention by God in human affairs. Here is a profounder kind of approach to the text than concerns of a strictly literary-critical nature. The latter are not invalid. Neither, however, should they be allowed to invalidate the reading of Hebrews, which has given a new kind of life to the passage. It is not just that 'we' have our kinds of concerns and 'they' had theirs, though it is partly that. Hebrews' reading of Genesis is also a function of its reception of Scripture as Word of God, and its expectation that in it is found the way of life.

6

ABRAHAM, AKHENATEN, MOSES AND MONOTHEISM

Alan R. Millard

Summary

Israel's faith in one God only arose comparatively late in her history according to many biblical scholars, and so is inconceivable for a Moses or an Abraham. Yet the religious revolution of Akhenaten proves a form of monotheism was possible in the second millennium BC. The nature of the evidence for that belief, and for other religious concepts in the ancient Near East which continued over many centuries, shows there is no logical reason to deny monotheism could have existed among Israel's ancestors.

Introduction

The period 1350-1250 BC. was 'ideally suited to give birth to monotheism' wrote W.F. Albright in his famous book *From the Stone Age to Christianity*.[1] So far as Albright was concerned, Israel's faith in a single god began then, but many others do not see it emerging until the eighth century BC or later, so that W.G. Dever can write, 'the overwhelming scholarly consensus today is ... that true monotheism developed only late in Israel's history, probably not until the Exile and Return'.[2] Whatever opinions about the date of monotheism appearing in Israel are held, the fact remains that her faith is unique in the ancient world. No other beliefs current there have affected so many people over so large a part of the world for so long a time. A unique phenomenon is awkward for historians since they have no standard way to explain or assess it, so they make strenuous attempts to fit it with a pattern of known features in the same general category. For Israel's devotion to her one God that means bringing its date as late as possible, the time when the great passages in Isaiah 42-46, etc., declaring there is no God but the Lord, were written, and those chapters are commonly dated in the 6th century BC, the period which is seen as the acme of Israelite religious development. Yet H.H. Rowley remarked, 'It is indeed surprising, and not easily to be accounted for on simple evolutionary lines, that Israel attained a monotheistic faith.'[3] Following the usual view about the progress of Israelite religion and the dating of the Pentateuchal sources which accepts it, there is relatively little problem in accommodating the statements of Genesis and Exodus: they are retrojections from theological thought of the 1st millennium BC. The usual view, however, fails to treat the Pentateuch as a group of ancient Near Eastern writings and to examine it in its context. There is a constant need for that contextual study if the Pentateuch, or any part of the Old Testament, is to receive an historical assessment which may begin to approach reality. The purpose of this paper, therefore, is to explore the historical and logical possibility of

---

[1](2nd ed; New York, Doubleday 1957) 12.

[2]'What Remains of the House That Albright Built?', *BA* 56.1 (1993) 25-35 [33].

[3]*The Faith of Israel* (London, SCM 1956) 73.

monotheism, or at least the exclusive worship of a single god, at the time of Moses and even of Abraham.

I. Moses and Akhenaten

Two famous declarations to Moses establish the identity of the God who will lead Israel from Egypt to the Promised Land with the God who led Abraham from Mesopotamia and promised the land to his posterity: 'I am the God of your father, the God of Abraham, the God of Isaac and the God of Jacob' (Ex. 3:6) and 'I am the Lord. I appeared to Abraham, to Isaac and to Jacob as God Almighty, but by my name the Lord I did not make myself known to them' (Ex. 6:3).

In the song at the crossing of the Red Sea, that God is described as incomparable:

> Who among the gods is like you, O Lord ?
> Who is like you -
> majestic in holiness,
> awesome in glory,
> working wonders ? (Ex. 15:11).

If those words do not deny the existence of other gods, they certainly imply they are not worth attention.

Moses lived, we suppose, in the 13th century BC, less than a hundred years after the well-known Egyptian 'heretic' pharaoh, Akhenaten, who reigned *c.* 1352-1336 BC. Under his rule Egypt experienced a revolution in religion and art. The pharaoh declared the sun-disk, Aten, to be the only divinity, changing his own name from Amenhotep (IV) to mark his new allegiance. Hitherto Egyptians had worshipped a large pantheon, with Amen-Re, identified with the sun, at its head. By the 15th century BC some theologians hailed Re as 'the Universe who has assimilated all the other gods in his being'.[4] The Aten was unique, without consort or family. Other gods were no longer countenanced, many of their names were erased from visible monuments and their cults stopped, especially in the cases of Amen-Re and Osiris. Even the plural word 'gods' was changed to 'god' where it stood in inscriptions. Images were apparently condemned as futile, the product of human speculation, contrasting with the sun-disk

[4]C. Aldred, *Akhenaten, King of Egypt* (London, Thames and Hudson 1988) 239.

who renewed and revealed himself every day. Egyptologists from the time of J.H. Breasted describe the king and his faith straightforwardly: 'the earliest monotheist';[5] 'Atenism ...was a genuine monotheism';[6] 'Where the idea of Akhenaten differed from the Re of the new [Eighteenth Dynasty] sacred books was that, instead of incorporating all the old deities in a comprehensive henotheism, it rigidly excluded them in an uncompromising monotheism.'[7] This unparalleled change in Egypt's worship was the king's doing. He was 'the beautiful child of the Aten', so his divine father may have revealed his nature to him. Certainly, the king announced Aten revealed to him the site for the new capital city which was to perpetuate the god's name, Akhetaten, modern El-Amarna.[8] A corollary of this relationship between the single god and the pharaoh was the king's position as sole intermediary between the deity and his worshippers. While historians can trace some movements in Egyptian religion towards the concept of a single god in the decades before Akhenaten ascended the throne, the cult he imposed was most likely his own creation. 'Where Akhenaten's ideas of monotheism came from in a world which widely tolerated so many diverse forms of godhead is unknown, but the inference is that they were his own, the logical outcome of regarding the Aten as a heavenly king, whose son was the pharaoh. Like the latter, he could only be regarded as "unique, without a peer".'[9] Not only religion stemmed from him. Another scholar has affirmed, 'The entire period, its art, its religion, its denial of accepted forms bears the imprint of a powerful mind, and it is surely unnecessary to look for this powerful mind elsewhere than with the pharaoh.'[10]

Akhenaten's revolution lasted little longer than he did; his successor changed his own name from Tutankhaten to

---

[5]J.H. Breasted, *A History of the Ancient Egyptians* (London, Hodder and Stoughton 1909) 264-265.

[6]Sir Alan Gardiner, *Egypt of the Pharaohs* (Oxford, Clarendon 1961) 227.

[7]C. Aldred, 'Egypt: the Amarna Period and the End of the Eighteenth Dynasty', *CAH* II.2 (3rd ed; London, CUP 1975) 88.

[8]Aldred, *Akhenaten, King of Egypt*, 44-49, 269-270; Gardiner, *Egypt of the Pharaohs* , 221-222.

[9]Aldred, 'Egypt', 89.

[10]J.D. Ray, 'Prophets without honour? Akhenaten: Ancient Egypt's Prodigal Son?' *History Today* 40 (January 1990) 26-32.

Tutankhamun, abandoned the city Akhetaten for the old capital at Memphis and re-instated the worship of the old gods. The names of Akhenaten, his queen and his god were obliterated from the monuments, and while their impact lingered somewhere in the country's memory the king was execrated as the perpetrator of 'The Wrong'. Formal lists of pharaohs omitted Akhenaten's name. Beyond the court and major temples, evidence suggests the Aten failed to displace the traditional gods in popular religion, for ordinary people continued to pray as they had always done to this deity or that with whom they felt a personal link.[11]

Since the revelation of Akhenaten's activities to modern eyes a century or so ago, many writers have attempted to explain the 'monotheistic' faith of Moses as derived from them. Whatever the similarities, the distinctions should also be given due weight. One Egyptologist has recently written, "...there is an important difference between the sun-god Aten of Akhenaten on the one hand and both the Judaeo-Christian-Islamic deity and the traditional Egyptian sun-god Ra on the other. The sun-god of Akhenaten is not engaged with humanity beyond dawning to give light and life, a task that it performs for every living being on earth as well, animal or vegetable. The course of the Aten across the sky has no moral content, and the king defends only the truth that Aten is sole god, not the moral or social order.'[12]

The example of Akhenaten proves that a 'monotheistic' faith could originate in the 2nd millennium BC, the product, experts declare, of a single man's mind. If there could be an Akhenaten, a monotheistic Egyptian, then logically there could be others. Albright's basic contention cannot be gainsaid: a Moses could have promoted the worship of one god only among his people, together with the appropriate cultic and festal observances.

---

[11]See Aldred, 'Egypt', 89, for the suggestion that a Semitic influence may have crept into the attitude evident in prayers.

[12]S. Quirke, *Ancient Egyptian Religion* (London, British Museum Press 1992) 42-43; *cf.* Gardiner, *Egypt of the Pharaohs,* 229: 'A defect of the Doctrine was its complete lack of ethical teaching.'

II. The Aten and the Divine Name

Although Akhenaten's religion was new, perhaps it was foreshadowed in the reign of his father Amenophis III (*c.* 1390-1352 BC) when the 'references to Aten as a solar divinity become more numerous'.[13] The Aten was an ancient concept as 'the sun's disk'. A famous earlier occurrence of this sort is in the Story of Sinuhe, that interesting account of an Egyptian finding refuge and living with a semi-nomadic chieftain in Canaan about the time of Abraham, a story, whether it be true or not, actually available to us in copies written only a century or so after the events it describes, demonstrating that such narratives could be created and preserved from the Middle Bronze Age. As the story opens, the Pharaoh who favoured Sinuhe has died, a moment conveyed by the expression 'the king ... went aloft to heaven and became united with the disk, the limb of the god being merged with him who made him.' Gardiner says, 'It is often difficult to tell when this term has or has not a religious implication', for it might mean simply 'the sun' or 'the sun-god'.[14]

Perhaps an analogy can be drawn between the interpretation and development the Aten underwent under Akhenaten and the revelation of YHWH which Moses received. In each case a term was given fresh significance, and the Aten was certainly an old term, as just noted. For a long known concept to gain an enlarged meaning and fresh currency is quite common (compare the use of 'flying' in 19th century English with its use to-day), and so the same could be true with a divine name.

The history of the Aten in Egypt may open a way to understand the revelation of the Divine Name in the Pentateuch. Beside the literal acceptance of Exodus 6:3 as commonly translated, 'I appeared to Abraham, to Isaac and to Jacob as God Almighty, but by my name the LORD I did not make myself known to them' (NIV), which G.J. Wenham defended positively in 1980,[15] stand the interpretations of W.J. Martin, taking the words as a question, '...for did I not let

---

[13]Aldred, *Akhenaten King of Egypt*, 239.

[14]Gardiner, *Egypt of the Pharaohs*, 217. For a translation of the story, see *ANET* 18-22.

[15]'The Religion of the Patriarchs' in A.R. Millard, D.J. Wiseman (eds.) *Essays on the Patriarchal Narratives* (Leicester, IVP 1980) 157-88.

myself be known to them by my name YHWH ?'[16] and of J.A. Motyer who, following earlier writers, takes 'name' to denote character.[17] Those two views assume the name was current long before the revelation to Moses, that it was the name of the God of the fathers.

III. The God of the Fathers

A. Alt's famous essay drew attention to the concept of the paternal god or gods among the Nabataeans and contemporary peoples in Syria in 1929 as a source for comparison with Israelite beliefs.[18] A few years later J. Lewy pointed to the existence of 'the god of the father' almost two millennia earlier in the Old Assyrian tablets from the merchant colony at Kanesh in central Anatolia.[19] The subject has continued to provoke discussion, with debate especially over the role and identity of the god(s).[20] It should be observed that the 'personal god', although often anonymous, could be a major deity such as Ashur or Adad.[21] Among the lately published documents from Emar on the Euphrates in Syria there are a number of wills dividing property among a man's family. They state, 'the gods belong to the principal dwelling; the principal dwelling is the share of the eldest son'. These activities are only documented long after the time of the Patriarchs, close to or contemporary with Moses, but they show there was a feeling that there were family gods which belonged to the eldest son.[22] Although slightly later in date

---

[16]*Stylistic Criteria and the Analysis of the Pentateuch* (London, Tyndale 1955) 18-19; *cf.* NIV footnote and G.R. Driver, 'Affirmation by Exclamatory Negation', *Journal of the Ancient Near Eastern Society of Columbia University* 5 (1973) *The Gaster Festschrift*, 107-14, esp. 109.

[17]*The Revelation of the Divine Name* (London, Tyndale 1959).

[18]A. Alt, *Essays on Old Testament History and Religion* (ET of 1929 original; Oxford, Blackwell 1966) 1-77.

[19]'Les textes paléo-assyriens et l'Ancien Testament' *RHR* 110 (1934) 19-65, although, as Alt remarked (*The God of the Fathers*, 32, n. 77) these do not contain the expression 'god of PN'.

[20]See recently J.-M. Heimerdinger, 'The God of Abraham', *Vox Evangelica* 22 (1992) 41-55.

[21]Examples cited in *CAD* I-J (1960) 94-97.

[22]Examples in D. Arnaud, *Textes syriens de l'Age du Bronze Récent* (Aula Orientalis Supplementa 1; Barcelona, Editions AUSA 1991) no. 42:13; *cf.* nos. 41:12, 26; 46:10; 72:10; 73:7; 48.

than the tablets of Nuzi, these Emar references may be relevant to the interpretation of statements about gods in some of the Nuzi texts formerly brought into the discussion of patriarchal customs.[23] What those gods were may be revealed by the many terra-cotta figures found at Emar and other sites, sometimes placed beneath the threshold, presumably to protect the occupants of a house from evil.[24]

The major question about the patriarchal religion is the identity of the God of the Fathers. Again, ancient texts have refreshed the discussion, leading many to assume the God of Abraham was the El of the Canaanites and the texts from Ugarit, found in various guises, El Olam, El Shaddai, El Bethel, etc. Now while every attempt to set biblical reports in their ancient context is welcome, those reports should receive due weight themselves. Either the Patriarchs worshipped several gods under various names, or they worshipped one who had several names.[25] The former position suits the ancient context well and so has many adherents. Still, it is the easier solution and for that reason deserves to be treated with caution; the text critic's principle of *lectio difficilior* may be apt in this area of research also. A variety of names for a single deity is by no means rare in the societies which have left a considerable range of documents. One god could absorb the attributes of others in a syncretistic way, as Amun did in Egypt before Akhenaten's revolution, or could be known in many guises.

IV Abraham and Akhenaten

Many centuries elapsed between the age of Abraham and the time of Moses. Could the worship of the same god continue over so long a period in a tribal society ? In the Near East most

---

[23]See M.J. Selman, 'Comparative Customs and the Patriarchal Age' in *Essays on the Patriarchal Narratives,* 110; *idem,* 'The Social Environment of the Patriarchs', Tyndale *Bulletin* 27 (1976) 114-36.

[24]Examples in M. van Loon, '1974 and 1975 Preliminary Results of the Excavations at Selenkahiye near Meskene, Syria', *AASOR* 44 (1977) 97-112.

[25]See J. Barr, 'The Problem of Israelite Monotheism', *Transactions of the Glasgow University Oriental Society* 17 (1957-58) 52-62. Barr also argued there for a pre-Mosaic knowledge of the Divine Name, but as an expression of God's presence and action rather than as a proper name.

ancient written records come from urban populations rather than groups, such as the patriarchal families, who were virtually landless, or such as their descendants living in Goshen. Even when Israel became an entity in Canaan, occupying the towns as well as villages, where they could know and use writing and its products more readily, little is likely to last three thousand years for modern scholars to read, for all except the briefest and most ephemeral documents will have been written with ink on perishable papyrus.[26] However, occasional glimpses afforded by different writings from other areas show what could happen. North Arabian tribes of the first centuries of our era left numerous inscriptions and graffiti in Syria, Jordan and Arabia which mention their gods. A deity whose name occurs in Nabataean, Palmyrene, Safaitic and Thamudic texts is Rudâ, apparently an astral deity, perhaps Mercury.[27] In the 5th century BC, Herodotus mentioned Orotalt as one of the deities the Arabs worshipped (Book III 8), and that name is an etymologically satisfactory form of Rudâ. In 1957 the Assyriologist R. Borger identified the name of the same god in an inscription of Esarhaddon, king of Assyria (*c.* 681-669 BC), where it is written Ruldayu.[28] The god Rudâ is well-attested in the early Roman period, Herodotus and Esarhaddon prove his cult existed respectively four and seven hundred years earlier. Notice, however, that nothing is known of him at those earlier periods from documents produced by his own devotees. Had the Assyrian army of Esarhaddon's father, Sennacherib, not removed the statues of Arab gods and Esarhaddon then returned them, refurbished and suitably inscribed, had there been no Greek whose curiosity led him to amass and compile an immense store of information, there would be no means of knowing about Rudâ's antiquity to-day.

---

[26]A.R. Millard, 'The Ugaritic and Canaanite Alphabets, Some Notes', *Ugarit-Forschung* 11 (1979) 613-16.

[27]See J. Teixidor, *The Pagan God* (Princeton, Princeton UP 1977) 88.

[28]R. Borger, 'Assyriologische und altarabistische Miszellen', *Orientalia* (NS) 26 (1957) 1-11, esp. 10.

There are doubtless other cases, a few demonstrable,[29] many entirely lost. The ancient Near Eastern context, therefore, was suitable ground for tribal worship centred upon a particular god or gods to flourish for many generations. Where there is documentation of continuing reverence for a certain deity by the same group at points many centuries apart, no-one doubts the fact. Since examples like that are known, the possibility of others has to be allowed, thus authorising anyone who wishes to suppose the worship of Abraham's God, named YHWH, could have continued in his family until the Exodus. The interval separating those two points in time is little greater than the centuries between the earliest witness to Rudâ by Esarhaddon and the plentiful occurrences of the Roman period.

In Egypt 'Atenism' died with Akhenaten. As the 'heretic pharaoh' had treated the old gods, so his successors treated him and his god. The fact that a new form of belief could become dominant, then disappear so completely, points to a small yet extremely powerful body of promoters, centred on the pharaoh; without his active support no major traditional customs could be changed so radically. The rapid reversal after his death shows how closely the changes were associated with the king, and neither the faith itself nor its followers had sufficient attraction or influence to resist the tide of traditionalism which rose again. Were it not for the chance retrieval of monuments and objects in the abandoned ruins of Akhetaten, the smashed sculptures, the carved blocks re-used as ordinary stones, the tombs of some of Akhenaten's courtiers and material in Tutankhamun's tomb, modern scholarship would be as ignorant of this episode in Egypt's history as Akhenaten's successors wanted their people and their posterity to be: there would be no vestige of the now celebrated 'heretic pharaoh' nor of his monotheistic interruption to Egypt's long-lived religious traditions.

Now Akhenaten was a powerful ruler imposing his new faith on his realm, celebrating it in monumental style and

---

[29]The case of Apladad is one, see E. Lipiński, 'Apladad', *Orientalia*.(NS)45 (1976) 53-74.

with great artistry. Were there not powerful rulers able to have monuments erected or priestly establishments having books copied, what trace of other distinctive religious innovations would survive in a form clearly intelligible now ? As the first hundred years of Christianity have left no traces that would be understandable without the New Testament writings, so the possibility has to be allowed that in the 2nd millennium BC there was a family, then a people worshipping one God alone in the Levant and Egypt, then in Canaan, without leaving any trace apart from the traditions preserved in writings formed at a later date.

The purpose of this study is simply to argue that there are no satisfactory grounds for ruling out of consideration the biblical assertions about the faith of the Patriarchs and Moses in one and the same God. Ancient Egyptian and Near Eastern history is more favourable to those assertions than many recognise, and the revolution of Akhenaten demonstrates that one man could conceive and establish a new mode of faith. Neither his claim to a revelation from Aten, nor the biblical claims to revelations from God can be tested by historical study. It is evident that Akhenaten had a strong conviction which he expressed in that way, and if he could have that experience, there is no reason why others could not have similar experiences, although they were not in a position to leave concrete testimonies to them.

7

SHARED VOCABULARY IN THE PENTATEUCH AND THE BOOK OF DANIEL

Terence C. Mitchell

Summary

There are a limited number of technical terms used in connection with episodes in The Pentateuch and the Book of Daniel, in which Hebrews, Joseph (Gen. 40-41), Moses (Ex. 7-8) and Daniel (Dan. 1-5) have encounters with the officials of rulers or other superiors. Principal among these are פשׁר/פתר, *'to interpret',* פעם, *'to trouble',* חַרְטֹם, *'reciting priest', and* מְכַשֵּׁף,*'sorcerer'. A study of these suggests that the writer of Daniel may have consciously selected individual terms from the Pentateuch for use in appropriate contexts in his book.*

Much of the vocabulary of the Old Testament is distributed, so to speak, throughout the text. There are however some technical terms which have a more limited distribution. As might be expected, such terms are usually found only in the specific contexts which require them, but in such contexts vocabulary sometimes changes with the passage of time. A well known example of this is the case of 'linen' for which the earlier texts have the word שֵׁשׁ while in the later texts this is superseded by בּוּץ.[1] This example is also typical of many in that both שֵׁשׁ and בּוּץ are probably foreign loan-words, in this case Egyptian.[2]

I shall be concerned here with some words and phrases which are found in specific contexts in both the Pentateuch and the Book of Daniel, texts separated by a considerable gap in time, and I will concentrate mainly on words which are not much attested elsewhere.

The contexts in question are ones in which Hebrews have dealings with rulers or other superiors: in the Pentateuch with the Egyptian Pharaoh or the official Potiphar; and in Daniel with the king of Babylon. In the Pentateuch there are two relevant episodes, that in which Joseph acts as a dream interpreter for Pharaoh (Gen. 40-1), and that in which Moses contends with the magicians of Pharaoh (Ex. 7-8). In Daniel there are the episodes where Daniel acts as dream interpreter for Nebuchadnezzar (Dan. 1-5).

A parallel usage can be seen between Genesis and Daniel in the use of חלם, 'to dream', not particularly significant in view of its frequency elsewhere, but perhaps more significant in the wording of the sequels where, of both the Pharaoh and Nebuchadnezzar, it is said that 'his spirit was troubled'; וַתִּפָּעֶם רוּחוֹ (Gen. 41:8); וַתִּתְפָּעֶם רוּחוֹ (Dan. 2:1), passages differing only in that in Genesis the Niphal and in Daniel the Hithpael stem is used; though in Daniel 2:3, where Nebuchadnezzar speaks of himself, the Niphal is used (וַתִּפָּעֶם רוּחִי). This is perhaps a not very remarkable parallel, though the verb פעם only occurs five times in the Old Testament, in

[1]M.F. Rooker, *Biblical Hebrew in Transition. The Language of the book of Ezekiel* (JSOTS 90; Sheffield, JSOT Press 1990) 159-161.

[2]T.O. Lambdin, 'Egyptian Loan-words in the Old Testament' *JAOS* 73 (1953), 145-55; see pp. 155 and 147-8 respectively.

the three passages already quoted (Gen 41:8; Dan. 3:1,3) where the רוּחַ of the principal is the subject, in one (Judg. 13:25) where the רוּחַ of Yahweh is said to 'trouble' Samson, and in one other (Ps. 77:5) without רוּחַ.

After a dream comes interpretation, and there is some parallelism in this, with the cognate forms פתר, 'to interpret', and פִּתְרוֹן, 'interpretation', in the context of the dreams of Joseph's fellow prisoners the butler and baker (Gen. 40:5, 8) and of the Pharaoh (Gen. 41:8, 12), and פשׁר, 'to interpret', and פִּשְׁרָא, 'interpretation', in connection with Nebuchadnezzar's dreams in the Aramaic part of Daniel (verb, 5:12, 16; noun, 2:4 and frequently). It has been argued that פִּתְרוֹן/פִּשְׁרָא signifies not simply 'interpretation', but 'presage, prognostication' in the sense 'prefiguring of the future',[3] but this does not affect the present point. Both the Hebrew and Aramaic forms are presumed to derive from Akkadian *pašāru*, 'to loosen, solve',[4] but this raises a question concerning the *t* in the Hebrew form. Analogous differences in spelling are found in the place-name Aššur which occurs in early Aramaic inscriptions as *'šwr* but in the fifth century Tale of Ahiqar as *'twr*, and also in the word for 'table', Akkadian *paššuru*/5th century Aramaic *ptwr*,[5] the change presumed to be by way of **ṯ* (th). In the case of the present word, the change did not take place universally, as is shown by the fact that both *pšr* and *ptr* 'to interpret' are attested in later Aramaic,[6] nevertheless the form with *t* appears to

[3]I. Rabbinowitz, '"PESHER/PITTĀRÔN". Its Biblical Meaning and its Significance in the Qumran Literature' *Revue de Qumran* 8 (1972-75), 219-232.

[4]W. von Soden, *Akkadisches Handwörterbuch* (Wiesbaden, Harrassowitz 1959-81) 842-7; S.A. Kaufman, *The Akkadian Influences on Aramaic* (Assyriological Studies 19; Chicago and London, University of Chicago Press 1974) 81; see also D.C. Fredericks, *Qoheleth's Language: Re-Evaluating its Nature and Date* (Ancient Near Eastern Texts and Studies 3; Lewiston and Queenstown, Mellen 1988) 326.

[5]K. Beyer, *Die aramäischen Texte vom Toten Meer*(Göttingen, Vandenhoeck and Ruprecht 1984) 100, n. 1, who concludes that the change (*š*>*ṯ*) took place when followed by *r*. In Old Persian the name Aššur is transcribed *aṯur* (Athur), perhaps reflecting a stage in the Semitic shift *š*>**ṯ*>*t*, but it is also possible that it may represent a native Iranian shift *š*>*ṯ* (see e.g. W. Brandenstein and M. Mayrhofer, *Handbuch des Altpersischen* (Wiesbaden, Harrassowitz 1964) 108.

represent the later spelling, so it is necessary to account for its use in Genesis. Apart from speculations about the date of this part of Genesis (according to the traditional source-critical view it belongs to the supposed E document, dated not later than the 8th century), there is a possibility of spelling revision by a later scribe. Alternatively an explanation might be found in evidence from Akkadian that in the Old Babylonian period there may have been a dental spirant *ṯ (th) in the spoken language which was represented in the script sometimes as *š* and sometimes as *t*,[7] the form in Genesis perhaps in some way reflecting this.

Notable shared elements in the vocabulary of the Pentateuch and Daniel are the titles of officers at the courts of Pharaoh and Nebuchadnezzar. One of these, the title סָרִיס, 'official, eunuch', probably a loan from Akkadian *ša rēši*, '(he) of the head', was, however, fairly common elsewhere in the Old Testament (42 times: in Genesis, Samuel, Kings, Chronicles, Isaiah, Jeremiah and Esther),[8] and its meaning shifted in some contexts from 'official, chamberlain' or the like, in the 2nd millennium BC to the narrower 'eunuch' (e.g. Is. 56:3) in the 1st millennium.[9]

Again, the designation 'wise (man)' is found among the officials confronted in both the accounts of Joseph and Moses in the Hebrew form חָכָם (Gn. 41:8, 33, 39; Ex. 7:11) and of Daniel in the Aramaic form חַכִּים (Dan. 2:12ff; 4:3, 15; 5:7, 8, 15), but this is common elsewhere in the Old Testament,[10] and the root

---

[6]M. Sokoloff, *A Dictionary of Jewish Palestinian Aramaic* (Ramat Gan, Bar-Ilan UP 1990) 454, 456.

[7]W. von Soden and W. Röllig, *Das Akkadische Syllabar* (Analecta Orientalia 42, 4th ed; Rome, Pontifical Biblical Institute 1991), xix-xx; and see Kaufman, *Akkadian Influences*, 81-2, 116-9.

[8]Statistics in F.I. Andersen and A.D. Forbes, *The Vocabulary of the Old Testament* (Rome, Pontifical Biblical Institute 1992) 385, no. 5342.

[9]K.A. Kitchen, *JEA* 47 (1961), 160; *Ancient Orient and Old Testament* (London, The Tyndale Press 1966), 165-6; J.A. Brinkman, *A Political History of Post-Kassite Babylonia 1158-722 BC* (Analecta Orientalia 43; Rome, Pontifical Biblical Institute 1968), 309-11; A.L. Oppenheim, *JANES* 5 (1973) 325-34. Oppenheim (329) has pointed out that no reference in the Neo-Babylonian texts requires the meaning 'eunuch', and the same is true of the references in Daniel, so the chief סָרִיס, Ashpenaz, was presumably a normal official and not a eunuch.

[10]Statistics in Andersen and Forbes, *Vocabulary of the Old Testament*, 317, no. 2329.

ḥkm is found widely in West Semitic (Ugaritic, Phoenician, Aramaic and indeed also in Arabic and Ethiopic),[11] so it is not particularly significant on its own.

Probably more relevant for the present purpose are the words חַרְטֹם, 'reciting priest', and מְכַשֵּׁף, 'sorcerer'.

The word חַרְטֹם, plural חַרְטֻמִּים, is applied to the members of the household of the Egyptian Pharaoh in the time of Joseph (Gen. 41:8, 24) in the context of the interpretation of dreams; of Moses (Ex. 7:11, 22; 8:3, 14, 15; 9:11) in magical contexts; and in its Hebrew and Aramaic forms (חַרְטֹם, plural חַרְטֻמִּין), to officials in the court of Nebuchadnezzar in the time of Daniel (Dan. 1:20; 2:2, 10, 27; 4:4, 6; 5:11). It has been suggested that the term חרטם is a loan from the Egyptian title *ḥry-tp*, 'who (is) over' or 'chief', which occurs usually, but not exclusively, in conjunction with the title *ẖry-ḥbt*, 'lector priest', from the Middle Kingdom onwards.[12] An example of the two titles together is found in a cycle of stories known from a papyrus of the Hyksos period, but probably composed in the 12th Dynasty (early 2nd millennium BC), and purporting to relate to the time of Khufu (Cheops) of the 4th Dynasty.[13] It has usually been assumed that the phrase *ẖry-ḥb(t) ḥry-tp* used in this and other texts is to be rendered 'chief lector priest',[14] but it has been convincingly argued that these should be taken as two separate titles, 'lector priest' and 'chief'.[15] This analysis is

---

[11]See e.g. H.P. Müller in *TDOT* 4.364-7.

[12]B.H. Stricker, *Acta Orientalia* 15 (1937) 6, 20; A. Gardiner, *JEA* 24 (1938) 164-5; J.M.A. Janssen, *JEOL* 14 (1955-56) 65-6; J. Vergote, *Joseph en Égypte. Genèse Chap. 37-50 a la lumière des études égyptologiques récentes* (Louvain, Louvain UP 1959) 66-73; H.P. Müller, *TDOT* 5.176-9; A.L. Oppenheim, *The Interpretation of Dreams in the Ancient Near East* (Transactions of the American Philosophical Society. New Series 46/3; Philadelphia, 1956) 238; H. Ranke, *Keilschriftliches Material zur altägyptischen Vokalisation* (Berlin, Königliche Akademie der Wissenschaften, 1910) 37.

[13]Papyrus Westcar, Berlin 3033. Translations in A. Erman, *The Literature of the Ancient Egyptians*(ET; London, Methuen 1927) 36-47; W.K. Simpson in *The Literature of Ancient Egypt* (New Haven and London, Yale UP 1972) 15-30.

[14]E.g. Erman (Blackman), *Literature*, 36-47, 316, 'chief kherheb'; Simpson, *Literature* 15-30, 'chief lector'.

[15]J. Quaegebeur, '*La designation (p3-) ḥry-tp : phritob*' in J. Osing and G. Dreyer (eds.) *Form und Mass. Beiträge zur Literatur, Sprache und Kunst des alten Ägypten. Festschrift für Gerhard Fecht* (Wiesbaden, Harrassowitz 1987)

supported by the fact that in at least one instance of Middle Kingdom date these two titles appear in the reverse sequence *ḥry-tp ẖry-ḥb.w*, 'chief and lector priest'.[16] Concerning the equation of Egyptian *ḥry-tp* with Hebrew חַרְטֹם, a variant spelling of *ḥry-tp* as *ḥr(y)-'idb*, which probably shows its actual pronunciation,[17] may bear on the emphatic *ṭ* in the Hebrew form. Though *ṭ* was not represented separately in the Egyptian script, it has been suggested that there was a *ṭ* in spoken Egyptian represented by the value transcribed as *d*.[18] It might be, therefore, that the representation of Egyptian *t* by Hebrew (and Aramaic) *ṭ* simply reflects what a scribe heard. Again the representation of Egyptian *b* by *m* in Hebrew and Aramaic could be an example of interchange between voiced bi-labial consonants of which there are examples in the Semitic languages.[19] That the final consonant was pronounced as *b* rather than *p* is further suggested by the Greek form *phritob* (from *p'-ḥry-tb*, *p* being the definite article) common in the Ptolemaic period.[20] The development *ḥr(y)-tp* > *ḥr(y)-db* > (Hebrew) *ḥr-ṭb* > *ḥr-ṭm* therefore seems reasonable.[21]

The form *ḥry-tp* further appears to have been borrowed in Neo-Assyrian where a list of the names of officials of the 7th century BC from the so-called Library of Ashurbanipal (Kuyunjik Collection in the British Museum) includes a section listing three individuals summarised by the designation 'total (*napḫaru* (PAP)) 3 *ḫar-ṭi-bi*'.[22] That *ḫarṭibi* may reflect Egyptian

---

368-94, esp. 368-70, 377-8, 383-4. I am indebted to Professor K.A. Kitchen for drawing my attention to this article, and providing me with a photocopy.

[16]Quaegebeur, *Festschrift Gerhard Fecht*, 377-8.

[17]J. Quaegebeur, 'On the Egyptian Equivalent of Biblical *ḥarṭummîm*' in S. Israelit-Groll (ed.) *Pharaonic Egypt. The Bible and Christianity* (Jerusalem, Magnes 1985) 162-72, esp. 167-9. I am again indebted to Professor Kitchen for knowledge of this article.

[18]W. Schenkel, *Einführung in die altägyptische Sprachwissenschaft* (Darmstadt, Wissenschaftliches Buchgesellschaft 1990) 46-7.

[19]S. Moscati *et al.*, *An Introduction to the Comparative Grammar of the Semitic Languages* (Wiesbaden, Harrassowitz 1964) 25-6, section 8.8.

[20]Quaegebeur, *Festschrift Gerhard Fecht*, 388-93.

[21]Private communication from Professor Kitchen to whom I am again indebted.

[22]Tablet BM.WA.K.1276: column iv line 2; C. Bezold, *Catalogue of the Cuneiform Tablets in the Kouyunjik Collection of the British Museum* I, (London, British Museum 1889).

ḥry-tp is supported by the fact that of the three personal names so designated, while the first is damaged, the other two *Ra-aʾ-si-i* and *Ṣi-ḫu-u* are probably Egyptian,[23] and this identification is further supported by a following section, again of three names, *Ḫu-u-ru, Ni-ḫar-a-u* and *Ṣu-u-a-ṣu*, who are summarised as 'three Egyptian scribes' (3 *tupšarrū* (A.BA.MEŠ)) *m u-ṣur-a-a*). The three names are generally interpreted as Egyptian.[24] It thus seems likely that *ḫarṭibi* in the Assyrian text was an Egyptian word. The sign read *ṭi* also had the values *di* and *de* (as well as *ṭe*), but it may perhaps be assumed on the basis of the Hebrew/Aramaic transcription ט that the Assyrian scribe heard the emphatic sound, and that *ḫarṭibi* rather than *ḫardibi* is correct. A second possible occurrence of the word in the first column of a fragment of a cuneiform prism of Esarhaddon,[25] where a *ḫar-ṭi-...* (ḪAR.DI...) is listed among craftsmen and other professionals, now seems uncertain. The text may relate to Esarhaddon's campaign against Egypt, but this is not certain,[26] and the damaged text can only be read with

---

[23]K.1276: iii:13-iv:1; Ranke, *Keilschriftliches Material*, 37,38 ('Vielleicht Ägyptisches'); K.L. Tallqvist, *Assyrian Personal Names* (ASSF 43.1 [1914]; repr. Hildesheim, G. Olms 1966) 186, 205.

[24]K.1276: iv:3-7; Ranke, *Keilschriftliches Material*, 29, 31, 33 ('Sicher Ägyptisches'); Tallqvist, *Assyrian Personal Names*, 90, 173, 206.

[25]Text BM.WA.91-5-9,218; H. Winckler, 'Bruchstücke von Keilschrifttexten' in *Altorientalische Forschungen, 1898-1900* (Leipzig, E. Pfeiffer 1901) 1-26, no. 16 (pp. 21-3; wrongly quoted as 91-2-9,218), with a copy of the text; transliteration in R. Borger, *Die Inschriften Asarhaddons, Königs von Assyrien* (AfO Beiheft 9; Osnabrück, Biblio-Verlag 1967) 114, no. 80; translation, A.L. Oppenheim in J.B. Pritchard, *Ancient Near Eastern Texts* (3rd ed. with Supplement; Princeton, Princeton UP 1969) 293-4, no. 7; and quoted as LU *ḫar-ṭi-[bi]* in *CAD* 6, Ḫ, 116.

[26]Winckler (*Altorientalische Forschungen,*, 22) suggests that cities mentioned as renamed by Esarhaddon in the second column of the prism were actually Egyptian, but it cannot necessarily be assumed that the text in the second column has anything to do with that in the first. Oppenheim, however, associates the text with Egypt on the basis of a parallel enumeration of craftsmen and specialists from Egypt in the Nahr al-Kalb inscription (Oppenheim, *ANET*, 293, no. 6), and Borger tentatively associates this text with the prism fragment BM.WA.80-7-19,15 his Nineveh E (*Asarhaddon*, 38-9 and 65-6), which refers to the campaign against Egypt (short extract translated by Oppenheim, *ANET*, 293, no. 4).

difficulty *ḫar*-DI-*e* (*??i???*)-*bi*,[27] so it cannot be counted as a reliable witness.

It is reasonable, on the basis of the evidence quoted above, to conclude that the word ***ḫarṭibi*** was borrowed directly from Egyptian into Assyrian, and gives added weight to the suggestion that earlier חַרְטֹם was a loan from *ḥry-tp*.

The form מְכַשֵּׁף is an intensive (Piel) participle of the verb כשׁף, 'to practice magic, sorcery' which is found in the Old Testament only in the intensive stem. מְכַשֵּׁף occurs in Exodus 7:11 in the context of the practitioners (who also include חַרְטֻמִּים, 'reciting priests') summoned by the pharaoh to match the miracles of Aaron, and in the book of Daniel where the מְכַשְּׁפִים are among the officials summoned by Nebuchadnezzar to interpret his dreams (Dan. 2:2). It is also found in Deuteronomy 18:10 in a condemnatory passage,[28] and in 2 Chronicles 33:6 and Malachi 3:5 in Israelite contexts. Since the verb ***kašāpu***, "to bewitch, cast an evil spell', is found in Akkadian from the early second millennium BC onwards,[29] the Hebrew verb may well have been a loan from Akkadian, and therefore its use in the Pentateuch need not be seen as anachronistic. The noun כַּשָּׁף, 'sorcerer', which occurs in Jeremiah 27:9 among those who will falsely tell the Israelites not to submit to Nebuchadnezzar, is probably a direct loan from the Akkadian derived noun ***kaššāpu***, 'sorcerer', found in first millennium BC Babylonian texts.[30]

What is to be made of these observations? It should be noted that in these passages not all similar events are expressed with similar vocabulary. This is shown by the passages which deal with Joseph and Daniel finding favour with superiors. In Genesis it is said וַיִּמְצָא יוֹסֵף חֵן בְּעֵינָיו 'and Joseph found favour (חֵן) in his eyes' (Gn. 39:4), 'his' referring to Potiphar; while in

---

[27]Borger, *AfO* 18 (1957-8) 116, reproducing all his interrogation marks.

[28]See O. Eissfeldt, 'Wahrsagung im Alten Testament' in *La divination en Mésopotamie ancienne et dans les régions voisines* (XIVe Rencontre Assyriologique Internationale, Strassbourg, 2-6 juillet 1965; Presses Universitaires de France, Paris 1966) 141-6, specifically 145.

[29]*CAD* K, 284.

[30]*CAD* K, 292. A possible Ugaritic occurrence, ***kṯpm*** (C.H. Gordon, *Ugaritic Textbook* (Analecta Orientalia 38; Rome, Pontifical Biblical Institute 1965), 424, no. 1334a; L. Koehler, W. Baumgartner and J.J. Stamm, *Lexicon in Veteris Testamenti Libros* (3rd ed; Leiden, Brill 1967-90) II, 479, is uncertain.

Daniel it is said וַיִּתֵּן הָאֱלֹהִים אֶת־דָּנִיֵּאל לְחֶסֶד וּלְרַחֲמִים לִפְנֵי שַׂר הַסָּרִיסִים 'God gave Daniel favour (חֶסֶד) and compassion (רַחֲמִים) in front of the chief officer' (Dan. 1:9); two very different ways of expressing the same thing.

Moreover the use of חלם is not in itself significant since in the Old Testament no other word is used to express the meaning 'dream, dreaming', and the root was indeed probably Common West Semitic, being found also in Ugaritic and Aramaic.[31]

Equally there is perhaps not much significance in the title סָרִיס in view of its frequent use elsewhere in the Old Testament, and particularly in view of the fact that in Daniel the word is, so to speak, at home and not unexpected in the context (compare also the use of רַב־סָרִיס to refer to Assyrian [2 Ki. 18:17] and Babylonian [Jer. 39:3, 13] officials); while in Egypt (Genesis) and Israel it was a loan word. A question on which there might be speculation is whether its use in Genesis might be due to a back influence from Daniel or one of the other later books. I shall return to this speculation below.

In a similar way, as has been mentioned, the Hebrew form חָכָם, 'wise (man)', is not particularly significant on its own since it is common elsewhere in the Old Testament.

There thus remain four lexical items where the parallelism may be more significant: פשׁר/פתר ('to interpret'), פעם ('to trouble'), חַרְטֹם ('reciting priest') and מְכַשֵּׁף ('sorcerer'). Of these perhaps the most significant is חַרְטֹם, since its occurrence in Daniel seems to show a conscious use by the scribe of the vocabulary of the Pentateuch, while the Neo-Assyrian example shows that a recognisably related form was used in Assyrian by the seventh century BC, and could have been known in Babylonia in Neo-Babylonian times, and might have encouraged a harking back to Pentateuchal language. This observation suggests that the other parallels may be interpreted in the same light, that is to say, the writer of Daniel, knowing the Pentateuch well, as he presumably did, and remembering the parallel situations confronted in earlier times by Joseph and Moses, and having recognised the counterpart of חַרְטֹם in *ḫarṭibi*, might have consciously made use of the vocabulary

---

[31]See M. Ottosson in *TDOT* 4.462-7.

stock in Genesis and Exodus. He knew this would be familiar to his readers/hearers, and would represent technical titles in Babylonia, coming near when possible to the Babylonian forms. If this is correct, it would appear to have been a case of the scribe selecting individual words rather than taking lists of titles. The following tabulations give the sequences in which the titles are listed, citing them in their singular or plural forms as they appear in the text. The enumerations begin either with חַרְטֹם as in Genesis, or with חָכָם as in Exodus:

Genesis 41:8	Daniel 1:20	Daniel 2:2	Daniel 2:10
חַרְטֻמֵּי מִצְרַיִם	חַרְטֻמִּים	חַרְטֻמִּים	חַרְטֹם
	אַשָּׁפִים	אַשָּׁפִים	אָשַׁף
חֲכָמֶיהָ			
		מְכַשְּׁפִים	
		כַּשְׂדִּים	כַּשְׂדָּי

Exodus 7:11	Daniel 2:27
חֲכָמִים	חַכִּימִין
מְכַשְּׁפִים	
	אָשְׁפִין
חַרְטֻמֵּי מִצְרַיִם	חַרְטֻמִּין
	גָּזְרִין

These show that only in the second tabulation is there any comparability, and that only very tenuous. Nevertheless the trend of the evidence suggests some minimal use of the Pentateuchal vocabulary by the writer of Daniel. The inclusion of the other terms אַשָּׁף ('exorcist'), כַּשְׂדָּי ('augur') and גָּזְרִין ('soothsayer')[32] in the above tabulations shows that he did not rely entirely on the Pentateuch for his technical terms.[33] This

---

[32]The precise renderings of these terms are uncertain. They will be discussed in my commentary on the Book of Daniel, in preparation.

[33]There were other terms in the Old Testament available to the writer of the Book of Daniel: אוֹב, 'necromancer (?)', מְעוֹנֵן, 'magician', חֹבֵר, 'exorcist', מְנַחֵשׁ, 'magician', קֹסֵם, 'diviner', שֹׁאֵל, 'enquirer', יִדְּעֹנִי, 'soothsayer' (again, the precise meanings are uncertain). Several of these are listed in the condemnatory passage in Deuteronomy (18:10-11) mentioned above in connection with מְכַשֵּׁף, 'sorcerer' - namely (in the order in which they are mentioned) קֹסֵם, מְעוֹנֵן, מְנַחֵשׁ, מְכַשֵּׁף, חֹבֵר, שֹׁאֵל, אוֹב, יִדְּעֹנִי. The fact that, apart

further shows that the earlier suggestion that there might have been back influence on a reviser of the text of Genesis in the case of סָרִיס seems less likely, though in view of the frequent use of this term in the historical and prophetic books, this should not be entirely ruled out, Daniel, of course, being only one of the sources which might have suggested such a revision. In suggesting such a possibility, I am simply speculating that a scribe revising a text to make it more comprehensible, as for example one may perhaps assume the revision of spelling in Daniel (e.g. *z* >*d*), might have modified a word to bring it into line with what was known.[34]

I have great pleasure in offering this slight paper in honour of Donald Wiseman.

from מְכַשֵּׁף which has Akkadian overtones, none of these terms was used in Daniel supports the view that if the writer was selecting from the Pentateuch he only did so very judiciously.

[34]As an analogy I would suggest the possibility that the qualification 'of the Chaldaeans' after 'Ur' in Genesis 11:28,31 and 15:7 might have been taken over by a copyist from Nehemiah 9:7 where it was simply a contemporary statement.

8

CHRIST AS THE KEY TO SCRIPTURE

Genesis 22 Reconsidered

R.W.L. Moberly

Summary

A major problem for the Christian who reads the Old Testament is to know how to balance the two tasks of understanding the text in its ancient Israelite context and of relating the text to the context of Christian faith. It is argued that both tasks are necessary and must be held in constructive tension. Genesis 22 in its Old Testament context can be seen to resonate with the central traditions of both Sinai and Zion and to be a kind of hermeneutical key to the Old Testament. An interpretation in the light of Christ must do justice to these concerns. Traditional Christian typology is in danger of superficiality. Von Rad's powerful Lutheran Christological reading avoids this danger, but raises difficulties of its own. Some concluding reflections suggest directions for a renewed Christian engagement with the story of Abraham.

Introduction: the Problematic Role of Historical Criticism

The assumption that the whole of scripture ultimately points to, and should be interpreted by, Jesus Christ is a fundamental element of traditional Christian faith. It has not, however, been a fundamental element in most modern biblical exegesis and interpretation over the last 200 years or so. On the contrary, one of the recurrent concerns, at least in theory, has been to keep biblical interpretation separate from the dogmatic formulations of Christian theology, precisely so that the authentic voices of the biblical writers may be heard in their own integrity.

This concern, which is characterised at heart by a sense of the potential otherness of the past and a respect for that otherness, was in many ways a characteristically Protestant development. To be sure, the Reformers themselves did not have the kind of historical awareness that developed in the following centuries and they continued to maintain the hermeneutical principle of Christ as the key to scripture. Nonetheless, their sense of the difference of the Bible from the apparent corruptions of much medieval Christianity together with their Renaissance sense of the purity and superiority of antiquity led to an insistence on the role of the Bible as an authoritative norm which stands over against the traditions of the Church, an insistence which in certain important respects drove a wedge between Bible and Church. This opened the way to a subsequent enlargement of the wedge in ways that the Reformers themselves had not countenanced, as first became apparent in the 17th century in the Socinian controversy about the status of the doctrine of the Trinity. By the 18th and 19th centuries, the recovery of the original sense of the biblical text, appropriate to its ancient context, became separated from all the systematic theological interpretations put upon the text by the Fathers and their successors. The notion of Christ as the key to scripture, dependent as it is ultimately upon the doctrine of the Trinity, became an illegitimate hermeneutic. *Sola Scriptura* became separated from *solus Christus* (not to mention *sola gratia* and *sola fide*). And when it was discovered that the interpretations of the Church were present even in the biblical text itself, most obviously in the portrayals of Jesus in the gospels, then it seemed appropriate to move the wedge back and insert it within the very text in the attempt to recover the pure and normative original. The results, with the constant value-laden distinction between the authentic and the secondary, and the ever-renewed quest for the 'real' or 'genuine' Jesus of history, are well-known to anyone familiar with the literature of modern biblical scholarship. Although much 20th century scholarship has become more positive about the processes of theological tradition discovered within the biblical text, the notion that these traditions should still be firmly separated from post-biblical traditions remains largely unquestioned.

This whole approach to the Bible was largely carried out by liberal Protestant scholars and could be seen as a natural development of the original Protestant stance - an apologetic point regularly made by defenders of the historical-critical approach, at least against its less liberal Protestant detractors. Nonetheless, despite this milieu in which historical-critical study of the Bible developed, the basic insight is independent of religious stance. Once one has acquired a sense of genuine historical awareness, then there is something self-evidently valid about seeking to understand any ancient text, biblical or otherwise, in the kind of way in which it would have been understood in its ancient context.

Although no part of biblical interpretation has been unaffected by this historically-oriented approach, its results have perhaps been most striking with regard to a Christian understanding of the Old Testament. While it still might make some historical sense to see Christ as the key to the New Testament, since all its writers explicitly refer to Christ whose life, death and resurrection antedated their writings - although this historical approach would of course exclude the understanding of Christ in normative Christian theology as the second person of the Trinity - this could hardly apply to the Old Testament, which was all written before Christ's birth. Traditional Christian interpretation had not, of course, been unaware of this problem, but had resolved it, following the lead of the New Testament, by supposing that the real agenda of the Old Testament was Christ nonetheless. Old Testament writers had either explicitly anticipated Christ, in well-known messianic and predictive texts, or implicitly borne witness in ways which allegory, with its ability to move beyond the surface meaning of the text, could uncover.

But all this fell into disrepute with the development of historical awareness. The messianic and predictive passages could be seen to have meanings relevant to their ancient context with no intended reference to Jesus Christ, while allegory became the classic example of finding in the text what one wants to find there, simply reading the text on one's own terms, rather than submitting to the discipline of hearing the text on its own terms, eisegesis rather than exegesis. Whatever Christian scholars have made of the Old Testament subsequently, the notion that Christ should be the key has not usually featured prominently, though there have been exceptions.

This broad brush picture of course obscures numerous qualifications and distinctions that might be made, but it is intended simply to remind us of a general outlook that has, at least until recently, characterised the vast majority of biblical scholars of every persuasion. It is well known that recent hermeneutical debate has made the whole question of what counts as a good interpretation far more problematic than it was thought to be for a long time. New approaches are opening up, some bearing striking similarity to very old ones. Much recent literary criticism, concerned with the text as text rather than with its origins and composition, is akin to midrash. And if ancient Jewish approaches can be repristinated then so can ancient Christian approaches. David Clines, for example, has recently said that he foresees 'a new lease of life for Christological interpretations of the Old Testament'.[1] Nonetheless, the fact that much of the historical-critical work of the last two centuries may have been hermeneutically over-simple in no way invalidates its fundamental premise of the importance of understanding ancient texts as ancient texts and respecting their integrity as such. No account of Christ as the key to scripture will be, or deserves to be, taken seriously unless it does justice to these legitimate historical concerns.

---

[1]'Fashion being what it is, some day the interpretations of the past will come again into their own. I foresee, for example, a new lease of life for Christological interpretations of the Old Testament, not pre-critical any longer (for we cannot turn back the clock), but post-critically serving the pietism of the new Christian community' (D.J.A. Clines, 'Biblical Interpretation in an International Perspective', *Biblical Interpretation* 1 [1993], 67-87, quotation at 80-81).

The Status of Christian and Jewish Faith in Reading the Bible

One might perhaps try to focus things sharply by saying that the central problem posed by the modern historical-critical approach to the Bible is in what sense, if any, it remains valid to read the Bible as a Christian. In saying this I do not question that most modern biblical scholars have studied the text for reasons of faith; the issue is rather whether their theory and practice have been fully consistent. For on the one hand, the content and self-definition of all the mainstream branches of the Christian Church is provided, at the very least, by the Bible in conjunction with the theological formulations of the Patristic period - the creeds and councils with their Trinitarian and incarnational understandings of God, Christ and salvation. To accept the validity of these dogmas (however much they may need reformulation in contemporary concepts) is part of the definition of what it means to be a Christian, at least for the Roman Catholic and Orthodox churches, and also for those Protestant churches that belong to the World Council of Churches; and for most Christians there are normative post-Patristic formulations also. Yet on the other hand, because none of these dogmas were formulated by the biblical writers (although of course the biblical writers provide the material for which the Fathers were seeking to provide an appropriate conceptualisation), and are therefore technically anachronistic for an understanding of the biblical material in its original context, historical criticism has insisted that they be excluded from the pre-understanding the reader brings to the text. To be a Christian means, at least in part, accepting certain theological dogmas; to read the Bible historically means excluding those theological dogmas. How then should one read the Bible as a Christian?

The short answer is that one needs the hermeneutical sophistication both to bracket out one's theological dogmas and to bring them to bear appropriately upon the text. The interplay between these two perspectives is where most illumination for the Christian reader is likely to occur. This means, however, among other things, that particularly for Protestant theology the reformulation of the relationship between Bible and Church is a pressing problem. For however much scripture remains the supreme norm for Christian theology, it can only function normatively in the context of the life and traditions of the Christian Church to which it gave rise and which in important respects necessarily move beyond it. The all-important question is, of course, precisely how Bible and Church interrelate, but it is clear that it must be two-way traffic. The basic difficulty with the principle of *sola scriptura* is that it is in danger of sawing off the branch it is sitting on, a danger well exemplified by the history of modern biblical scholarship, which has all too often transformed holy scripture into a collection of interesting fragments about ancient religion.

This basic problem has been well addressed from a Jewish perspective by Jon Levenson, who has noted that 'the historical-critical method compels its practitioners to bracket their traditional identities, and this renders its ability to enrich Judaism and Christianity problematic'. He argues that: 'In the realm of historical criticism, pleas for a "Jewish biblical scholarship" or a "Christian biblical scholarship" are senseless and reactionary. Practising Jews and Christians will differ from uncompromising historicists, however, in affirming the meaningfulness and interpretative relevance of larger contexts that homogenise the literatures of different periods to one degree or another. Just as text has more than one context, and biblical studies more than one method, so Scripture has more than one sense, as the medievals knew and Tyndale, Spinoza, Jowett, and most other moderns have forgotten'. Further, 'unless historical criticism can learn to interact with other senses of Scripture - senses peculiar to the individual traditions and not shared between them - it will either fade or prove to be not a meeting ground of Jews and Christians, but the burial ground of Judaism and Christianity, as each tradition vanishes into the past in which neither had as yet emerged'. He concludes his discussion by saying, 'Bracketing tradition has its value, but also its limitations. Though fundamentalists will not see the value, nor historicists the limitations, intellectual integrity and spiritual vitality in this new situation demand the careful affirmation of both'.[2]

---

[2]'Theological Consensus or Historicist Evasion? Jews and Christians in Biblical Studies' in R. Brooks & J.J. Collins (eds.) *Hebrew Bible or Old Testament?* (Indiana, Notre Dame UP 1990) 109-45, quotations at 143-5. This essay is reprinted in *The Hebrew Bible, the Old Testament, and*

The Role of the Reader

How then should we proceed? It will be helpful to start with some reflections on the role of the reader or interpreter in determining meaning. Although this has the arguable advantage of being in keeping with current fashion, it is in fact a very ancient concern which was in a sense embodied in the patristic notion of the reader approaching the biblical text with the rule of faith as a hermeneutical key. The concern only became lost in the context of the Cartesian epistemological revolution, with its concern to achieve objectivity by eliminating personal subjectivity; a concern which was to prove enormously fruitful in the sciences and which became embodied in the humanities in the form of the historical-critical method.

The importance of the role of the reader is expressed most clearly by the simple recognition that the answers you get depend on the questions you ask, or, to change the metaphor, what you see depends on what you are looking for. To say this is not to suggest that all interpretation is somehow predetermined or circular, or to deny that often fresh and unexpected insights can be arrived at in surprising ways. It is rather to recognise that interpretation does not take place in a vacuum or with a *tabula rasa*, but that some kind of pre-understanding is always brought to the task of interpretation and in various ways conditions the results of the exercise. The pre-understanding is of course open to modification by the object of its study, and may then in turn set that object in a fresh light. One thus has the well-known hermeneutical spiral, of a constant interaction between pre-understanding and text leading, at least in theory, to an ever greater and fuller understanding.

The questions which set the interpretative process in motion are chosen by the interpreter and may differ greatly. But perhaps the crucial point to appreciate is that individual interpreters, however much they may produce fresh interpretations, do not operate on their own but always belong to some larger context, what one may call an interpretative community. This recognition of the importance of an interpretative community raises all sorts of interesting issues.

Historical Criticism: Jews and Christians in Biblical Studies (Louisville, Westminster/John Knox 1993) 82-105.

On the one hand there are questions about the community's internal workings and the various strategies it adopts to encourage or preclude particular types of understanding and practice; and on the other hand there are questions about the relationship between different interpretative communities and the ways in which it is possible for genuine dialogue to take place. For present purposes, however, the important point is that it is the fact of the Christian Church which sets the context for the Christian interpreter. Ultimately, the nature of questions and answers as Christian questions and answers depends on their relationship to the Christian Church; and the ultimate legitimacy (or otherwise) of those questions and answers is inseparable from questions about the legitimacy of the Christian Church.

Christ as the Key to Scripture

Since at the very heart of Christian self-definition is the person of Christ as the interpretative key to God and humanity, Christians naturally seek to use this interpretative key in all they think and do - or at least this is the goal towards which Christian growth and development moves. Although Christians continue to discuss extensively among themselves how to arrive at the truest understanding of Jesus Christ and how to apply that understanding, this does not prevent them from having some kind of understanding (however corrigible) and from using it accordingly. Given the historic importance of God's dealings with Israel as setting the context for the life, death and resurrection of Jesus, it is hardly surprising that something so basic as understanding the scriptural witness of Israel should be included in this Christ-centred interpretative process. How then might this process work?

First, and most obviously, it is an evaluative process. Christians use their understanding of Christ as a norm for assessing the witness of the Old Testament. Although sometimes the assessment may be carried out in such a way that its results may be disowned by the Christian community generally, as was the case classically with Marcion, that simply exemplifies one possible boundary for the undertaking. Thus throughout the last 2000 years Christians have recurrently been disturbed by aspects of the Old Testament, perhaps most obviously God's command to Israel to slaughter the

Canaanites. Although this can be seen as problematic on grounds other than those of Christian faith, the basic reason for Christian difficulty has been the apparent incongruity between the command to kill and the New Testament witness to Jesus, who took the part of the outsider, taught and exemplified the forgiveness and love of one's enemies, died for the sin of the whole world, and initiated a mission to all people, Jew and Gentile alike. Strategies for handling such problems vary, but the basic point is that it is the values, rooted in Christ, that Christians bring to the text that determine their evaluation of it. As far as this goes, such a Christian reading of the Old Testament need not be different in principle from a Christian reading of any other religious text such as the Qur'an or the Bhagavad-Gita, or some other existentially committed approach, other than Christian, to the biblical text. People naturally use their existing values to assess value-laden material; although obviously sometimes interesting and unexpected hermeneutical transformations take place.

It is at the level of basic values that interpreters may often be unaware of the extent to which their work is influenced. Wellhausen was hardly undertaking to offer a Christological reading of the Old Testament. Yet his exaltation of the early, free and religiously most authentic material in the histories and the prophets and his denigration of the deadening effect of the post-exilic covenantal and legal embodiment of religious faith is a clear analogue to his understanding of the free and authentic spirit of Jesus, which was overcome by the deadening hand of the institutional Church and was recovered by the Reformation and subsequent liberal Protestantism. Christian evaluations come so naturally to Christian scholars that they can often suppose themselves to display a kind of objectivity that in reality may be an illusion. This is usually most clearly seen by scholars who do not share the basic assumptions and stand within a different interpretative community. Jon Levenson has regularly made this observation from a Jewish perspective;[3] and the highlighting of unconscious assumptions is the bread and butter of feminist criticism. This, however, is not an argument

[3]See the essays collected in *The Hebrew Bible, the Old Testament, and Historical Criticism.*

against having interpretative values but rather for being clearer about what they are and why one holds them.

Beyond this rather obvious sense of Christ as an interpretative key, there are more subtle dimensions which relate to the dynamic of the Christian relationship to the Old Testament as an authoritative text, holy scripture, which is to be appropriated by believers as part of the process of shaping or reshaping their lives. For when Christians read the Old Testament, they assume that the God it speaks of is the same as the God in whom they believe. And yet at the same time, Christians do not understand God in the same way that the writers of the Old Testament did, for our understanding of God is mediated through Christ and the Holy Spirit with the result that we confess God as Trinity. When we read Genesis 22, whose writer did not have a Trinitarian belief, we appropriate what it says about God within the context of God as Trinity. The essential point, as already noted above, is that the Bible functions as scripture when it is related to, and appropriated within, a context of understanding that is continuous with, and yet moves beyond, the frame of reference of the Bible itself. This does not deny the historical awareness that 'God' in Genesis 22 meant something different from what the Christian means by that term - though precisely what understanding of God was presupposed by the text of Genesis 22 in its ancient context is a moot point - but it is in cases like this that the classic distinction between what a text meant and what it means is least helpful. For the Christian, when Genesis 22 refers to God, it refers to the God known in and through Jesus Christ - that is what the text means. Therefore even for the Christian with the most acutely developed sense of historical differentiation, such differentiation is in important respects overcome by subtle (and perhaps often unconscious) hermeneutical moves through the very act of reading the text as scripture.

The fact that the Christian reader brings a particular understanding of God and of the life of faith to the Old Testament when read as scripture has its essential corollary in the nature of the text itself. For the act of reading the text with Christian values and beliefs in order to appropriate the text within Christian faith would make little sense unless there was an intrinsic continuity of subject matter between Old

Testament text and Christian faith together with a use of language (to convey that subject matter) that was intrinsically resonant and open-ended. Thus, within Genesis 22, those verbs that convey the central concerns of the story - 'test', 'see/provide', 'bless', which have God as their subject, and 'fear', 'obey' which have Abraham as their subject - are all words related to the central dynamics of the life of faith in both Old and New Testaments. The meaning of these words, the realities to which they point, will be existentially explored by all those who seek to live that life of faith. A Christian who has some understanding of these realities through faith in Christ may still seek to discern as accurately as possible how these concepts were understood in their Old Testament context and thereby to encounter aspects which otherwise might have been missed - for example, the language of God testing and Abraham fearing as resonant with, and paradigmatic for, Israel's obedience to Torah, and the setting for this obedience in the place of Israel's worship in Jerusalem. But when there is further witness to the meaning of these concepts in the New Testament and in subsequent Christian tradition (and, in its own way, in Jewish tradition), interpreters whose concern is to understand these concepts and enter into their reality as fully as possible will naturally make use of whatever resource and insight is at their disposal. Their understanding of the nature of God's testing and providing and of human obeying may initially be drawn from specifically Christian tradition and experience. But if it helps illuminate the meaning of these terms in Genesis 22, then so much the better. The hermeneutical approach is shaped by the goal of the interpretation. The Christian who reads Genesis 22 as a Christian will not read it primarily as evidence for certain beliefs and assumptions in ancient Israel (though that will be an element in the interpretative process), but rather as a witness both to the way God may deal with his faithful servants and to the way in which a trustful and life-enhancing response to God's costly demands may be made in the context of contemporary reality. And, of course, the hermeneutical spiral between text and pre-understanding will continue to operate.

To sum up. Although I think it is still often meaningful and helpful to use the concept of authorial intention in a text, I see no reason to suppose that valid interpretation should be limited to a recovery of that intention. As has often been pointed out, a text as text may have meaning and significance beyond that intended by its originator. To be sure, the responsible interpreter will generally take seriously the originally intended meaning (where recoverable) as a guide to interpretation; and I think it would be a rare case indeed where what was accepted as a valid interpretation contradicted, rather than continued, the general tenor of that original meaning, unless one was being explicitly playful or imaginative. Moreover, it is not the case that every biblical text can have its original significance extended through Christological reflection, but only those whose content is intrinsically suitable. For example, it would be hard to imagine a Christological hermeneutic doing very much with the list in Ezra 2//Nehemiah 7 of those who returned from exile in Babylon (except on a wholly generalised level of reflection about those who constitute the people of God); and many of the individual proverbs in the Book of Proverbs offer only limited grist for the Christological mill. But Genesis 22 has traditionally been a focus for Christological interpretation precisely because its concerns resonate so profoundly with those of Christian faith; and it is reasonably clear that already in ancient Israel the story was the focus of intensive reflection on, in the light of experience of, the nature of God's dealings with his people, and that this 'lived' dimension has made the story what it now is. In general terms, an Old Testament text is amenable to Christological interpretation to the extent that its content engages with substantive issues that are contained within Christian faith - the nature of God and humanity, life and death, repentance and faith, and so on.

Genesis 22 in its Old Testament Context

It is time to turn to the interpretation of Genesis 22. As I have already elsewhere set out the exegetical basis for my understanding of the chapter,[4] I will offer a brief résumé here and then seek to extend my earlier observations.

---

[4]'The Earliest Commentary on the Akedah', *VT* 38 (1988) 302-23, reprinted in *From Eden to Golgotha: Essays in Biblical Theology* (USF Studies in the History of Judaism 52; Atlanta, Scholars Press 1992) 55-73; *The Old Testament of the Old Testament* (Overtures to Biblical

First, the two primary words for interpreting the story are 'test' in 22:1, the narrator's explicit guide to the nature of the story, and 'fear' in 22:12, the eliciting of Abraham's fear (in the sense of obedience, *cf.* Dt. 5:29, Jb. 1:1, 28:28)[5] being the purpose of the test. A conceptual linkage between divine testing and the obedience of Israel as a nation is well attested elsewhere (Ex. 15:25, 16:4, Dt. 8:2, 13:3 [Heb. 4], Judg. 2:22, 3:4), and the specific juxtaposition of 'test' and 'fear' comes in only one other passage, Exodus 20:20, in which Moses explains to Israel the purpose of God giving to Israel the Ten Commandments, the heart of Torah. The verbal and conceptual parallel between Genesis 22:1,12 and Exodus 20:20 is hermeneutically suggestive.

It is highly likely in general terms that the pre-Israelite patriarchal stories of Genesis 12-50 have been told from an Israelite perspective,[6] a point perhaps most clearly visible in the use of the name YHWH in Genesis (this basic hermeneutical point was implicit in the traditional ascription of Genesis to Moses, and is not affected by the critical recognition of a variety of post-Mosaic writers as responsible for Genesis). Further, the language of divine testing and human obedience is most at home (i.e., most used and probably originating) in the context of YHWH's dealings with Israel. It is likely, therefore, that the story of Abraham has been deliberately told in the language of Israel's obedience to Torah so that Abraham can be seen as a type or model of Israel. Such typology serves on the one hand to show that what was introduced at Sinai was not a complete novelty but was

---

Theology; Minneapolis, Fortress 1992), esp. 138-45, 188-90; *Genesis 12-50* (Old Testament Guides; Sheffield, JSOT Press 1992), chs. 3, 6.

[5]It is curious that this is still sometimes missed. In a recent study on Genesis 22 Phyllis Trible comments on v. 12 that 'the term "fearer of God" embodies awe, terror, and devotion in the presence of the *mysterium tremendum*' ('Genesis 22: The Sacrifice of Sarah' in J.P. Rosenblatt & J.C. Sitterson [eds.] *'Not in Heaven': Coherence and Complexity in Biblical Narrative* [Indiana Studies in Biblical Literature: Bloomington & Indianapolis, Indiana UP 1991] 170-91, quotation at 178). To read the text in these Otto-like categories is to skew it. In the religious language of the Old Testament 'fear' is primarily an ethical term to do with actions rather than feelings, although it can have other senses as well.

[6]See my *The Old Testament of the Old Testament*, chs. 1-4.

congruous with what preceded, since the story of Abraham was open to having its true meaning brought out by the theological conceptuality of Torah; and on the other hand Abraham now serves as the definitive example of the kind of obedient response that God seeks from Israel.[7]

Secondly, although many ancient and modern interpreters have found problematic the fact that God asks for the life of a child, it is vital to avoid anachronism in reading the story and not to insist in imposing natural but misleading assumptions upon it. The story's assumptions are patriarchal in a rather strong and narrow sense of that overused and complex term, that is that a man's children are seen as extensions of his own value and significance and are not considered as uniquely important human beings in their own right.[8] In Genesis 22, Isaac's value is spelt out in terms of what he means to Abraham (22:2, 12), not in terms of his own intrinsic individuality. What this means, therefore, is that Isaac is that which Abraham values and prizes the most, effectively his most precious possession, though with a greater existential significance than any ordinary possession, for the preceding narrative makes Isaac central to Abraham's story. Isaac represents both Abraham's past, as that gift from God for which he waited for years, and his future, as the bearer of God's promise of descendants. The natural interpretative

[7]I disagree, therefore, with proposals that the test in Genesis 22 should be seen as peculiar to Abraham. So, e.g. Brevard Childs comments that 'it is a "patriarchal temptation" and as such viewed as non-repeatable within the Bible' (B.S. Childs, *Biblical Theology of the Old and New Testaments* [London, SCM 1992] 334, *cf.* 327).

[8]In the earlier layers of the Old Testament, this assumption is reflected in various ways; on the one hand, fathers are assumed to be able to make life and death decisions about their children (Gn. 38:24; 42:37; Judg. 11:34-40); on the other hand the punishment of a man's whole family represents not the victimising of the innocent but rather the thorough punishment of that guilty man (Ex. 20:5; 34:7; Jos. 7:24). This particular form of patriarchy gradually faded within Israel, no doubt as a result of a growing sense of human individuality and of changing social patterns. In a canonical context, the notion of humanity as in the image of God, as formulated in Genesis 1:26, has rightly been seen by Jewish and Christian tradition as a strong pointer towards the unique value of every human being, including children. It is, however, unclear at how early a date the implications for children of the generalised nature of Genesis 1:26 would have been appreciated.

move, therefore, when Genesis 22 is presented as paradigmatic for the believing community, is to see Isaac as a metaphor for anyone or anything that is particularly valuable to those being tested; with the possibility that this valuable thing may even represent the very heart of what constitutes the person's faith in God. There is also the further corollary that the language of sacrifice becomes metaphorical for relinquishment to God; a metaphorical shift facilitated by the fact that the kind of sacrifice specified in Genesis 22:2, 13 is the burnt offering (עֹלָה) whose total consumption in the process of sacrifice (*cf.* Lev. 1) naturally symbolises total dedication to God.[9]

Another important emphasis in Genesis 22 is that God 'provides'/'sees' (ראה, 22:8, 14). The somewhat ambiguous use of the verb ראה is not without parallel elsewhere (e.g. 1 Sa. 16:1), but has particular significance in Genesis 22. The general theological point is well captured in English by the notion of providence, whose etymological basis in God's foresight is closely connected to its meaning in terms of God's practical care. This providence, however, is not just expressed as a general principle, as in 22:8, but it is also explicitly linked to one particular place, where the climax of the story occurs, as the name of that place (22:14a). Although the identity of this place has been much disputed, there can be little doubt that as the story stands the place is none other than Jerusalem, as rabbinic tradition has always recognised.[10]

There are three main reasons for this identification. First, the use of the verb ראה is probably to be connected with the name Moriah, understood as a noun from the verbal root ראה with the regular nominal preformative מ.[11] Moriah thus

---

[9]Trible ('Genesis 22') sees the relinquishing of attachment as central to the story, but interprets it rather curiously in that she sees paternal bonding (and Sarah's maternal bonding) as an idolatrous problem. Surely the point is not that attachment to other humans is wrong, but rather that it must always be subordinate to one's attachment to God; though it may simply be that I find her terminology misleading.

[10]See e.g. C.T.R. Hayward, 'The Present State of Research into the Targumic Account of the Sacrifice of Isaac', *JJS* 32 (1981) 127-50, esp. 132.

[11]Probably the main difficulty with this suggestion, and the reason why it has often not been accepted, is the lack of an א, the middle radical of ראה, in the Masoretic spelling of Moriah (מֹרִיָּה), although it is attested in

means 'place of seeing'. If one asks in the light of the rest of the Old Testament where is the place of seeing, where God both sees (22:14a) and is seen (22:14b), the answer is either Sinai (Ex. 24:9-11) or Zion (2 Sa. 24:15-17, Is. 6:1, Ps. 84:5,8 [Heb. 6,9]). Since the story envisages the site as three days' journey from Beersheba (22:4),[12] which is appropriate for Jerusalem, but too short a journey for Sinai, it is therefore Jerusalem which is indicated.

Secondly, the saying in 22:14b about the 'mount of YHWH' (הַר יהוה) most naturally refers to the place named in 22:14a. Since the phrase הַר יהוה elsewhere in the Old Testament regularly refers to Jerusalem (Ps. 24:3, Is. 2:3, Zc. 8:3), with only one reference to Sinai (Nu. 10:33), a reference to Jerusalem is most likely in Genesis 22.

Thirdly, the concerns of Genesis 22 naturally resonate with those of the Temple in Jerusalem. Abraham is told to go to a place to which God will direct him, there to offer sacrifice, just as Israel is to offer its sacrifices at the place which YHWH chooses for them (Dt. 12:5-6,13-14), a place interpreted as Jerusalem (1 Ki. 14:21). The place Abraham goes to is called Moriah, which is only elsewhere referred to as the site of the Temple (2 Ch. 3:1). At Moriah Abraham offers a burnt offering, just as Israel does in the Temple. The obedience which Abraham shows as he comes to sacrifice is what Israel should show when it comes to sacrifice in the Temple (Pss. 15, 24:3-6, *cf.* Je. 7:1-15). Thus, Abraham's sacrificial worship on Moriah is readily seen as the archetype of Israel's worship in the Temple in Jerusalem, and is presumably to be understood as ultimately the basis for it.[13]

---

some of the versions (see BHS *ad loc.*). This lack does not invalidate our interpretation, but it does make it more debatable.

[12]Admittedly the story does not explicitly say that Abraham set out from Beersheba. However, that is where Abraham is located at the end of the previous story (21:33), and that is where he goes when he leaves Moriah (22:19). A starting point in Beersheba remains therefore the most natural assumption.

[13]It should be noted, however, that another story of the choice of the site of the Temple is given in 2 Samuel 24, a link made more explicit in the retelling in 1 Chronicles 21, esp. 1 Chronicles 22:1. Given the intrinsic importance of the site of the Temple, it is natural that it should be related to more than one of the key figures in Israel's story.

If one reflects further on the main concerns of the story, it can be seen that in it there are brought together arguably the two central traditions of the Old Testament, Sinai and Zion; Sinai with its concern for Torah-centred obedience to God, and Zion as the place chosen by God for God to be specially present with Israel as they come to worship in the Temple. Another way of looking at it, with a slightly different emphasis, is to see the story as the paradigmatic union of morality and religion, as Abraham shows supreme obedience to God precisely in the context of offering sacrificial worship in the prescribed place. Either way, the story can be seen as a kind of hermeneutical key to interpreting the rest of the Old Testament. Of course, the relationship between the Sinai and Zion traditions, or between ethical and ritual emphases, in the course of the actual history of Israelite religion was hardly always harmonious; and the story itself may not always have had precisely the significance that it now has; indeed, if its origins are genuinely ancient, from a pre-Israelite patriarchal period, then it could not originally have had the kind of resonances it now has which must make the story as it stands at least subsequent to the building of the Temple under Solomon; and it is possible that disagreements as to the significance of Jerusalem may still be reflected in the textual variants in 22:2, 14. But the crucial point is that Genesis 22 is designed to function as a normative interpretation of Israel's traditions, certainly arising out of Israel's history, but in no way to be equated with it; rather, it is a way of seeing the deeper significance of Israel's traditions, so that they may be more effectively appropriated by ongoing generations of Abraham's descendants.

One possible objection is that it is inappropriate to tie the story so closely to Sinai and Zion traditions when neither Sinai nor Zion are actually mentioned. Certainly, our interpretation has depended on being open to what I have taken to be deliberate hints and clues in the text which make most sense when related to other parts of the Old Testament, and it is possible that not everything suggested was intended by those responsible for Genesis 22 as it now stands. That would not, however, invalidate the interpretation, but simply be a way of saying that what it now means in the context of the Old Testament transcends authorial intention. Nonetheless, the lack of specific mention of either Torah or Jerusalem should still be given full interpretative weight.

In compositional terms, the primary reason is probably a respect on the part of the writers for the particularity of the patriarchal context as prior to the context of Israel. Lack of direct reference is consonant with Torah and Jerusalem not yet having the significance which they subsequently came to have; hints and allusions, for those who have ears to hear, may have been seen as the most appropriate way for the story in its Genesis context to anticipate and adumbrate the traditions of Israel. In terms of interpretation, the allusive language makes it possible to some extent to loosen the links between Genesis 22 and Sinai and Zion. That is, although hitherto I have highlighted and emphasised the links, to show what I believe are the primary resonances of the story in its Old Testament context, the fact remains that it is possible to interpret the language of the story without reference to Torah and Jerusalem. Although the language of testing and fearing is given distinctive content by its association with God giving Torah to Israel, it remains intrinsically meaningful in its own right. Likewise, although the place where God sees and provides is intended to be Jerusalem, the notion of God seeing and providing remains intrinsically meaningful without reference to Jerusalem. Thus, the language of the story is such that it is open to have meaning in contexts other than that to which it is primarily related. It is this that helps make the story open to a Christological interpretation, insofar as a Christological interpretation genuinely engages with the kind of issues already discerned as present within the text.

One final element within Genesis 22 is the second address by the angel of YHWH in 22:15-18. This is generally ignored in interpretations of Genesis 22, for the not unnatural reason that the dramatic climax has been reached and the main issues of the story resolved by 22:14. If the story ended at 22:14, simply being rounded off by 22:19, many might not notice the loss of 22:15-18. Nonetheless, as I have argued elsewhere,[14] these extra verses add an important dimension to the story. The angel renews God's promise of descendants to Abraham, formulating the promise with unique emphasis and relating it specifically to Abraham's obedience in a way that is otherwise

[14]See my 'The Earliest Commentary on the Akedah' (n. 4).

unprecedented. Hitherto, the promise has been a wholly gratuitous offer by God; now it is given to Abraham because he has been obedient (22:16b, 18b). If special significance is to be seen in this conceptual change, as is surely natural in context, then it is probably best to avoid the overworked and overladen categories of merit or faith and works,[15] and attempt rather a fresh formulation of the value of a faithful human response to God. As I put it in my earlier article:

> Abraham by his obedience has not qualified to be the recipient of blessing, because the promise of blessing had been given to him already. Rather, the existing promise is reaffirmed but its terms of reference are altered. A promise which previously was grounded solely in the will and purpose of YHWH is transformed so that it is now grounded *both* in the will of YHWH *and* in the obedience of Abraham. It is not that the divine promise has become contingent upon Abraham's obedience, but that Abraham's obedience has been incorporated into the divine promise. Henceforth Israel owes its existence not just to YHWH but also to Abraham.
>
> Theologically this constitutes a profound understanding of the value of human obedience - it can be taken up by God and become a motivating factor in his purposes towards humanity. Within the wider context of Hebrew theology I suggest that this is analogous to the assumptions underlying intercessory prayer. Here too faithful human response is taken up and incorporated within the purposes and activity of God'.[16]

This interpretation of the value of Abraham's obedience resonates with some of the fundamental assumptions about the relationship between God and humanity in the Old Testament, assumptions which continue into the New Testament and subsequent Christian tradition. The concerns of the passage are therefore intrinsically open to be related to the wider context of Christian theology and read from a Christological perspective.

Classic Christian Approaches to Genesis 22

The New Testament explicitly engages with the story of Genesis 22 in two passages, Hebrews 11:17-19 and James 2:18-

---

[15]Unfortunately Childs solely cites Calvin and uses the categories of faith and works in his own recent interpretation (*Biblical Theology*, 335).

[16]*VT* 38 (1988) 320-1 = *From Eden to Golgotha*, 71.

24. It seems, however, that it was Paul's possible allusion in Romans 8:32, 'He who did not spare his own son but gave him up for us all...', that was historically most influential. Whether or not Paul intended an allusion to Genesis 22 is unclear,[17] but Paul's language naturally lends itself to a typological parallel between Abraham and Isaac and God the Father and God the Son. The theme of a father giving up a son to sacrificial death, with consequent blessing for all the nations of the earth (Gn. 22:18), readily resonates with the Christian story of God the Father giving his Son to die with a consequent Christian mission to proclaim salvation to the whole world. When one adds to this the imaginatively suggestive parallel of incidental detail that just as Isaac bore the wood for the sacrifice (Gn. 22:6) so Christ carried his cross (Jn. 19:17), not to mention that both stories are located in Jerusalem, it is not difficult to see why Genesis 22 came to be considered by Christians as one of the clearest anticipations in the whole Old Testament of the Christian story of salvation. There is of course the important difference that Isaac was never in fact put to death as Christ was, and this difference has often been noted. But the fact that a ram was sacrificed, and that the ram also could be seen as a type of Christ, meant that despite a certain looseness the imaginative parallel with the death of Christ could be maintained.

Although this basic outline of a Christological interpretation of Genesis 22 was developed in numerous ways by the Fathers, and provides a fascinating study in its own right, I do not propose to discuss it here. Partly this is because I am not sufficiently at home in the literature.[18] However, it is also because I wish to avoid the danger that the classic Christological reading could be relatively superficial in the extent of its engagement with the issues that the Old Testament text poses. Although, for example, the parallel carrying of the wood of sacrifice or the cross is imaginatively

---

[17]The issue is uncertain primarily because there are not the precise verbal links that one might have expected. The Hebrew adjective qualifying 'son' in Genesis 22:2,12, 16, יָחִיד, is appropriately rendered by Paul's ἴδιος, but the LXX, which might be expected to have influenced Paul had he had the text in mind, uses ἀγαπητός.

[18]For an introduction, see e.g. J. Daniélou, *From Shadows to Reality: Studies in the Biblical Typology of the Fathers* (London, Burns & Oates 1960) 115-130.

suggestive, it has no bearing on the issues of moral or theological importance in the text. Likewise, discussions about the ways in which both Isaac and the ram could represent Christ are ultimately somewhat arbitrary and leave me at least not much the wiser. This is not to discount such concerns altogether, but simply to say that they are secondary issues which should not be allowed onto centre stage.

The Typological Interpretation of von Rad

I propose, therefore, to focus initially on what is the outstanding modern Christological interpretation of Genesis 22, which is in the work of the scholar who is widely recognised to be the acutest theological interpreter of the Old Testament in the 20th century, Gerhard von Rad. Von Rad had a particular interest in Genesis 22, as he even wrote a small popular book devoted to it.[19] However, I shall concentrate on the interpretation offered in von Rad's Genesis commentary, which itself was aimed to appeal to an audience beyond that of the academic specialist.[20]

The key to understanding von Rad's Genesis commentary is given in the introduction, which von Rad concludes as follows:

> Franz Rosenzweig once remarked wittily that the sign 'R' (for the redactor of the Hexateuch documents, so lowly esteemed in Protestant research) should be interpreted as Rabbenu, 'our master', because basically we are dependent only on him, on his great work of compilation and his theology, and we receive the Hexateuch at all only from his hands. From the standpoint of Judaism, that is consistent. But for us [i.e. Christians], in respect to hermeneutics, even the redactor is not 'our master'. We receive the Old Testament from the hands of Jesus Christ, and therefore all exegesis of the Old Testament depends on whom one thinks Jesus Christ to be. If one sees in him the bringer of a new religion, then one will consistently examine the chief figures of the patriarchal narratives for their inward religious disposition and by, say, drawing religious 'pictures from life' will bring into the foreground what comes close to Christianity or even corresponds with it. But this 'pious' view is unsatisfactory because the principal subject of the account in the Genesis stories is not the religious characteristics

[19] *Das Opfer des Abraham* (Munich, Chr. Kaiser 1971).

[20] *Genesis* (rev. ed.; London, SCM 1972; ET of 9th German edition). For von Rad's intended readership, see p. 11.

of the patriarchs at all. Any mention of them is almost an aside. Often the details have to be drawn from the reader's imagination. The real subject of the account is everywhere a quite definite act of Yahweh, into which the patriarchs are drawn, often with quite perplexing results. So the first interest of the reader must be in what circumstances and in what way Yahweh's guidance is given, and what consequences result from it. In all the variety of the story, can we perhaps recognise some things that are typical of the action of God towards men? Then we must go on to raise the chief question: can we not recognise a common link even between the revelation of God in the old covenant and that in the new, a 'type'? The patriarchal narratives include experiences which Israel had of a God who revealed himself and at the same time on occasions hid himself more deeply. In this very respect we can see a continuity between the Old Testament and the New. In the patriarchal narratives, which know so well how God can conceal himself, we see a revelation of God which precedes his manifestation in Jesus Christ. What we are told here of the trials of a God who hides himself and whose promise is delayed, and yet of his comfort and support, can readily be read into God's revelation of himself in Jesus Christ.[21]

Whether von Rad's dismissal of 'religion' as contrasted with the acts of YHWH really does justice to the relationship between the human and the divine dimensions in the text seems to me doubtful but does not affect the key fact that von Rad is explicitly identifying his work of commentary with the classic Christian stance of reading the Old Testament in Christological terms. On the one hand, understanding of the Old Testament follows, rather than precedes, an understanding of Jesus Christ; the historical sequence from Israel to Christ may be reversed hermeneutically when it comes to reading Israel's scripture as Christian scripture. On the other hand, the interpretative exercise relates not to secondary issues but to the most fundamental issue of all, that of the nature of God and of his self-revelation as perceived by humans.

How then does this work in practice? Although the Christological perspective is not always readily apparent, it comes strongly to the fore in the interpretation of Genesis 22. First, we may note von Rad's methodological comments in the epilogue to the interpretation:

---

[21]*Genesis*, 42-43.

In the case of a narrative like this one, which obviously went through many stages of internal revision, whose material was, so to speak, in motion up to the end, one must from the first renounce any attempt to discover one basic idea as *the* meaning of the whole....Such a mature narrator as this one has no intention of paraphrasing exactly the meaning of such an event and stating it for the reader. On the contrary, a story like this is basically open to interpretation and to whatever thoughts the reader is inspired.[22]

Thus von Rad emphasises that the nature of the material is intrinsically such that it is open to reflection from a Christological perspective.

With regard to the central concerns of the story von Rad writes:

It is decisive for a proper understanding of what follows that one leave to the statement in v.1 its entire weight (the word 'God' is particularly emphasised in the syntax), and that one does not try to resolve it by a psychologising explanation....One must indeed speak of a temptation (*Anfechtung*) which came upon Abraham but only in the definite sense that it came from God only, the God of Israel....The narrator has not caused his reader any premature excitement regarding a horrible experience. The subject that now engages excited interest is rather Abraham's (and Isaac's) demeanour. For Abraham, God's command is completely incomprehensible: the child, given by God after long delay, the only link that can lead to the promised greatness of Abraham's seed (ch. 15.4f) is to be given back to God in sacrifice.....One must be careful not to interpret the story in a general sense as a question about Abraham's willingness to obey and accordingly to direct all interest to Abraham's trial. Above all, one must consider Isaac, who is much more than simply a 'foil' for Abraham, i.e. a more or less accidental object on which his obedience is to be proved. Isaac is the child of promise. In him every saving thing that God has promised to do is invested and guaranteed. The point here is not a natural gift, not even the highest, but rather the disappearance from Abraham's life of the whole promise. Therefore, unfortunately, one can only answer all plaintive scruples about this narrative by saying that it concerns something much more frightful than child sacrifice. It has to do with a road out into Godforsakenness *(Gottverlassenheit)*, a road on which Abraham does not know that God is only testing him. There is thus considerable religious experience behind these nineteen verses: that Yahweh often seems to contradict himself,

---

[22]*Genesis*, 243.

that he appears to want to remove the salvation begun by himself from history. But in this way Yahweh tests faith and obedience! One further thing may be mentioned: in this test God confronts Abraham with the question whether he could give up God's gift of promise. He had to be able (and he was able), for it is not a good that may be retained by virtue of any legal title or with the help of a human demand. God therefore poses before Abraham the question whether he really understands the gift of promise as a pure gift'.[23]

This interpretation of Genesis 22, especially its key sentence about Abraham being on a road out into Godforsakenness, has been much appreciated by Old Testament scholars. For example, John Scullion, the translator of Westermann's great Genesis commentary, in his own recent Genesis commentary cites von Rad at the climax of his interpretation;[24] though remarkably he leaves von Rad's 'moving reflection' entirely without comment, presumably either because he considered its significance self-evident or because he failed to see what its significance is. James Crenshaw is more to the point when he says that, 'Von Rad writes that God led Abraham to Golgotha!'[25] (though he himself has 'grave doubts about the legitimacy of such a procedure', that is seeing Christian significance for Old Testament texts).[26] Since the significance of von Rad's interpretation is not instantly self-evident, it is worth spelling it out and then reflecting on it a little.

First, von Rad was a Lutheran, and at the heart of Lutheran theology stands a theology of the cross which centres upon the cry of dereliction upon the lips of Jesus in Matthew 27:46, Mark 15:34: 'My God, my God, why have you forsaken me?' (rendered in German by Luther as 'Mein Gott, mein Gott, warum hast du mich verlassen?'). So if Abraham is on a road into Godforsakenness (Gottverlassenheit), the primary intended resonance is with the crucifixion of Christ. In the light of what von Rad says in his introduction about types, it seems clear that Abraham is being understood as a type of Christ.

---

[23]*Genesis*, 238-239, 244; the italicised German words have been added to emphasise the key concepts.

[24]J.J. Scullion, *Genesis: A Commentary for Students, Teachers and Preachers* (Collegeville, Liturgical Press 1992) 174; *cf.* R. Davidson, *The Courage to Doubt* (London, SCM 1983) 52-3.

[25]J.L. Crenshaw, *Gerhard von Rad* (Makers of the Modern Theological Mind; Waco, Word 1978) 120.

[26]*Gerhard von Rad*, 184, n. 11.

Secondly, the significance of Luther's theology of the cross is that it conveys a particular understanding both of the way in which God reveals himself and of the way in which he works in human lives. On the one hand, there is the notion of the hidden and paradoxical way in which God works - the test of Abraham comes 'from God only' and is 'completely incomprehensible'; on the other hand, the process of God's working within people is depicted by the complex and elusive term *Anfechtung* - which is the term von Rad uses to depict God's test of Abraham in v. 1. These interrelated concepts of the hiddenness of God and of *Anfechtung* are well described by Alister McGrath:

> For Luther, the sole authentic *locus* of man's knowledge of God is the cross of Christ, in which God is to be found revealed, and yet paradoxically hidden in that revelation....In that it is God who is made known in the passion and cross of Christ, it is *revelation*; in that this revelation can only be discerned by the eye of faith, it is *concealed*....The concept of a hidden God (*absconditus Deus*) lies at the centre of the theology of the cross....
>
> God is particularly known through suffering....Luther regards God himself as the source of *Anfechtung*: God assaults man in order to break him down and thus to justify him....The 'theologian of the cross' regards such suffering as his most precious treasure, for revealed and yet hidden in precisely such sufferings is none other than the living God, working out the salvation of those whom he loves....As Luther remarks, *Anfechtung*, 'in so far as it takes everything away from us, leaves us nothing but God: it cannot take God away from us, and actually brings him closer to us'. It is through undergoing the torment of the cross, death and hell that true theology and the knowledge of God come about.[27]

Thus the process of testing which Abraham undergoes is interpreted by the dynamics revealed at Calvary and recapitulated in the lives of Christians.

Thirdly, when von Rad speaks of Abraham having to understand the gift of promise as a 'pure gift' which cannot be held onto 'by virtue of any legal title or with the help of a human demand', the language resonates with the Lutheran interpretation of Paul's concept of faith and works; humanity should not make, and cannot have, a claim on God, but rather must receive from God that which can only be received as a gift

[27]*Luther's Theology of the Cross* (Oxford, Blackwell 1985) 149-52.

of grace. Thus Abraham displays the kind of response to God that should characterise the Christian.

This interpretation by von Rad is imaginatively powerful and theologically profound. How might one evaluate it? In the first place, it is important to appreciate that in essence von Rad is not doing with the story of Abraham anything different from what the Genesis writer has done. That is, just as the Genesis writer has taken the story of Abraham and interpreted it from the perspective of Israel's relationship with God centred on Torah obedience and worship in Jerusalem, so von Rad has interpreted it from the perspective of the Christian understanding of God centred on Christ crucified. In each case a theological perspective from a context other than that of the story in itself has been used to bring out its meaning. And these theological perspectives are not arbitrary, but rather are those which the historic communities of faith, both Jewish and Christian, have recognised as central to their existence. The difference, of course, is that Israel's interpretation has become embodied in the text and has become integral to its canonical form, while von Rad's depends entirely on the resonances of the text when read in a wider New Testament and Christian context. This is not a difference between valid and invalid or between better and worse, but rather between different phases of a continuing quest to relate the paradigmatic stories of Abraham to the ongoing life of faith of the various descendants of Abraham.

Secondly, von Rad has abandoned the classic Christian pattern of seeing Abraham and Isaac as typifying God the Father and God the Son, and instead has made Abraham the type of Christ. This is surely a positive development since it means that the relationship is between those two figures on whom the Genesis and New Testament texts most concentrate and whose dynamics are intrinsically open to be linked to each other. It ensures that the typology focuses on the genuine existential issues present in the biblical text.

Thirdly, von Rad's interpretation is not as deeply rooted as it might be in an exegesis of the biblical text. On the one hand, although he offers special excursuses on the two key concepts of testing and the fear of God, in neither instance does he note the crucial linkage with Exodus 20:20. Even when he notes the concept of testing as applied to all Israel in e.g.

Deuteronomy 13:3, Judges 2:22, he only uses this to make a historical observation about the notion of the testing of all Israel being older than that of the testing of an individual, an observation which is left hermeneutically mute. Thus the linkage with Torah is missed. On the other hand, von Rad misses the linkage with Jerusalem (except as a possibly late and marginal development).[28] He appears to be deliberately reacting against Gunkel's famous interpretation of the story as originally the cult legend of Jeruel, and insists on working with the text in its canonical form. He notes how strange it is that despite all the importance attached to the naming of the place in v. 14 no place name is given, but simply sees this as a loss caused by the story's lengthy history of tradition.[29] If von Rad had seen that Gunkel was right to fix on the wordplay in the story and only questionable in relating it to the insignificant Jeruel, he might have reflected on it afresh and seen that the resonances with Jerusalem are deeply embedded in the story. Quite apart from the fact that this would be congenial to his typology - Golgotha being in the heart of Jerusalem - it might have led to reflection on the possible significance of the seeing motif beyond noting that 'the reader is here to be summoned to give free reign to his thoughts'.[30] Ironically, therefore, although von Rad stresses the depth dimension of the text he largely misses the significance of this dimension, and therefore his own interpretation lacks a certain depth in relation to the Old Testament context. In particular, it means that his interpretation of testing as *Anfechtung* relates somewhat uneasily to the notion of testing as a means of enhancing obedience to God's revealed will in Torah.

---

[28]'The name Moriah was perhaps inserted into our story from 2 Chronicles 3.1 only subsequently in order to claim it as an ancient tradition of Jerusalem' (*Genesis*, 240).

[29]'It may have become clear that the supposedly oldest version of the narrative was a cult saga of a sanctuary and as such legitimised the redemption of child sacrifice, actually demanded by God, with the sacrifice of an animal. This idea is quite foreign to the present narrative. One sees it most clearly in the loss of the name of the cultic centre. When the narrative lost its connection with its ancient cultic point of contact, any particular interest in the name also disappeared. What was once the most important point has now become an accessory to the narrative in the form of a pun' (*Genesis*, 243).

[30]*Genesis*, 242.

Fourthly, although von Rad initially renounces a psychologising explanation and notes how 'the narrator refrains from giving us an insight into Abraham's inner self',[31] his introduction of the notion of Godforsakenness surely moves in an opposite direction. The notion of forsakenness in general terms naturally draws attention to the psychology of the person so afflicted, for forsakenness is a particular interpretation of, with corresponding feeling about, an experience of being alone. And when the forsakenness is linked with the Godforsakenness of Jesus on the cross, with his loud cries of anguish as depicted by Matthew and Mark (Mt. 27:46, 50, Mk. 15:34, 37), it is difficult not to move into a psychological mode and reflect on the inner awareness of the sufferer, whether Jesus or Abraham. Von Rad's central concept relates more readily to a subjective state of feeling than to an objective act of obedience, and so again is subtly moving away from the concerns of the Genesis text. One may wish to argue that ultimately this enriches the appropriation of the text, at least for many a modern reader, and that may be so. But if one takes that path, it is vital to be aware of what one is doing.

Towards a Fresh Christological Interpretation

In a final section I would like to propose a few preliminary outlines for a fresh Christological reading of Genesis 22. This will retain von Rad's typology of Abraham and Christ but develop it differently.

I suggest initially that the best New Testament analogue to God's test of Abraham is not in the first instance the crucifixion, vital though that is, but rather the call to discipleship at Caesarea Philippi (Mt. 16:24-28, Mk. 8:34-9:1, Lk. 9:23-27); although the call to go the way of the cross as a metaphor is indeed linked to the literal crucifixion of Jesus, it is helpful to retain a distinction between the two.

If one sets the Caesarea Philippi episode alongside Genesis 22 a number of common concerns emerge. Each passage presupposes the characteristic logic of biblical monotheism, for each sees the call of God as the supreme claim on a person's life beside which all other value is relativised. As a result of this, the language about denying self and losing

[31] *Genesis*, 240.

one's life to find it correlates readily with God requiring Abraham to relinquish that which is most precious to him. And each passage explores the paradox that it is precisely the willingness to let go in trust of that which is most precious, which one most wants to preserve, that leads to the fullest realisation of human hope for life and entering into unparalleled blessing.

A further point to notice is that the gospel text, like Genesis 22, does not draw attention to the subjective feelings that may accompany discipleship, but focuses entirely upon what is involved in the objective act of obedient response. Each time it is actions, not feelings, that count. The importance of this emphasis is of course the fact that the feelings accompanying costly obedience may vary greatly. This is particularly striking if one considers the portrayal of the crucifixion as the culmination of Jesus' obedience to God. For example, in a study of the crucifixion narratives in Mark and Luke I argued that:

> In Mark, Jesus is an anguished figure, abandoned by both people and God, speaking only in loud cries. There is absolutely nothing to relieve the agony except perhaps the centurion's words, by which time Jesus is already dead. In Luke, Jesus is a compassionate figure, forgiving people, trusting God, and peaceful throughout. The nature of the difference may be well expressed by an artistic analogy. Mark's portrayal is like Grünewald's famous crucifixion in the Isenheim altarpiece - a stark, agonising, disturbing picture. Luke's portrayal is like any of the crucifixion scenes of Fra Angelico - always peaceful, dignified, moving.[32]

The natural implication of the differing gospel portrayals is that the subjective, inward dimension of obedience even to death may be anguished but may be calm. Although commentators on Genesis 22 are frequently tempted to speculate on Abraham's inner anguish,[33] the text not only gives no hint of it, but, in the words of Abraham cited in v. 8, suggests, if anything, the opposite; a portrayal of Abraham

---

[32]'Proclaiming Christ Crucified: Some Reflections on the Use and Abuse of the Gospels', *Anvil* 5 (1988) 31-52, reprinted in *From Eden to Golgotha*, 83-104; quotation at pp. 39 and 91-2 respectively.

[33]It is striking that even Robert Alter, usually so sensitive to the reticence of the biblical narrative, cannot resist depicting Abraham in Genesis 22 as 'an anguished father' (R. Alter, The *Art of Biblical Narrative* [London & Sydney, George Allen & Unwin 1981] 182).

that is perhaps closer to the crucifixion of Jesus as portrayed by Luke (or John) rather than by Mark (or Matthew).

In general terms both God's test of Abraham and Jesus' call to discipleship display the characteristic biblical and Judaeo-Christian understanding that human life finds its fulfilment in moral and spiritual commitment. This commitment is not something arbitrary, although it must be consciously chosen, but rather is a response to a sense of that ultimate reality which is God, a God who is personal and moral and reveals himself in gracious challenge. This means that life is always necessarily a process of growing, and often struggling, towards subordinating natural desires and inclinations to that supreme good which is God. This process, as already noted, is intrinsically paradoxical as God may require that which runs counter to one's deepest natural inclinations. The paradox is intrinsic to the process and its possible implications are differently developed in Old and New Testament.

In the Old Testament, God's gift of Torah to Israel is at the same time a test. The purpose of the test is good, that Israel should grow in moral stature, but it recognises that a choice is involved on Israel's part and that therefore Israel's obedience may not be forthcoming. However, despite the recognition, most marked in the most extensive theology of Torah, i.e., Deuteronomy, that Israel may be stiff-necked and rebellious (e.g. Dt. 9:4-6, 7-8, 22-24; 31:27-29) it is a characteristic note that obedience is a real possibility. 'This commandment which I command you this day is not too hard for you, neither is it far off....But the word is very near you; it is in your mouth and in your heart, so that you can do it' (Dt. 30:11,14). This possibility of obedience is what Abraham supremely exemplifies; obedience can be a reality even when it takes its most demanding form.

In the New Testament, this understanding is in some ways simply presupposed and continued. Jesus himself, like Abraham, shows complete obedience to God, and even surpasses Abraham in the constant and unbroken nature of his obedience. And when Jesus calls his disciples to follow, both initially and at Caesarea Philippi, he clearly presupposes that it is possible to do what he says. However, the New Testament moves beyond the Old in at least two ways.

On the one hand, the call to discipleship is explicitly linked with the suffering and death of Jesus. This means, among other things, that although losing one's life to find it is primarily a metaphor, it is given special meaning by its literal enactment in the death and resurrection of Jesus; for disciples too, the metaphor may sometimes require an outworking that may mean that the life which is gained may be as much, if not more, in an order of existence beyond this present one. Although the notion that obedience to God may entail death is certainly present in the Old Testament (e.g. Is. 52:13-53:12, Dn. 3:16-18), and was much developed in Jewish tradition in reflection on the role of Isaac in Genesis 22,[34] the concept of death as the key to life acquires a centrality in the New Testament that is unparalleled in the Old.

On the other hand, the paradigmatic passion narrative in which Jesus is faithful to death is marked by the unfaithfulness of all his disciples, an unfaithfulness characterised as much by Peter's unreflecting desire for self-preservation in the courtyard of the high priest, as by the more blatant failure to pray and subsequent flight of all the disciples in Gethsemane. It is only the forgiveness made possible by the resurrection that makes it possible for the disciples to be fully restored to their discipleship. Implicit in this story appears to be an understanding not just of the capacity of human faithfulness to fail at the crucial moment but also of the willingness of God to offer forgiveness and seek reconciliation in a way that entails transcending even the apparently final limit of death. Again, this pattern of death and resurrection as intrinsic to the call of God offers a witness to a reality towards which the Old Testament points more tentatively.

Much remains to be said. But I hope the above gives some indication of possible ways in which a Christological reading of the Old Testament might begin to be reformulated afresh. The responsible Christian use of the Old Testament has always been a fundamental concern of Donald Wiseman, and it is a pleasure to dedicate this essay in his honour.

---

[34]See S. Spiegel, *The Last Trial* (New York, Behrman 1979) *passim*.

9

GENESIS 32: LIGHTEN OUR DARKNESS, LORD, WE PRAY

David F. Pennant

Summary

Many attempts have been made to render the account of Jacob wrestling with God by night more acceptable. Whether early rabbinic, early Christian or from the 20th century, these have tended to rewrite the story to some degree. But the desire to 'make sense' of this story is deceptive, as is the quest for scientific certainty in biblical studies which may lie behind these attempts. A more helpful approach might be to take the incident as it stands, and ask what light might be shed on other parts of the Old Testament that seem to be related to it if we take this line.

Some passages in the Old Testament seem obscure to us at first sight. Jacob's unexpected wrestling match at night with an unknown foe, recorded in Genesis 32:23-33 [MT; English 22-32], is one of these. Much has been written about this story, and we will begin by looking at some of the approaches taken up by early commentators.

We start in the Old Testament itself. The Genesis account states that the adversary was a man, and that Jacob believed it was God that he had seen face to face (vv. 25, 31 [24, 30]). Hosea 12:4 states that Jacob's struggle was with an angel. Whether the discrepancy between the title 'God' and 'angel' would have been seen as significant in those times may be hard to discern. In an earlier generation, Abraham, sitting by his tent in the heat of the day, looked up and saw three 'men'; these later turned out to be the Lord and two angels (Gn. 18:2, 19:1). The words of the angel of the Lord in Genesis 22:15-17 are very similar to God's word in 17:1-2. A few generations later, Moses encountered the Lord at the burning bush (Ex. 3:6), which was later reported by Stephen as meeting an angel (Acts 7:35). Manoah considered that to see the angel of the Lord was to see God (Judg. 13:21-22). It seems to me that a case can be made for these terms being somewhat interchangeable in the Old Testament era.[1]

Be that as it may, with the passing of time, early rabbinic commentators had difficulty with the idea that God himself had been present. They drew a distinction between God and his representative. In fact, the entire corpus of rabbinic writings chose to follow Hosea, in ascribing the attack to an angel, ignoring Genesis 32:29 [28].[2] Moreover, because the story tells of Jacob being wounded in the fight, leaving him limping, they found the attack hard to attribute even to an angel. In one view, the assailant was declared to have assumed the shape of a shepherd or brigand chief (Gn. Rab. 910). Another view was that the attacker was Samael, celestial guardian of Edom, who attempted to destroy Jacob (Yalkut Reubeni *ad* Gn. 32:35).[3] We may notice that it is not stated in the text itself that the assailant's aim was to kill Jacob; this is an interpretation. Once

---

[1]D. Kidner, *Genesis* (TOTC; IVP 1967) 33-34. See also Jos. 5:13-15.

[2]W.T. Miller, *Mysterious Encounters at Mamre and Jabbok* (Brown Judaic Studies 50; Scholars Press, Chico 1984) 114-5.

[3]R. Graves & R. Patai, *Hebrew Myths* (Cassell, London 1963) 227.

this idea had gained a footing, it had the effect of relegating God from his place in the story, since how could God want to destroy Jacob (*cf.* Gn. 31:3)? The possible parallel with Genesis 22 had not been noted, it seems.[4]

Christian commentators also introduced new ideas. It was Justin Martyr (*c.*100 - *c.*165 AD) who first said that the angel was the Christ in human form.[5] Later, Hippolytus of Rome (*c.* 170 - *c.* 236 AD) said that the new name Israel could be understood as 'A man who sees God'; (אִישׁ רָאָה אֵל, pronounced 'eesh raah el').[6] Both ideas were widely followed by later writers. Origen (*c.* 185 - *c.* 254 AD) later declared that there were two angels; one wrestled against Jacob, and one wrestled with him, in the sense of being on Jacob's side in the struggle.[7]

These are just a few of the many proposals made over the course of centuries. Our purpose is not to examine the ideas in themselves, but to ask what the motive behind them might be. One suggestion is that the midrashic views were prompted by 'pious embarrassment'.[8] The thinking might run along these lines: how could God struggle with a man? The idea seems to lack credibility, so sense somehow needs to be made of the story. It is a short step from these instincts, which may have been barely discerned by the commentators in question, to adapting the story to fit better with preconceived ideas.

A final example will make this point clear to us. Didymus the Blind (*c.* 313 - 398 AD), a teacher in the catechetical school in Alexandria, declared that the name Jacob means 'He who mentally sees God'.[9] The phrase has a curious ring to it; we ask, why is the word 'mentally' employed here?

---

[4]R.S. Hendel, *The Epic of the Patriarch. The Jacob Cycle and the Narrative Traditions of Canaan and Israel* (Harvard Semitic Monographs 42; Scholars Press, Atlanta 1987) 105-6.

[5]Miller, *op. cit.* 119, citing *Trypho* 58:10.

[6]*Ibid.*, 120, citing *Pentateuch Fragment 16* on Genesis 49:7. However, P.L. Sachsse, 'Die Etymologie und älteste Aussprach des Namens Israel' (*ZAW* 34 [1914]) 2 attributed this to Philo (1st century AD). Along similar lines, Steuernagel suggested in 1901 that the name Israel might have come from אִישׁ רָחֵל, 'a man from the Rachel tribe' (Sachsse, p. 4).

[7]*Ibid.* 124, citing *De Princip*. 3.2-5.

[8]Graves, *op. cit.*, 228. These views arise from an assumption, which I share, that the account deals with events that took place.

[9]Miller, *op. cit.*, 124.

The answer is not far to seek. Didymus himself was blind, so the only way he could see anything was 'mentally'. This restriction has been imposed on Jacob in turn, probably unwittingly.

We detect a tendency in the history of comment on this passage. Commentators, in applying their minds to this text, have done precisely that; they have applied their minds to the text, and something has tended to stick. The result has been that when reading their writings, we may feel wiser about the outlook of the people who wrote, even if we do not always feel clearer about the original story they were writing about.

This process, in which the text is massaged into a shape acceptable to the commentator, rather as a potter moulds clay, did not cease in the early era. It seems safe to assume that it continues to this day. An example might be cited from Gunkel, who found it 'evident' that the contents of Genesis were legends handed down by oral tradition.[10] Reflection shows that this statement is far from evident. Another view expressed in our century is that the opponent was originally some kind of alien god, even a demon.[11] We may feel that here the plain statement of the text has been side-stepped to a marked degree, but it would be a mistake, in my view, for anyone to imagine that they are altogether immune from this tendency.

There is another avenue to explore, namely that of biblical allusion. Our story does not exist in a vacuum, but is part of the book we call Genesis, which in turn introduces that wider corpus that Christians call the Old Testament.

Several points of contact between our passage and others have been noted. We have already alluded briefly to Genesis 22, where God apparently orders the death of Isaac, the child of promise, at the hand of his father. This is presented as a test of Abraham. A few chapters later, another nocturnal struggle is recorded, where God approaches Moses intending to kill him (Ex. 4:24-6); this despite the commission laid on Moses in the previous chapter.[12]

---

[10]H. Gunkel, *The Legends of Genesis* (Schocken Books, New York 1964) 4. See also G. Von Rad, *Genesis* (OTL; 2nd edition, SCM, London 1972) 319-20 for a confident account of the prehistory of the text.

[11]J.G. Frazer, *Folk Lore in the Old Testament* Vol. 2 (Macmillan, London 1919) 410-25.

[12]Hendel, *op. cit.*, 105-6.

Other elements of the story have echoes elsewhere. The name-change from Jacob to Israel recalls the earlier name-change from Abram to Abraham (Gn. 17:5).[13] It also foreshadows the later name-change from Gideon to Jerubbaal (Judg. 6:32). Indeed, the name Jerubbaal suggests something similar to 'He struggled with God', inviting us to compare Gideon and Jacob (ריב, to struggle, בַּעַל, god).[14] It has also been noted that Leah's remark at the birth of Naphtali 'I have had a great struggle with my sister and I have won', highlights a struggle between the two sisters which is not dissimilar to Jacob's struggle with God and man (Gn. 30:8).[15]

Contact with other passages also arises from the issue of Jacob in relationship to others. The danger he is conscious of is from Laban in the preceding chapter, and from Esau in the next (though at the Jabbok, these are seen to be less than the danger from the mysterious attacker). The link between the Jabbok incident and what follows is brought to our attention by Jacob's remark to Esau, 'To see your face is like seeing the face of God' (Gn. 33:10).[16]

This alerts us to another Old Testament theme that appears in our text, namely the danger of seeing God face to face. Moses learned expressly from God what he had already known instinctively, that no-one could look on God's face and live (Ex. 3:6; 33:20). Other passages in the Old Testament where this point is an issue may be compared with ours (Gn. 16:31; Is. 6:1).

Even the focus on Jacob's hip may have its parallel elsewhere. Abraham had earlier made his servant swear loyalty over the matter of his son's marriage by placing his hand under his hip (Gn. 24:2, 9). This action, and the Old Testament phrase for progeny as being one that springs from the hip (יֹצְאֵי יְרֵכוֹ Gn. 46:26) suggest that the family line may be in mind, both there and here, in the reference to Jacob's hip being touched (32:26 [25]).[17]

---

[13]G.J. Wenham, *Genesis 16-50* (Waco, Word [forthcoming]) *ad. loc.*
[14]M. Buber, *Kingship of God* (London, Allen & Unwin 1967) 71.
[15]F.I. Andersen, 'Note on Genesis 30:8', *JBL* 88 (1969) 200.
[16]Wenham, *op. cit. ad. loc.*
[17]Miller, *op. cit.* 103; S.A. Geller, 'The Struggle at the Jabbok: The Use of Enigma in a Biblical Narrative', *JANES* 14 (1982) 50.

We should note also that this passage is rich in word-plays on names. Jacob is similar to Jabbok, and we have the etymologies for Israel and Peniel, all within a few verses. In addition, the rare word used for fight (אבק) employs two of the consonants in Jacob's name. A play on 'bless' (ברך) and 'hip' (יָרֵךְ) has been suggested.[18] The significance of the Old Testament's fondness for such alliteration is not clear, but it may have to do with God's normal method of communication with his prophets, which is by means of riddles (Nu. 12:8). Maybe the presence of so many verbal plays in such a short space should alert us to the thought that God is particularly speaking through these events.

Further points of similarity with other Old Testament themes could probably be found. It seems, then, that our passage is not in a vacuum. Perhaps by studying related passages of the kind we have listed, we could use insights from them to make sense of our story in Genesis 32.

The approach of comparing biblical passages which contain similar material has much to commend it. But I submit that we are in danger of making the same mistake as the earlier commentators we considered above. Once again, our natural desire to 'make sense' of a 'difficult' passage needs to be checked.

In what follows we will consider possible links with some other Old Testament passages, with the aim, not of 'ironing out' all the difficult aspects of our story, but rather of throwing them into relief, paying particular attention to the fact which some of the commentators noted above sought to downplay, that this passage explicitly says that it was God whom Jacob encountered at the Jabbok. We will use the passage to interpret other parts of the Old Testament that seem to be related to this event, in which God's direct involvement is less obvious.

First let us address the fact which the early commentators could not easily accept, that God, in blessing Jacob, also appeared to oppose him, and caused him pain. This turns out to be a recurring pattern in Scripture. Abraham, called the friend of God (Is. 41:8), suffered much anguish in waiting years for the promised son, only to find himself driving

---

[18]B. Weber, '"*Nomen est Omen*": Einige Erwägungen zu Gen. 32:23-33 und seinen Kontext', *BN* 61 (1992) 79-80.

off Hagar and Ishmael twice at his wife's insistence, and then discovering he was commanded to kill Isaac (Gn. 16; 21; 22). Moses was not only in danger of death from God, as we have seen, but in accepting God's call, ran danger of death from Pharaoh (Ex. 10:28) and even from the people of God (17:4). Job, one of God's special favourites, actually had Satan's attention drawn to him by God himself, which resulted in great suffering and harassment (Jb. 1:8). Jeremiah, spokesman for God, was bitterly opposed by his generation (Je. 20:7-8), as was Jesus himself in his turn (Mt. 27:41-4). Paul, outstanding missionary, was made aware at his call of how it would mean suffering for him (Acts 9:16; see 2 Cor. 1:5; ch. 12).

We can now appreciate more easily why it was considered death to see God face to face. It seems from Scripture that the more intimate the relationship between God and one of his people, the more suffering that person would experience. The fact that this may seem hard to understand does not give us licence to attempt to change such a prominent theme of Scripture.

We wondered whether the wounded hip spoke of God's hand on future generations. Despite appearances that Jacob has the upper hand over God, for which, surprisingly, he is commended, Israel is clay in the Lord's hands (Je. 18:10-6), and God's hand is seen to be shaping the future. This had already been envisaged before Jacob's birth, where he and Esau were spoken of as nations in the womb (Gn. 25:23).

This thought alerts us to Jacob in a prophetic role, copying his grandfather before him (Gn. 20:7). Perhaps we should consider the life of Jacob as pointing to the nature of the emerging Israel. So the connection with Naphtali may be representative, suggesting that not just that one, but all the children's names are somehow prophetic; perhaps readers of Genesis 29-30 can reflect on the future course of the nation as much as when they read chapters 48 and 49. The link with the attack on Moses in Exodus 4 perhaps invites us to compare Moses' life with the life of Jacob. To give just one example, this thought may help us in considering the comparison between the hostility of Laban to Jacob, and Pharaoh to Moses, which has been noted.[19] We observed Gideon's name-change to

---

[19]Originally a rabbinical insight; see W. Brueggemann, *Genesis* (Atlanta, John Knox 1982) 258.

something very similar to Jacob's new name. Gideon may perhaps be seen as a representative of the Judges, encouraging us to compare not just his exploits, but all the accounts of the Judges with that of Jacob. This exercise proves particularly fruitful in the case of Samson. Moreover, the destruction of Benjamin in the closing chapters of Judges, who in the light of events there should perhaps have kept his original name of Benoni after all (Gn. 35:18), does appear in that context to herald the imminent demise of Israel, as the old patriarch had feared so long before (Gn. 42:38).[20]

Once again, our aim here is not to examine these ideas in detail, but rather to suggest that, whereas trying to make 'sense' of the Jabbok incident seemed counter-productive, seeing it as a foundational passage, in which profound communication between God and man takes place, proves fruitful. Our few brief reflections suggest that there is considerable scope for enquiry in this direction. I believe this approach to be truly theological, because it recognises, in the spirit of Isaiah 55, that God intervenes in his world in ways that surprise us, and it attempts to take his words and deeds seriously by noting their consequences. Furthermore, seeing this passage as foundational seems reasonable in the light of its context. Jacob the patriarch is here re-entering the promised land on his return home after a long period away, recalling his vow at Bethel (Gn. 28:21). It is a moment of no small significance.

We will end by thinking in this way in a little more detail about one incident from Genesis 32, namely the 'two companies' passage. Jacob encountered angels of God, made a remark about there being two companies, and called the place Mahanaim, meaning 'two camps' (32:2-3 [1-2]). While Peniel and Mahanaim may be geographically different,[21] the text seems to apply the idea of two companies right through our section.

Jacob divides his parties into two groups (v. 8 [7]). Then, the account speaks of another grouping - Jacob's wives and children on the one hand, and Jacob himself on the other (v. 12 [11]); these two parties end up on different sides of the

---

[20]D.F. Pennant, *The Significance of Rootplay, Leading Words and Thematic Links in the Book of Judges* (Unpublished Ph.D. thesis, CNAA, 1988) ch. 8.
[21]Wenham, *op. cit. ad loc.*

Jabbok (vv. 23-25 [22-24]). In chapter 33, there are two groupings, of Jacob and company, facing Esau with four hundred men.

It is not difficult to see these varying divisions along different lines as being prophetic for aspects of Israel's future life as a nation. First we have the quarrelling in Genesis which arose among Jacob's children, suggesting potential for division. After the Exodus, two and half tribes would settle down without crossing over the Jordan. We have already referred to the inter-tribal disharmony in the era of the Judges. The nation would divide after Solomon. The enmity between Jacob and Esau would continue between the two nations that came from them. Indeed, bearing in mind also the hostility with Laban, we observe that Israel would end up at odds with all her neighbours in the region. Finally, some might suggest that the tendency for God's chosen family group to split into two anticipates God's people being found among both Jewish believers and Gentile Christians. On this scenario, Jacob's remark to Esau about his face being as the face of God might anticipate that final glorious acceptance of the Gospel by the Jews, and a recognition of Gentile believers as brothers (Rom. 11:25-6).

Some details of this final presentation may find greater acceptance than others. But its purpose has not been to propose a detailed outworking of our theme. Rather, our aim has been to suggest that theological comment on this passage, as indeed on the rest of the Old Testament, should focus on allowing God to be God, and seeing where this leads, rather than on refashioning the accounts, however subtly, to suit our opinions better. The closing verses of Psalm 19 make a fitting conclusion to our thoughts as we attempt to comment on Scripture:

Who can discern his errors?
Forgive my hidden faults. . .
May the words of my mouth and the meditation of my heart be pleasing in your sight,
O Lord, my Rock and my Redeemer (vv. 12, 14).

10

THE FACE AT THE BOTTOM OF THE WELL

Hidden Agendas of the Pentateuchal Commentator

Gordon Wenham

Summary

Commentators on Genesis tend to differ in their portraits of the patriarchs. To some extent these portraits reflect the theological and critical stance of the commentator. This is illustrated by a review of the work of Genesis Rabbah, Calvin, Gunkel, von Rad, Westermann, and Sternberg. It is argued that the approaches of von Rad and Sternberg come closest to recovering Genesis' own view of the patriarchs as sinners saved by divine mercy, who are expected to live in faithful obedience to God's commands.

Introduction

How far are commentators on the Bible reading their own ideas into the text? How far are they bringing out of the text the author's ideas? For many years commentators and preachers have been aware of the danger of doing eisegesis rather than exegesis. No-one made the point more sharply than Albert Schweitzer in *The Quest for the Historical Jesus*. After surveying the 19th-century attempts to build up a picture of Jesus through a critical reading of the gospels, Schweitzer concluded that scholars were creating a Jesus in their own image. 'As formerly in Renan the romantic spirit created the personality of Jesus in its own image, so at the present day the Germanic spirit is making a Jesus after its own likeness'.[1] Claiming to be objective, these scholars were looking into the well of history and simply seeing their own reflections at the bottom and supposing it to be the historical Jesus. Do commentators on the Old Testament do any better?

There is a strong school of thought today, which claims that they do not do any better, indeed that we cannot do any better, that it is the interpreter rather than the author who gives the text meaning, and that we should accept the situation and simply set about producing the most interesting readings that we can.[2]

Christian readers of Genesis have consciously or unconsciously been guided by St Paul's dictum that whatever was written in former days was written for our instruction (Rom. 15:4) and for training in righteousness (2 Tim. 3:16). Yet what lessons commentators draw from the stories in Genesis differ widely. For example in Genesis 12:10-20 Gunkel[3] and Vawter[4] regard Abraham's action in passing off Sarah as his sister as a demonstration of shrewdness, whereas Delitzsch[5]

[1]A. Schweitzer, *The Quest of the Historical Jesus* (ET of 3rd ed; London, Black 1954) 307.

[2]This serious challenge to the authority of Scripture is addressed at a more theoretical level by A.C. Thiselton, *New Horizons in Hermeneutics* (London, Harper and Row 1992).

[3]H. Gunkel, *Genesis* (3rd ed; Göttingen, Vandenhoek and Ruprecht 1910 [reprinted 1977]) 169.

[4]B. Vawter, *On Genesis: A New Reading* (Garden City, Doubleday 1977) 181-2.

[5]F. Delitzsch, *A New Commentary on Genesis* (ET; Edinburgh, T. & T. Clark 1888) I.385.

and Westermann[6] among others regard it as showing a lack of faith. The verdicts of two early 20th-century English commentators could hardly be more different. Driver[7] says: 'the narrator is clearly conscious that (Abram) fell below the standard which he might have been expected to attain, and contrasts him unfavourably with the upright and straightforward heathen king'. Skinner[8] states: 'It is assumed that in the circumstances lying is excusable. There is no suggestion that either the untruthfulness or the selfish cowardice of the request was severely reprobrated by the ethical code to which the narrative appealed'. Jewish commentators also disagree among themselves, but in general seem more concerned to justify the patriarch's conduct. Jacob[9] for example sees Abraham being at fault only for his lack of explicitness, while Sarna[10] insists that Abraham should not be judged by the standards of chivalry, but by morality which would justify his lies as the lesser evil.

It is partly the lack of explicit moral comment within this story and many others within the Old Testament that leads to this great diversity of interpretation about what the narrator's standpoint is to the episodes he relates. Occasionally he shows his hand as in 34:7, where commenting on the rape of Dinah, he says, 'Such a thing ought not to be done'. But what does he think about the following events? Does he endorse the brothers' massacre or Jacob's condemnation of their behaviour? Surprisingly few commentaries discuss the moral problems raised by this story. Perhaps they are so appalled by it that it seems safer to concentrate on the source-critical issues the chapter raises.

However I think the moral and theological outlook of the commentator also has its part to play in the different evaluations of the narrator and his tales. Some commentators note the difference between their outlook and the Bible's.

---

[6]C. Westermann, *Genesis 12-36: A Commentary* (ET; London, SPCK 1986) 164.

[7]S.R. Driver, *The Book of Genesis* (London, Methuen 1904) 148.

[8]J. Skinner, *A Critical and Exegetical Commentary on Genesis* (2nd ed; Edinburgh, T. & T. Clark 1930) 249.

[9]B. Jacob, *The First Book of the Bible: Genesis* (ET of 1934 original: New York, Ktav 1974) 355.

[10]N.M. Sarna, *The JPS Commentary: Genesis* (Philadelphia, Jewish Publication Society 1989) 95.

Driver says: 'it would be manifestly unjust to measure Abram by a Christian standard'.[11] At other times the commentator's outlook emerges in passing, but is not addressed explicitly. For example what happened to Sarah when she entered Pharaoh's harem? Some commentators are as discreet as the narrator allowing us to surmise what went on, but others, e.g. Calvin, Jacob, Ross go to great lengths to prove that the LORD protected Sarah's purity by sending the plagues.[12]

But it is not just at the level of individual acts that the narrator's reticence and the commentator's assumptions leave the interpretation rather open. If the patriarchs are intended as paradigms, we must ask not just about particular episodes, but about the pattern of their lives. Are they viewed as basically models of virtue who sometimes slip, or are they sinners saved by grace, whose actions sometimes are praiseworthy, sometimes reprehensible? Why were they chosen by God initially, and why does he maintain his relationship with them? Are they rewarded for acts of obedience and punished for their sins, or does the relationship continue irrespective of their behaviour? These are issues that continually confront the commentator or the preacher who believes that Scripture was written for our instruction. That they are so rarely addressed by mainline critical commentators is a measure of the distancing, indeed the detachment, of many writers in this tradition. Nevertheless the new literary critics in their discussions have shown that even if we do not wish to preach from Genesis, these theological and ethical issues are of great interest if we wish to understand the text fully.

In this paper I want first to draw attention to some of the recurrent emphases in a variety of commentators, which I suggest give a clue to their basic theological and ethical stances. I shall do this by looking at a series of problematic passages, 12:10-20; chapter 16 (the birth of Ishmael), chapter 22 (the sacrifice of Isaac) chapter 27 (Jacob obtains Esau's blessing), and chapter 34 (the rape of Dinah). I shall then declare my own biases, and conclude by asking which of these outlooks comes

---

[11] *The Book of Genesis*, 148.

[12] See *ad loc.* J. Calvin, *A Commentary on Genesis* (1847 ET of 1554 original; reprinted London, Banner of Truth 1965); Jacob, *The First Book;* A.P. Ross, *Creation and Blessing: A Guide to the Study and Exposition of the Book of Genesis* (Grand Rapids, Baker Book House 1987).

closest to the narrator's I shall argue that the opening chapters show most clearly his fundamental theological and ethical convictions, and they should inform our reading of the patriarchal narratives.

Genesis Rabbah

Genesis Rabbah, dating from about 400 AD,[13] is not really a commentary in the modern sense, so much as an anthology of early rabbinic remarks about Genesis. Nevertheless it gives some interesting insights into their approach to the text. There is a definite tendency to put the best possible gloss on the patriarch's behaviour, and to blame foreigners or women for anything that goes wrong. For example in chapter 27 there is barely a hint of criticism for Isaac or Jacob, indeed two angels are said to have supported Jacob's trembling legs as he approached Isaac. His dish smelled like the garden of Eden, whereas Esau's smelled of Gehenna! Esau is described as wicked, even demonic; he symbolises Rome the destroyer of the temple. In 22:5 where Abraham disingenuously tells his servants 'we will come again to you', Midrash Rabbah takes it as a confident prediction of a triumphant return. In chapter 34 all the men are exculpated. Simeon and Levi act with reason (736); when the text says they spoke deceitfully, the Midrash (741) says: 'What think you; that we have a case of deceit here? No, for the Holy Spirit states, "Because he had defiled Dinah their sister".' In other words Shechem's behaviour justified their deceit. Jacob is praised as a man of discernment and is alleged to have helped his sons in the sack of the city (739, 743). Indeed there is no explicit condemnation of Shechem in the Midrash, though it clearly regards the vengeance wreaked on him as deserved. It is Dinah who is blamed over and over again. The narrative's opening comment, 'Dinah went out' is taken to mean 'Dinah acted like a harlot', and is repeatedly cited throughout the narrative. To underline the point of the

[13]So J. Neusner, *Genesis Rabbah: The Judaic Commentary to the Book of Genesis. A New American Translation*, Vol. I. (Atlanta, Scholars Press 1985) ix-x. Neusner provides an analysis of the themes and ideas running through Genesis Rabbah in *Genesis and Judaism: the Perspective of Genesis Rabbah: An Analytical Anthology* (Brown Judaic Studies 108; Atlanta, Scholars Press 1985). Quotations from Genesis are from H. Freedman's translation, *Midrash Rabbah* (3rd ed; London, Soncino 1983).

woman's perversity, God's reasons for creating Eve out of Adam's rib are explained.

I will not create her from Adam's head, lest she be frivolous; nor from the eye, lest she be a coquette, nor from the ear, lest she be an eavesdropper, nor from the mouth, lest she be a gossip; nor from the heart, lest she be prone to jealousy, nor from the hand lest she be light-fingered; nor from the foot, lest she be a gadabout. But I will create her from the modest part of man. . . (to) be a modest woman. Yet in spite of all this. . . I did not create her from the head, yet she is frivolous (Is. 3:16); nor from the eye, yet she is a coquette (Is. 3:16); nor from the ear, yet she is an eavesdropper (Gn. 18:10); nor from the heart, yet she is prone to jealousy (Gn. 30:1); nor from the hand, yet she is light-fingered (Gn. 31:19); nor from the foot, yet she is a gadabout: And Dinah went out' (738).

Not every passage is as blatantly sexist as this. Sarah is quite positively treated in Genesis 16. Her suggestion to Abraham that he should go into Hagar (16:2) is said to be 'the voice of the Holy Spirit' (380). And the comment that she 'dealt harshly, oppressed' Hagar is explained as slapping her face with a slipper, or making her carry a towel to the baths. This would seem to minimise the harshness of Sarah's actions. It is part of a general attempt to view the nation's ancestors in the best possible light.

John Calvin

Calvin's long commentary on Genesis (1554) written more than a thousand years after the Midrash Rabbah, is very different. It is the first modern commentary on Genesis, and in some ways is much more modern than most of the commentaries written this century. It combines attention to the overall theme of Genesis, the fulfilment of the promises to the patriarchs in a manner reminiscent of von Rad and Clines, with discussion of the psychological motivation of the actors as practised by the new literary critics such as Alter and Sternberg. If at times the interpretations are capricious and superficial, one certainly feels Calvin is addressing issues that our generation feels are important. That is not to say that he has not his own axes to grind, as I shall now illustrate.

For Calvin the promises to the patriarchs are the key to interpreting the stories in Genesis, indeed he sees the promises as motivating the patriarchs at almost every step. When Abram enters Egypt, it is not simply fear of the Egyptians that prompts him to describe Sarah as his sister, but concern that the hope of salvation should not be extinguished by his death. Abraham's motives were laudable, even though the means he chose to protect himself were deplorable. 'It follows that Abram's end was right, but he erred in the way itself'. 'If he was solicitous about his own life, which he might justly be, yet he ought to have cast his care upon God'.[14] Similarly Sarah's desire to have children showed her faith in the promise, but trying to hurry along its fulfilment by having a child through Hagar was nothing less than bigamy, clean contrary to the law of God:

The desire of Sarai proceeds from the zeal of faith; but because it is not so subjected to God as to wait his time, she immediately has recourse to polygamy, which is nothing else than the corruption of lawful marriage.[15]

The command to sacrifice Isaac was especially painful for Abraham not just because Isaac was his much loved only son, but because

God. . . requires the death of the boy, to whose person He himself had annexed the hope of eternal salvation. So that his latter command was, in a certain sense, the destruction of faith.[16]

Even more striking is Calvin's evaluation of the motives of Isaac, Rebekah and Esau in chapter 27. He sees Isaac and Rebekah as driven by the birth-oracle, 'The elder shall serve the younger' (25:23). In Isaac's case, 'Wonderfully was the faith of the holy man blended with a foolish and inconsiderate carnal affection'.[17] It was faith activated by the Holy Spirit that prompted him to bless Jacob, but blind love of his first-born that made him intend to bless Esau. Rebekah's consternation at the prospect of Esau being blessed was fully justified, for 'The inheritance promised by God was firmly fixed in her mind'.[18] This faith was over-zealous leading her to injudicious behaviour, but her intentions were excellent:

---

[14] *A Commentary on Genesis*, I.360.
[15] *A Commentary on Genesis*, I.425.
[16] *A Commentary on Genesis*, I.560.
[17] *A Commentary on Genesis*, II.83.
[18] *A Commentary on Genesis*, II.85.

She ought rather to have waited till God should bring relief from heaven, by changing the mind and guiding the tongue of Isaac, than have attempted what was unlawful.[19]

Jacob for his part is criticised by Calvin not for his reluctance to join in his mother's deceit, because it was deceit, but because his reluctance showed lack of faith in the promises made to him. 'Jacob by debating with himself, shows that he was deficient in faith'.[20] However once he agreed to participate in his mother's scheme, he sinned yet more by mixing pious sentiments with falsehood, e.g. in claiming the cause of the quick preparation was that 'the LORD your God granted me success' (27:20).

Usually Calvin wants to think the best of people. When the men of Sodom say they wish to know Lot's visitors, they are not speaking of sexual intimacy, but are merely curious about their identity. The patriarchs are generally portrayed as very committed religious enthusiasts, who want to do the best, but liable to be led astray by temptation or too much zeal. One suspects there were many like this among Calvin's supporters. However Jacob is portrayed without many redeeming features in the commentary on chapter 27, whereas Esau's character is commended:

Esau obeys his father, brings him the produce of his hunting, prepares for his father obtained by his own labour, and speaks nothing but the truth; in short, we find nothing in him which is not worthy of praise. Jacob never leaves his home, substitutes a kid for venison, insinuates himself by many lies, brings nothing which would properly commend him, but in many things deserves reprehension.[21]

For Calvin this contrast demonstrates the freedom of God's election, which is based not on works but on grace. Similarly commenting on 22:16-18, where the promises to Abraham are enhanced 'because you have obeyed my voice', Calvin is at pains to point out that this does not mean Abraham's virtue was rewarded but that 'what is freely given, is yet called the reward of works'.[22]

---

[19] *A Commentary on Genesis*, II.88.
[20] *A Commentary on Genesis*, II.86.
[21] *A Commentary on Genesis*, II.93.
[22] *A Commentary on Genesis*, I.572.

Hermann Gunkel

With Gunkel we breathe a quite different air. His great commentary on Genesis was published in 1901. Whereas Calvin read Genesis theologically, convinced that the stories show the fulfilment of the promises to the fathers and illustrate the doctrines of grace and human sinfulness Gunkel sees them as ancient sagas embodying the ideals of primitive Israelites. He was a romantic like Herder, almost a deist who preferred to think of God as the ultimate cause, rather than intervening in human history.[23] He was profoundly interested in the techniques of the biblical storytellers and his work shows many sharp insights into their characterisation of the actors in the story.

However he is determined to read the stories as he thinks they were originally intended, as separate sagas told round the fires of ancient Israel. He dismisses the context within the book as a whole.[24] From such a reading we may build up a picture of Israelite folk heroes, a world in which religion and morality had not yet been linked:

> The God of whom these old sagas originally told is not the majestic Yahweh, the giver of the Ten Commandments, but a much more primitive figure, a God who protects his favourite and his clan in all his ways however crooked.[25]

Thus 12:10-20 celebrates the beauty of the tribal mother and her loyalty.[26] The narrator is not troubled by Abraham's lies: he 'silently rejoices that Abraham had lied so extraordinarily well and made a virtue out of a necessity'.[27] As for the danger Abraham placed his wife in, Gunkel remarks: 'The ancient Israelite did not know the chivalrous duty of protecting his wife or daughter even to death.'[28] In chapter 16 Abraham is

---

[23]For a discussion of Gunkel's background see H.-J. Kraus, *Geschichte der historisch-kritischen Erforschung des Alten Testaments von der Reformation bis zur Gegenwart* (Neukirchen, Neukirchener Verlag 1956) 316-7, and more fully in W. Klatt, *Hermann Gunkel: zu seiner Theologie der Religionsgeschichte and zur Entstehung der formgeschichtlichen Methode* (FRLANT 100; Göttingen, Vandenhoeck und Ruprecht, 1969) esp. 264-71.

[24]E.g. *Genesis*, 171.

[25]*Genesis*, 308.

[26]*Genesis*, 169.

[27]*Genesis*, 170.

[28]*Genesis*, 170.

amiable and upright, a man who listens to his wife. Indeed Abraham, Sarah and Hagar are all typical Israelites. 'That they behave as they do, the naive saga finds very natural, for this is how one behaves in Israel'.[29]

Gunkel finds a similar glorification of the patriarchs and indifference to moral issues in Genesis 27. He dismisses attempts to see the subsequent sufferings of Jacob as divine punishment:

> The substance of this story is that a deception finally had a happy ending: the rogue Jacob really gained the blessing for himself. . . and the listeners are the fortunate heirs of the deceiver. ... It is quite impossible to think that the devotees or descendants of Jacob would have wanted to relate something scurrilous about their hero or ancestor and thereby band themselves with an ugly characteristic as their hallmark.[30]

When Jacob foresees that his father may not be deceived if he takes food in, and Rebekah suggests counter measures, Gunkel comments:

> We are meant to be pleased about the cleverness of son and mother. Jacob is clever in that he foresees that his father will touch him; but his mother is even cleverer in knowing a way of deceiving him nevertheless.[31]

When Jacob takes God's name in a lie, 'the old saga does not regard it as especially evil, but thinks, "that was a good lie"'.[32] From reading Gunkel's commentary it is not clear how far he identifies with the attitudes he ascribes to the storytellers: from time to time he contrasts the narrator's view with that of modern readers. But Gunkel's comments on patriarchal society and its attitudes certainly enshrine a romantic vision of what primitive societies were like: they were characterised by spontaneity and a lack of stultifying rules. Whether the author of Genesis would have recognised Gunkel's description is another matter.

---

[29]*Genesis*, 186.
[30]*Genesis*, 307.
[31]*Genesis*, 310.
[32]*Genesis*, 311.

Gerhard von Rad

The two great commentaries of the latter twentieth century are those of von Rad (1949)[33] and Westermann (1968-82). Von Rad has more in common with Calvin's approach, while Westermann resembles Gunkel, though neither is as extreme as their prototypes. Like Calvin, von Rad insists on reading the narratives in sequence and in the light of the promises. At many points he rejects Gunkel's interpretations, which he thinks only work if you read the stories in isolation from each other. But the collectors

> ...give meaning to a narrative from the overlapping whole. They do not see merely single stories which contain their own meaning, but they see a great divine event with the patriarchs.[34]

Thus 12:10-20 must be interpreted in the light of the programmatic statement in 12:1-3:

> One must remember that the jeopardising of the ancestress called into question everything that Yahweh had promised to do for Abraham. But Yahweh does not allow his work to miscarry right at the start; he rescues it and preserves it beyond all human failure.[35]

Von Rad suggests that the moral problems posed for us by this story were not felt so acutely by the author. Nevertheless he probably regarded Abraham as guilty of unbelief. He is more outspoken when he comments on chapter 16. Though Sarah's action in proposing surrogate marriage was quite proper by the mores of the patriarchal age, the narrator probably saw a great delinquency in it:

> Chapter 12:10ff told of the jeopardy of the promise, a disregard of the kind that springs from unbelief; the story of Hagar shows us to some extent the opposite, a fainthearted faith that cannot leave things with God and believes it necessary to help things along. All persons of the drama appear in a bad light. The narrator seems to be most sympathetic toward Hagar, although she offended most obviously against right and custom.[36]

In chapter 27 he agrees with Gunkel that Rebekah's ploy has a comic aspect. But

---

[33]G. von Rad, *Genesis: A Commentary* (ET of 2nd ed; London, SCM 1972)
[34]*Genesis*, 169.
[35]*Genesis*, 169.
[36]*Genesis*, 196; *cf.* 191.

the whole style of the narrative is much more exalted and serious. The crime against the blind man, the blasphemy against Yahweh (especially v. 20), the outbreaks of terror in the scene between Isaac and Esau, and finally at the end the bankruptcy of the whole family - none of that would have caused an ancient leader to laugh. But how are we moderns to answer the obvious question about motives, especially about Rebekah?[37]

Was she trying to further the divine plans, or being magnanimous? Or is Jacob's lifestyle regarded as more meritorious? Having posed these questions von Rad continues:

The narrative ... does not completely exclude such motives, but it does not hasten to direct our thoughts in such a direction ... The narrator is convinced that ultimately in the human struggle for the blessing of the dying man divine plans are being worked out, and he intends to show it. And Isaac cannot retract the blessing because God himself has acted in and through him and has accomplished his will ... The story reckons with an act of God that sovereignly takes the most ambiguous human act and incorporates it into its plans. The guilty one becomes the bearer of the promise! To be sure, the narrator draws a powerful picture of the most extraordinarily entangled guilt, but his view of what God has decreed and accomplished keeps him from being ruffled before the question of the personal guilt and subjective motives of the individual persons. If one wants to ask the narrator what his thoughts are concerning these men who act in the story, his concern, in our opinion, will be this: he intends to awaken in the reader a feeling of sympathetic suffering for those who are caught up mysteriously in such a monstrous act of God and are almost destroyed in it.[38]

Like most modern commentators von Rad is nonplussed by chapter 34. He spends a considerable time on the source-critical issues, and never discussed how the material relates to the patriarchal promises. Nevertheless he does venture more moral comment than most on this appalling episode. On the phrase 'he had wrought folly in Israel' (34:7) he observes

Israel thought very severely in these matters and knew herself to be uncompromisingly distinct from the Canaanites in the sexual realm.[39]

---

[37]*Genesis*, 280.

[38]*Genesis*, 280-1.

[39]*Genesis*, 332.

He notes that Jacob's passivity after the rape is remarkable. After the massacre he dismisses Jacob's reaction:

> His censure is more a peevish complaint. By contrast the answer of the two sons is proud and implacable; and the ancient reader, who felt more than we do the burning shame done to the brothers in the rape of Dinah, will not have called them wrong.[40]

His final judgement is that the massacre is a

> morally ambiguous deed ... which could perplex the reader if he did not know that this event also belongs to a course of history subject to God's special plans.[41]

The seriousness of von Rad's approach is in sharp contrast to the lightheartedness of Gunkel. How far I wonder does this reflect the time they were writing, Gunkel before the First World War and von Rad in the immediate aftermath of the Second World War? Reading von Rad, I hear the voice of one who has clung on to faith in God through very dark days.[42]

Claus Westermann

But with Westermann the pendulum swings back towards Gunkel in two respects. First, he tends to view each story in Genesis in isolation rather than as part of a long narrative in which the whole sheds light on the parts. This has very big consequences in his interpretation of the opening chapters of Genesis, where he rejects the traditional picture of the fall or what von Rad terms the avalanche of sin.[43] Each story in the primeval history or the patriarchal narrative tends to describe a typical human or family problem. Thus while commenting on 12:1-3 Westermann pays lip-service to this passage's significance for the patriarchal narratives as a whole, but in the immediately following episode the promises are virtually ignored. Secondly, he sees the Genesis stories as describing typical human predicaments. 12:10-20 is a story about choosing whether to surrender something which ought not to be surrendered, in this case his wife, or facing death.[44] This,

---

[40]*Genesis*, 334.

[41]*Genesis*, 335.

[42]For a review of von Rad's life and work see J.L. Crenshaw, *Gerhard von Rad* (Waco, Word 1978).

[43]See G.J. Wenham, 'Original Sin in Genesis 1-11'. *Churchman* 104 (1990) 309-28.

[44]*Genesis 12-36*, 167

Westermann observes, is a perennial issue and Abraham shows lack of faith in God's ability to rescue him. And yet God does. Similarly chapter 16 is basically understood as a story describing a typical conflict between women:

The writer gives expression with amazing skill to something which is part of life in common as long as people exist ... A feels disadvantaged by B; A is liberated from the disadvantage; A disadvantages B. This happens in every area of human life, most notably in the political area; the oppressed when liberated becomes the oppressor. The narrative of Genesis 16 is saying that this phenomenon is already present in the basic human community, the family. Such conflicts are part of human existence; they cannot be abolished.[45]

Similarly chapter 22 is essentially about God testing a man just as Job was tested. It is the potential loss of his son that matters, and this has nothing to do with the promises, for verses 16-18 are a secondary addition to the story. 'The narrative reaches its goal with the naming of the mountain.' It is the story of 'a father's path of suffering'.[46] For Abraham the angel's message and the substitution of the ram for Isaac does not mean that he has passed the test, but: "'My child is saved; thanks be to God!' the narrative looks not at the praise of a creature, but to the praise of God'.[47]

Similarly Westermann reads chapter 27 as a family conflict story setting out the rivalry between the generations and between siblings. It reflects an ancient even magical view of the way blessing is handed on from generation to generation.[48] Westermann makes few comments about the morality of the actors: he reads the story as a picture of how life is rather than as having a didactic or theological purpose. A complicated literary analysis dominates his exegesis of chapter 34, and moral comment is even more notable by its absence. Only the latest layer has a moral concern to condemn intermarriage with the Canaanites and illustrate the implementation of the law of Deuteronomy 7:2-3. But

..the narrative is secular in all its three constituent parts; only once, 35:5, is there any indication of the action of God, when the attackers

[45]*Genesis 12-36*, 241.
[46]*Genesis 12-36*, 364.
[47]*Genesis 12-36*, 365.
[48]*Cf. Genesis 12-36*, 440.

are protected from vengeance by a 'terrible fear (fear of God)' as they depart with their booty. But even this mention of God's action, though it is only a hint, is in contradiction to Jacob's works in 34.30 where he fears annihilation because of the violence of his sons.[49]

How far, it may be asked, is Westermann's interpretation a reflection of much Christian piety today: no long-term hope in the coming of the kingdom; no deep conviction about moral values, but an acquiescence in life as it is; and a belief that God may rescue us if we really find ourselves in deep water. For all the acuteness of his critical discussions and the detail of his exegesis I find Westermann's commentary disappointing. Though three times as long as von Rad's work, it contains less insight into the character of the patriarchs and little attempt to see Genesis in its entirety as a piece of literature, let alone as a significant piece of theology. One feels he has missed the wood for the trees.

Meir Sternberg

Before turning to my own approach to Genesis, I should like to say a little about Sternberg,[50] who, though he has not produced a commentary on Genesis, has written very insightfully about some of the chapters I have focused on so far. Sternberg displays an interest in characterisation and moral issues that surpasses all his predecessors. His studies of different stories involve such depth of analysis that inevitably those brought up on traditional commentaries must wonder how far he is reading his own ideas into the text and how far he is bringing out the narrator's. So before discussing some of his proposals, I should like to outline the assumptions that underlie his approach.

The first is that words are used precisely, so that we should be attentive to the precise nuances of each term. 'In a miniature narrative ... as in poetry, every word counts and every echo resounds.'[51] Thus the description of Dinah's rape is significant in its choice of verbs. 'The verbs selected (saw, took,

---

[49]*Genesis 12-36*, 545.

[50]M. Sternberg, *The Poetics of Biblical Narrative. Ideological Literature and the Drama of Reading* (Bloomington, Indiana UP 1985). R. Alter, *The Art of Biblical Narrative* (New York, Basic Books, 1981) is a less detailed work but on similar lines to Sternberg's.

[51]*Poetics*, 456.

lay with, abused) to describe the crime project a sharp judgement on the highest authority.' 'Lie with' is normally intransitive but is here transitive and 'reduces the victim to a mere object ..."abused" speaks for itself'.[52] Not only must the commentator be aware of the exact flavour of the term, but he must look out for where the term has been used before in the narrative. For example 27:1 'Isaac was old' echoes the earlier comments about Abraham being old, especially 24:1, and should awaken certain expectations in the reader: old age is associated in Genesis with admirable character, happiness and success.[53] Sternberg also pays close attention to the syntax of sentences, holding that unusual constructions may well draw attention to the author's intentions.[54]

The second important assumption is the unity of the biblical books. Sternberg does not reject source criticism on principle, but as far as interpreting Genesis is concerned, it is justifiable to use any passage in the book to shed light on any other, for they all come from the same author or have been edited by the same redactor. Thus knowledge of Jacob's unhappiness about his marriage to Leah helps explain his indifference to the rape of her daughter Dinah, which in turn fanned the sense of outrage felt by her full brothers Levi and Simeon.[55]

The third assumption made by Sternberg is that the moral outlook of the biblical writers is enshrined in the laws and ethical statements in the Pentateuch. Thus though the Bible storytellers rarely make explicit their attitudes to the deeds they describe, they and their first readers intuitively made judgements about the morality of events which it is the commentator's task to reconstruct. For a fuller discussion of other methodological principles enshrined in Sternberg's approach other literary critics need to be consulted.[56] But the points I have mentioned seem to me the most important and generate some rich exegesis.

For example Sternberg devotes a long section to explaining the motives and male reactions to the rape of

---

[52]*Poetics*, 446.
[53]*Poetics*, 350.
[54]E.g. *Poetics*, 454, 460.
[55]*Poetics*, 462-463.
[56]A. Mintz, 'On the Tel Aviv School of Poetics', *Prooftexts* 4 (1984) 215-35.

Dinah.[57] Interestingly he, unlike the rabbis, makes no comment on Dinah's behaviour. The narrator as we have seen outspokenly condemns the rape through the terms he uses to describe it, but then mitigates our judgement on Shechem by drawing attention to his fondness for Dinah. According to Sternberg Jacob's reaction is particularly deplorable. First, he just does not react to his daughter's plight; contrast his grief at the disappearance of Joseph, or David's anger at the rape of Tamar. This enrages Dinah's brothers, who then take the law into their own hands. Lest we think the Shechemites the purely innocent victims of a feud between Jacob's family and Hamor's, the narrator points out their greed in accepting the proposal of free intermarriage with Jacob's family. Sternberg is in no doubt that the massacre and subsequent looting of the city was viewed by the narrator as quite disproportionate revenge and contrary to natural justice, so he is not trying to exculpate Jacob's sons entirely. But Jacob's final comment to his sons, 'You have brought trouble on me' reveals him to be the

..tale's least sympathetic character. The cowardice betrayed. . . is less damning than the immorality. If Jacob reproached the pair for the massacre or the abuse of the rite of circumcision or even the breach of contract, he would gain a measure of understanding and support from the reader. But he does not even remotely protest against any of these offences.[58]

He is only worried about the potential revenge by the Canaanites:

His approach, like the words of the Hivites and the deeds of his other sons, is informed by those pragmatic considerations against which the narrative has levelled so much of its rhetoric.[59]

In other words Sternberg thinks the narrator is blaming all the actors in the story to different degrees for the incident.

Similarly in a much briefer discussion of chapter 27 Sternberg thinks all those involved misbehave by the narrator's norms. Isaac's physical and spiritual blindness trigger off the great catastrophe recounted here, but that does not justify Rebekah and Jacob's trickery or Esau's planned fratricide:

---

[57]*Poetics*, 445-75.
[58]*Poetics*, 473.
[59]*Poetics*, 473.

thus we leave the second patriarch: sightless, baffled ... ill at ease with every single member of his family, all (like himself) sinning and sinned against as a result of his folly ... In his old age Isaac has made such a mess of a hitherto uneventful career, patterned on his father's, as to jeopardise his whole heritage. And it is none of his doing that Jacob survives, prospers, *and* returns. Nor that the brothers are at last reconciled.[60]

Sternberg's book is essentially about narrative technique: it is not a commentary. So it does not give an overview of the book of Genesis as a whole and its themes. I should very much like to see how he would handle the book of Genesis as a coherent piece of literature in its own right. Where do the divine promises fit in? Would Sternberg regard them as central to the books as von Rad and his disciples have held, and how would he relate the patriarchal stories to the preceding material in chapters 1-11? Perhaps one day he will write more.[61]

Towards a Synthesis

Now at last I should like to try and sum up my approach to commenting on Genesis. I suppose I have been trying to use the methods of Sternberg within a framework akin to von Rad's. Certainly these are the two modern writers I feel most affinity with. I have tried to be as careful as Sternberg in determining the meaning of words and sentences, and have explored the character and motives of the different actors. But like von Rad I see Genesis as an account of saving history, whose purpose and direction is summed up in the promises to Abraham as in 12:1-3. I think David Clines has offered the best definition of the theme of the Pentateuch to date:

The theme of the Pentateuch is the partial fulfilment - which implies also the partial non-fulfilment - of the promise to or blessing of the patriarchs. The promise or blessing is both the divine initiative in a world where human initiatives always lead to disaster, and a re-affirmation of the primal divine intentions for man.[62]

---

[60]*Poetics*, 350.

[61]Mintz (*Prooftexts* 4 [1984] 232) argues that this is a deficiency in Sternberg's approach: 'In the Bible meaning involves a story's didactic function in Scripture's scheme of sacred history and not just its narrative mechanisms'.

[62]D.J.A. Clines, *The Theme of the Pentateuch* (JSOTS 10; Sheffield, JSOT Press 1978) 29.

However it seems to me that von Rad and Clines' understanding of the promises as tripartite, descendants, land and blessing of Israel, fails to pay sufficient attention to the climax of the promise that 'in you all the families of the earth shall find blessing'.[63] Genesis is an outward-looking book that expects Abraham's descendants to bring blessing to the whole human race. I agree with von Rad and Sternberg that Genesis expects its heroes to live by the law, so far as they knew it, but that very often they fell far short. They are saved by grace, not by merit, as chapters 12, 27, 34 and many other episodes demonstrate. Many a story shows the sinful guilt of the patriarchs, who despite their sin survive. This is put most explicitly in 45:5-8 and 50:20: 'You meant evil against me; but God meant it for good, to bring it about that many people should be kept alive, as they are'.

But grace and forgiveness does not mean freedom from punishment. Many commentators have pointed out that Jacob's deceit in obtaining the blessing from his brother Esau leads him into the hands of Laban, who cheats him out of his chosen bride Rachel. That this is not just a figment of commentators' imaginations is proved by the terminology used.[64] Isaac said 'your brother came with deceit' (מִרְמָה) (27:35). Jacob protests to Laban with the words, 'Why have you deceived me? (רִמִּיתָנִי) (29:25), and Laban's retort is a cutting comment on Jacob's treatment of Esau: 'It is not done in our country to put the younger before the first-born' (29:26). That Jacob himself recognises the injustice that he has done to Esau is very clear in chapter 33, where he tries to return the blessing he had illicitly acquired from Esau. He and his sons repeatedly bow down to Esau (33:3, 6, 7) just as Isaac predicted in the blessing he thought he was bestowing on Esau, 'May your mother's sons bow down to you'. He describes himself as Esau's servant and Esau as his lord, again echoing the blessing formula, 'Be lord over your brothers' (27:29 *cf.* 32:18,20; 33:5, 8, 13, 14, 15). Even more striking is Jacob's description of the droves of animals that he presents to Esau to placate him: 'please accept my *blessing* which has been brought to you' (33:11). He is

---

[63]*Cf.* G.J. Wenham, *Genesis 1-15* (Waco, Word 1987) 278, 283.

[64]See S.K. Sherwood, *"Had God Not Been on My Side" An Examination of the Narrative Technique of the Story of Jacob and Laban Genesis 29:1-32* (Frankfurt, Lang 1990) 101-8.

deliberately giving back to Esau the blessing which he had cheated him out of. This whole episode is surely a paradigm of repentance and forgiveness in the Bible: forgiveness on Esau's part and repentance on Jacob's.

Interestingly, though, Genesis 33 does not end the consequences (or should we say the punishment?) of Jacob's sin in chapter 27. His bigamous marriage, which is the consequence of his flight from home, is very unhappy, and this spills over into the next generation as we have seen in chapter 34. It also poisons feelings between Joseph, Rachel's son, and his brothers, Leah's sons, so that they sell him into Egypt. But it is Jacob who suffers most in this affair, refusing to be comforted. That his suffering may ultimately be traced back to his deception of his father is made clear by the narrator, who informs us that Jacob's sons use a goat to deceive him about Joseph's fate just as earlier Jacob had used a goat to deceive his father (37:31; *cf.* 27:9-16). Complete reconciliation within the family is not achieved until they all come down to Egypt in chapter 46.

If the patriarchs are saved by grace, yet punished for their sins, they are also rewarded for their obedience. This is clear in 12:7. No sooner has Abraham left home in obedience to his call than he arrives in Canaan, and is told: 'To your descendants I will give this land'. His return from Egypt and his generosity to Lot is rewarded by a yet greater enhancement of the promise (13:14-17). But the most striking example of obedience rewarded is chapter 22. Here after the last and severest test of Abraham he is told: 'By myself I have sworn, says the LORD, because you have done this ... I will indeed bless you ... because you have obeyed my voice (22:16-18)'. Not only is this the fullest statement of the promises, but the status of the promise is changed: it is now a sworn divine oath, and has as it were become a guarantee. From now on nothing is added to the promise; it is sufficient simply to refer back to the oath sworn to Abraham your father (26:3). Joseph's career is portrayed as a great success, because the LORD was with him and he feared God. He is one who passes through harsh and barely-merited suffering before being exalted to Pharaoh's right-hand man, and then becoming the agent of world-wide famine relief. Thus he could be described as one through whom many of the families of the earth found blessing. But there is here and throughout the Pentateuch a sense of incompleteness. Its theme is the partial fulfilment of the promises, which implies the partial non-fulfilment of the promises. This is most obviously true of the land promise, which is not achieved till the book of Joshua, but the promises of countless descendants and the blessing of Israel and the nations are only partially fulfilled too. These promises force the reader to look beyond his or her present, whether it be the reign of David, the exile, the New Testament era, or the late 20th century to the day when we shall no longer need to pray 'Thy kingdom come, thy will be done', for the kingdom will be come and God's will will be done on earth as in heaven.

As a commentator, then, I consciously read Genesis in the light of my Christian convictions. I believe there is a continuity between God's patterns of working in Genesis and his working under the new covenant. More than that, the writer of Genesis had a view of the relationship between God and man, sin, grace and salvation similar to that of the New Testament. This I suppose is a corollary of my belief in one divine author of Scripture who worked in and through its multiple human authors.

Now you have let the cat out of the bag, it will be said. You are just a Christian reading your own ideas into the text. I should like to conclude by taking up this challenge: am I bringing out the narrator's own views or imposing mine on him? I think this is a very difficult question to answer, but I shall try to make my case that I am doing exegesis not eisegesis.

First, I should like to make it clear that here I am only discussing the perspective of the author of Genesis, his views of the relationship between God and the world, not those of the actors in the story, i.e., the patriarchs. I think Walter Moberly[65] has drawn some very plausible distinctions between patriarchal religion and later beliefs that the text presupposes. Here I am concerned with the writer's convictions, not those of the men who lived centuries before him. Within a canonical perspective it is his views that are authoritative for later generations, and within a literary-critical perspective it is his outlook that critics like Sternberg and Alter are anxious to elucidate.

---

[65]R.W.L. Moberly, *The Old Testament of the Old Testament* (Minneapolis, Fortress 1992).

Perhaps the point to begin is with Sternberg and von Rad's assumption that the writer of Genesis shares the ethical outlook of other parts of the Pentateuch, particularly as expressed in the legal sections. This is surely an inevitable corollary of any view that sees an authorial connection between Genesis and the following books, whether that link be Moses, J, E, P or a deuteronomist. And every now and then their common outlook is made obvious by a remark such as 'he had wrought folly in Israel . . . for such a thing ought not to be done' (34:7) or 'he did not lie with her again' (38:26), an allusion to the rule in Leviticus 18:15. Even a heathen king recognises that adultery was a great sin (20:9). Further it seems likely that the Pentateuchal writers instinctively assume the canonical authority of the laws delivered at Sinai. Abraham is said to have 'kept my charge, my commandments, my statutes, and my laws' (26:5), terms later used of the Sinaitic legislation. Abel offers a model sacrifice. Noah distinguishes between clean and unclean animals, works on a seven-day cycle and presumably keeps the Sabbath. Later readers therefore would have noticed when and where their ancestors deviated from such norms and come up with some historical or theological explanation. A historical explanation would be that the patriarchs were not aware of the Sinaitic norms, a theological explanation that they were sinning, falling short of eternal moral standards.

In most cases it seems to me that the writers must have expected their readers to resort to a theological explanation of the patriarchs' moral deficiencies. It seems unlikely that writers or readers would have excused Jacob's lies, blasphemy and disrespect for his father on the grounds that he had not heard the Ten Commandments. Such fundamental norms of behaviour are surely taken for granted in every biblical era. Much earlier in the narrative Cain and Ham are condemned for their sins, even though they were not told murder or disrespect for parents were wrong. So how did the writers explain God's choice of their ancestors and his tolerance of their sins? Did they view their merits as outweighing their sins, or did they see it as an act of divine grace and continuing divine forgiveness? Did they see all human beings including the patriarchs as intrinsically sinful, only escaping the full consequences of their sin by divine mercy, or are there some who deserve to be treated well by God?

We know what St Paul thought; and Calvin, working within an essentially Pauline framework, certainly offers a fruitful reading of Genesis. But can we approach any closer to the narrator of Genesis than Paul? The book of Deuteronomy is fairly explicit. It insists that it was not the merits of the people that led to their salvation from Egypt. 'It was not because you were more in number than any other people that the LORD set his love upon you' (Dt. 7:7). Nor was it because of their righteousness (Dt. 9:4-6). In fact Deuteronomy goes to great lengths to prove the inveterately sinful nature of Israel, recalling their numerous rebellions in the wilderness and predicting that this pattern of stubborn rejection of God's way will eventually culminate in their expulsion from the land (Dt. 29:11-28). There is no suggestion in Deuteronomy that present or future generations deserve God's kindness. But there is also the conviction that despite it all God will not desert them, that when they repent they will return to the land (Dt. 30:1-10).

So why did God choose Israel in the first place? The only answer given by Deuteronomy is that he was keeping the oath made to the fathers (7:7; 9:5). But this only pushes the issue further back: why did God choose Abraham, Isaac and Jacob? Reading the narratives of Genesis through the spectacles of the Sinai lawgiving, one cannot think that their behaviour is very different from Israel's in the wilderness. Jacob, after whom the nation was named, behaved disgracefully. He certainly did not get where he did because he deserved it. Abraham's career oscillated between moments of faith and disobedient unbelief (*cf.* 12:1-9 and 12:10-20: ch. 15 and ch. 16; ch. 18 and ch. 20) Even Isaac, who lived a tranquil and blessed life, made a grave error on his death bed which set in train a series of events which overshadowed the lives of his sons and grandsons for more than a generation. Sternberg is surely right when he says: 'None of his (i.e. the narrator's) righteous men is perfect and few of the unrighteous wholly evil.'[66] On chapter 27 he observes that all sin and are sinned against; and that it is none of Jacob's 'doing that Jacob survives, prospers, *and* returns'.[67] Though he does not use the terminology, Sternberg thus comes close to saying that the narrator of Genesis believes in the universality of sin, from which man is saved only by grace. If

[66] *Poetics*, 493.
[67] *Poetics*, 350.

Deuteronomy says that the nation was not saved because of its righteousness, is not the writer of Genesis saying the same about the patriarchs through his portrayal of their very chequered careers?

That this is a valid reading of Genesis I think is confirmed by a close reading of the opening chapters. These may be compared with parallel texts from the ancient Near East, some of which tell the same events in a similar order (creation to the flood) but, as Jacobsen has pointed out, reach very different conclusions. The Sumerian Flood Story

> ..takes throughout ... an affirmative and optimistic view of existence; it believes in progress. Things were not nearly as good to begin with as they have become since. In the biblical account it is the other way around. Things began as perfect from God's hand and grew steadily worse through man's sinfulness until God finally had to do away with all mankind except the pious Noah who would beget a new and better stock.[68]

This transformation of traditional accounts of world origins in Genesis speaks volumes for its understanding of man and his relationship with God. But Genesis does not stop here. Noah may be introduced as blameless among his contemporaries, but Genesis makes it plain that his contemporaries were anything but perfect. God's verdict before the flood was that 'every imagination of the thoughts of his heart was only evil continually' (6:5); after the flood, when only Noah and his family survived, the verdict is almost the same: 'the imagination of man's heart is evil from his youth' (8:21). And to underline the universality of sin, the second father of the human race succumbs to wine and is shamefully treated by his son. Here we surely have a re-run of the fall, just as the restoration of the earth after the flood is a second creation. More precisely the minor transgression of the father (eating the forbidden fruit/drinking too much wine) is followed by the much more serious sin of his son (fratricide/mocking his father). If Adam and Noah, who had opportunities that none of their successors enjoyed, proved to be sinners, how much more those who lived after them.

The opening chapters of Genesis set out with particular clarity the writer's understanding of God, his relationship to the world, and his ideals for mankind. God is here disclosed as

---

[68]T. Jacobsen, 'The Eridu Genesis', *JBL* 100 (1981) 152.

one, omnipotent, benevolent towards his creation. Man is seen as the apex of the created order, whose every need is met by his creator. He is expected to be fruitful, marry one wife, care for the rest of creation, rest on the Sabbath, obey God's one undemanding law, and enjoy a life of intimacy with God. Here we have a picture of abundant divine grace, which Adam and Eve spoil by one act of disobedience. And this is a pattern which repeats itself as time moves on, though very often Adam's descendants prove even more perverse than their father. Yet in these opening chapters the writer has provided us a yardstick by which all the subsequent events in sacred history may be measured. Thus though there is no explicit comment on Abraham's actions in chapter 16, attentive readers will note parallels with Genesis 3, indicating how the narrator viewed them.[69] In Genesis 1-3 God's character and intentions are most clearly disclosed, and the writer presupposes in the rest of the story the same God and the same divine plan. That human beings so often frustrate it by their sinfulness does not nullify the plan: it remains in force. After one false start in Adam, another with Noah, there is yet a third with Abraham. He like his predecessors is not a perfect saint, yet God calls him, and through his obedience (however inadequate) begins the redemption of the human race. This is a process that will be complete when God and man are reconciled in a new Eden.[70] Genesis shows that the path to this goal will be winding and slow, but it is this hope which gives the book an optimism in the face of the tragedies of sin.

---

[69]W. Berg, 'Der Sündenfall Abrahams und Saras nach Gen. 16:1-6'. *BN* 19 (1982) 7-14.

[70]G.J. Wenham, 'Sanctuary Symbolism in the Garden of Eden Story'. *Proceedings of the 9th World Congress of Jewish Studies* (1986) 19-25.

INDEX OF SCRIPTURE PASSAGES

Exodus

Leviticus

INDEX OF MODERN AUTHORS